NEW CENTURY BIBLE

General Editors

RONALD E. CLEMENTS

M.A., B.D., PH.D. (Old Testament)

MATTHEW BLACK

D.D., D.LITT., D.THEOL., F.B.A. (New Testament)

Leviticus and Numbers

NEW CENTURY BIBLE

Based on the Revised Standard Version

Leviticus and Numbers

N. H. SNAITH

Formerly Principal of Wesley College, Headingley, Leeds

the Attic Press, Inc.

GREENWOOD, S. C.

OLIPHANTS, Marshall, Morgan & Scott, a member of the Pentos group, 1 Bath Street, LONDON EC1V 9LB. First published 1969, reprinted 1977. ISBN 0 551 00778 8.
The Bible references in this publication are from the Revised Standard Version of the Bible, copyrighted 1946 and 1952 by the Division of Christian Education, National Council of the Churches of Christ, and used by permission.
Printed in Great Britain by Butler & Tanner Ltd, Frome and London. 772020L20.

CONTENTS

LISTS OF ABBREVIATIONS vii

BIBLIOGRAPHY OF RECENT PUBLICATIONS xi

GENERAL INTRODUCTION TO LEVITICUS AND NUMBERS

1 The Titles of the Books 1

2 Arrangement and Contents of the Books 2

3 The Sources of the Books 6

4 The History of the Priesthood 11

5 The Temple Sacrifices 14

6 The Priestly Tradition (P) 18

7 The Holiness Code (H) 22

8 The Itinerary 23

COMMENTARY ON LEVITICUS

First Section (1–7):
The Laws of Sacrifice 28

Second Section (8–10)
The Priesthood 49

Third Section (11–16):
Ritual Uncleanness and Purification Rites 62

Fourth Section (17–26):
The Holiness Code 83

Fifth Section (27):
The Commutation of Vows and Tithes 116

COMMENTARY ON NUMBERS

First Section (1.1–10.10):
What Happened at Sinai 120

Second Section (10.11–20.13):
What Happened in the Wilderness 138

Third Section (20.14–36.13):
What Happened from Kadesh to the Plains of Moab 169

MAP: SINAI PENINSULA AND CANAAN 205

INDEX 207

LISTS OF ABBREVIATIONS

ABBREVIATIONS OF TEXTUAL TRADITIONS

J	the early Judaean traditions
E	the traditions of Old Israel (continuing in the north)
D	the Deuteronomic tradition
H	the Holiness Code
P	the Priestly traditions

ABBREVIATIONS OF STANDARD BIBLICAL TEXTS

Aq	Version of Aquila
AV	Authorized Version
AVm	Authorized Version margin
DV	Douay-Rheims Version
EVV	English Versions
Heb	Hebrew text
LXX	Septuagint
RSV	Revised Standard Version
RV	Revised Version
RVm	Revised Version margin
S	Syriac (*Peshiṭta*) Version
Sam	Samaritan Pentateuch
Sym	Version of Symmachus
T	Targum (Onkelos)
T (Pal)	Targum (Palestinian)
Theod	Version of Theodotion
V	Vulgate

ABBREVIATIONS OF THE BOOKS OF THE BIBLE

OLD TESTAMENT (*OT*)

Gen.	Jg.	1 Chr.	Ps.	Lam.	Ob.	Hag.
Exod.	Ru.	2 Chr.	Prov.	Ezek.	Jon.	Zech.
Lev.	1 Sam.	Ezr.	Ec.	Dan.	Mic.	Mal.
Num.	2 Sam.	Neh.	Ca.	Hos.	Nah.	
Dt.	1 Kg.	Est.	Isa.	Jl	Hab.	
Jos.	2 Kg.	Job	Jer.	Am.	Zeph.	

APOCRYPHA (*Apoc.*)

1 Esd.	Tob.	Ad. Est.	Sir.	S 3 Ch.	Bel	1 Mac.
2 Esd.	Jdt.	Wis.	Bar.	Sus.	Man.	2 Mac.
			Ep. Jer.			

NEW TESTAMENT (*NT*)

Mt.	Ac.	Gal.	1 Th.	Tit.	1 Pet.	3 Jn
Mk	Rom.	Eph.	2 Th.	Phm.	2 Pet.	Jude
Lk.	1 C.	Phil.	1 Tim.	Heb	1 Jn	Rev.
Jn	2 C.	Col.	2 Tim.	Jas	2 Jn	

ABBREVIATIONS REFERRING TO DEAD SEA SCROLLS

1QM	War of the Sons of Light against the Sons of Darkness
1QpHab	Habakkuk Commentary
1QS	Rule of the Community (Manual of Discipline)
1QSa (=1Q28a)	Rule of the Community (Appendix)
1Qsb (=1Q28b)	Collection of Benedictions
CD	Fragments of a Zadokite work (Damascus Document)

ABBREVIATIONS OF JEWISH WRITINGS

MISHNAH AND TALMUD

b. Babylonian Talmud   jer. Jerusalem Talmud

*

Arakh.	ʿArakhin	Ned.	Nedarim
B.Bath.	Baba Bathra (Kel.)	Neg.	Negaʿim
Bekh.	Bekhoroth	Nidd.	Niddah
Ber.	Berakhoth	Pes.	Pesaḥim
Bets.	Betsah	RH	Rosh hashShanah
Erub.	ʿErubin	San.	Sanhedrin
Ḥull.	Ḥullin	Shabb.	Shabbath
Kel.	Kelim	Sheb.	Shebuʿoth
Ker.	Kerithoth	Sukk.	Sukkah
Ḳidd.	Ḳiddushim	Taan.	Taʿanith
Meg.	Megillah	Tam.	Tamid
Men.	Menaḥoth	Tem.	Temurah
Midd.	Middoth	Yeb.	Yebamoth
Naz.	Nazir	Zeb.	Zebaḥim

LIST OF BIBLIOGRAPHICAL ABBREVIATIONS

AI	Roland de Vaux, *Ancient Israel* (English translation, 1961)
AJSL	*American Journal of Semitic Languages and Literatures*
BA	*The Biblical Archaeologist*
BASOR	*Bulletin of the American Schools of Oriental Research*
BDB	*Hebrew and English Lexicon of the Old Testament* (edited by Brown, Driver, and Briggs)
CBQ	*The Catholic Biblical Quarterly*
DB	*Dictionary of the Bible* (2nd ed., 1963, edited by F. C. Grant and H. H. Rowley)
DIOT	N. H. Snaith, *The Distinctive Ideas of the Old Testament* (1944)
DOTT	*Documents from Old Testament Times* (1958, edited by D. Winton Thomas)
EB	*Encyclopaedia Biblica*
ERE	*Encyclopaedia of Religion and Ethics*
ET	*Expository Times*

HDB	Hastings' *Dictionary of the Bible* (5 vols.)
HPN	G. Buchanan Gray, *Hebrew Proper Names* (1896)
HUCA	*Hebrew Union College Annual*
ICC	International Critical Commentary
JA	*Journal Asiatique*
JBL	*Journal of Biblical Literature*
JEn	*Jewish Encyclopedia*
JNYF	N. H. Snaith, *The Jewish New Year Festival* (1947)
JSS	*Journal of Semitic Studies*
JTS	*Journal of Theological Studies*
KAT[3]	E. Schrader, *Die Keilinschriften und das alte Testament* (3rd ed., 1903, edited by H. Winckler and H. Zimmern)
MI	The Moabite Stone. See *DOTT* (E. Ullendorff), pp. 195–9
NSI	G. A. Cooke, *North Semitic Inscriptions* (1903)
OED	*Oxford English Dictionary*
OTT	G. von Rad, *Old Testament Theology* (1962)
QSPEF	*Quarterly Statement of the Palestine Exploration Fund*
RAPLA	S. A. Cook, *The Religion of Ancient Palestine in the Light of Archaeology* (Schweich Lectures, 1925)
RB	*Revue Biblique*
RS[2]	W. Robertson Smith, *Religion of the Semites* (2nd ed., 1901)
SOTS	R. de Vaux, *Studies in Old Testament Sacrifice* (1964)
VT	*Vetus Testamentum*
ZAW	*Zeitschrift für die alttestamentliche Wissenschaft*

BIBLIOGRAPHY OF RECENT PUBLICATIONS

INTRODUCTIONS

A. Bentzen, *Introduction to the Old Testament*, English ed., 2 vols., 1948–49, Copenhagen.

O. Eissfeldt, *Einleitung in das Alte Testament*, 3rd ed., 1964, Tübingen. English translation, Oxford, 1965.

R. H. Pfeiffer, *Introduction to the Old Testament*, 1941, New York.

A. Weiser, *Einleitung in das Alte Testament*, 5th ed., 1963, Göttingen. English translation of 4th ed., 1961, London.

Shorter and more popular:

G. W. Anderson, *A Critical Introduction to the Old Testament*, 1959, London.

C. R. North, 'Pentateuchal Criticism' in *The Old Testament and Modern Study*, 1951, edited by H. H. Rowley, Oxford.

R. H. Pfeiffer, *The Books of the Old Testament*, 1957, London.

H. H. Rowley, *The Growth of the Old Testament*, 1950, London.

H. H. Rowley, 'Introduction to the Old Testament: the Law' in *A Companion to the Bible*, 2nd ed., 1963, edited by H. H. Rowley, Edinburgh.

COMMENTARIES

H. Cazelles, *Le Lévitique*, 1951; *Les Nombres*, 1952 (Jerusalem Bible), Paris.

A. T. Chapman and A. W. Streane, *The Book of Leviticus*, rev. ed., 1914 (Cambridge Bible), Cambridge.

A. Drubbel, *Numeri uit de grondtekst vertaald en uitgelegd*, 1963 (*De Boeken van het Oude Testament*), Roermond en Maaseik.

K. Elliger, *Leviticus*, 1966 (Handbuch zum Alten Testament), Tübingen.

L. E. Elliott-Binns, *The Book of Numbers*, 1927 (Westminster Commentary), London.

G. B. Gray, *Numbers*, 1903 (*ICC*), Edinburgh.

J. H. Greenstone, *Numbers*, 1938 (Soncino Bible), Hindhead, Surrey.

P. Heinisch, *Leviticus*, 1951; *Numbers*, 1952 (Bonner Bibel), Bonn.

H. Kalt, *Genesis, Exodus, Leviticus*, 1947 (Herders Bibelkommentar), Freiburg.

A. R. S. Kennedy, *Leviticus and Numbers* (Century Bible), Edinburgh.

A. H. McNeile, *Numbers*, 1908 (Cambridge Bible), Cambridge.

J. Marsh and A. G. Butzer, *Numbers*, 1962 (Interpreter's Bible, vol. 2), New York and Nashville.

N. Micklem, *Leviticus*, 1962 (Interpreter's Bible, vol. 2), New York and Nashville.

M. Noth, *Das dritte Buch Mose, Leviticus übersetzt und erklärt*, 1962 (Das Alte Testament Deutsch), Göttingen. English translation, 1965, London.

H. Schneider, *Exodus, Leviticus, Numbers*, 1952 (Echter Bibel), Würzburg.

N. H. Snaith, 'Leviticus, Numbers' in *Peake's Commentary on the Bible*, rev. ed., edited by H. H. Rowley, 1962, Edinburgh.

J. G. Vink, *Leviticus uit de grondtekst vertaald en uitgelegd*, 1962 (De Boeken van het Oude Testament), Roermond en Maaseik.

SPECIAL STUDIES

W. F. Albright, 'The Oracles of Balaam', *JBL* 63 (1944) 207–33.
H. Cazelles, 'A propos du Pentateuque', *Biblica* 35 (1954) 279–98.
O. Eissfeldt, 'Die Komposition der Bileam-Erzählung', *ZAW* 57 (1939) 212–41.
O. Eissfeldt, 'Sinai-Erzählung und Bileamsprüche', *HUCA* 32 (1961) 179–90.
K. Elliger, 'Das Gesetz Leviticus 18', *ZAW* 67 (1955) 1–25.
L. E. Elliott-Binns, 'Some Problems of the Holiness Code', *ZAW* 67 (1955) 26–40.
G. B. Gray, *Sacrifice in the Old Testament*, 1925, Oxford.
M. Haran, 'The Uses of Incense in the ancient Israelite ritual', *VT* 10 (1960) 113–29.
A. R. Johnson, 'ḤESEḎ and ḤĀSÎḎ' in *Interpretationes ad VT pertinentes*, 1955, (Mowinckel Festschrift), 100–12.
K. Koch, *Die Priesterschrift von Ex. 25 bis Lev. 16*, 1959, Göttingen.
S. Mowinckel, 'Der Ursprung der Bilʿāmsage', *ZAW* 48 (1930) 233–71.
M. Noth, *Die Gesetze im Pentateuch*, 1940, Halle.
J. van der Ploeg, 'Studies in Hebrew Law', *CBQ* 12 (1950) 248–59, 416–27; 13 (1951) 28–43, 164–71, 296–307.
R. Rendtorff, *Die Gesetze in der Priesterschrift*, 1954, Göttingen.
H. Graf Reventlow, *Das Heiligkeitsgesetz*, 1961, Neukirchen.
R. de Vaux, *Les Institutions de l'Ancien Testament*, 2 vols., 1958 and 1960, Paris. English translation, *Ancient Israel, Its Life and Institutions*, 1961, London.
R. de Vaux, *Studies in Old Testament Sacrifice*, 1964, Cardiff.

INTRODUCTION TO THE BOOKS OF

LEVITICUS AND NUMBERS

INTRODUCTION

1. THE TITLES OF THE BOOKS

The official titles of these two books in the Authorized Version (AV), the Revised Version (RV) and the Revised Standard Version (RSV) are, 'The third/fourth book of Moses commonly [AV omits this] called Leviticus/Numbers.' The common names of all the five books of Moses are derived from the titles in the Septuagint (LXX) through the Vulgate (V). They are latinized Greek words, like the technical names of flowers, except for 'Numbers', which is a translation of a translation. Normally the LXX title was latinized by the Vulgate and the Vulgate title was continued in the English Versions. 'Leviticus' is the Vulgate's latinization of LXX *Leveitikon*, the Levitical (book). 'Numbers' is an English translation of Vulgate's *Numeri*, itself a translation of the Greek *Arithmoi*, but this is the exception. LXX sought in the titles of these five books to describe the contents: *Genesis*—the Beginning; *Exodos*—the Going Out (of Egypt); *Leveitikon*—the Levitical (book); *Arithmoi*—the Numbers; *Deuteronomion*—the Second law, due to the LXX rendering of Dt. 17.18, which in fact means 'a copy of this law'.

There is a reason for all this. It is not generally realized that up to *c.* A.D. 400 the Christian Bible was a Greek Bible, composed of LXX and the Greek New Testament. After the time of Jerome and until the Reformation, the Bible for all Christians in the West was Jerome's Latin Bible, and this still is the Bible of Roman Catholics in the edition authorized by Pope Clement VIII in the Papal Bull of 1592. The English edition of this is the Rheims-Douay Version of 1582 and 1609. For Protestants, the Bible is the Hebrew Old Testament and the Greek New Testament. Thus the history of the translation of the Bible into English is reflected in the titles of the first five books of the Old Testament. This is why the English titles are anglicized forms of latinized Greek words. Because of the way in which the Bible has come down to us, more attention than usual has been given in this commentary to the way in which LXX and V have interpreted the original Hebrew text. Further, since there are two main traditions of the exegesis of the Old Testament—Jewish and Christian—attention has also been given to Jewish exegesis, especially to the commentary of Rashi (A.D. 1040–1105), the greatest of all popular Jewish commentators.

The Jewish custom is to name the books by the first (or first significant) word: *Bᵉrēʾšîṯ* (in the beginning of), *Šᵉmôṯ* (names of), *Wayyiḵrāʾ* (and summoned), *Bᵉmiḏbar* (in the wilderness of), *Dᵉḇārîm* (words), and all five are known as the Law (*Tôrāh*), or 'the five-fifths of the Law' (*b. San.*, 44a). The word Pentateuch is from the Greek, 'the five-volume (book)', again through the Latin.

2. THE ARRANGEMENT AND CONTENTS OF THE BOOKS

To facilitate the study of the contents of these books, it is convenient to divide them into sections and sub-sections according to the nature of their contents.

LEVITICUS

The Book of Leviticus is best considered as consisting of five sections, four of which are from the Priestly tradition (P) and one from the Holiness Code (H). These sections can be summarized as follows:

FIRST SECTION. CHAPTERS **1–7** THE LAWS OF SACRIFICE
(All this section is from the Priestly tradition.)

A. **1.1–6.7.** *The manual for the people*
(a) **1.1–17.** The ritual of the whole-offering.
(b) **2.1–16.** The ritual of the grain-offering.
(c) **3.1–17.** The ritual of the shared-offering.
(d) **4.1–5.13.** The ritual of the sin-offering.
(e) **5.14–6.7.** The ritual of the compensation-offering.

B. **6.8–7.38.** *The manual for the priests*
(a) **6.8–13.** The ritual of the whole-offering.
(b) **6.14–18.** The ritual of the grain-offering.
(c) **6.19–23.** The ritual of the daily grain-offering.
(d) **6.24–30.** The ritual of the sin-offering.
(e) **7.1–10.** The ritual of the compensation-offering.

(f) **7.11–36.** The ritual of the shared-offering, including (verses 19–21) a digression on food *taboos* and (verses 22–27) a prohibition against eating any fat or any blood.
(g) **7.37–38.** Summary of the whole section.

SECOND SECTION. CHAPTERS **8–10** THE PRIESTHOOD

(All this section is from the Priestly tradition.)

(a) **8.1–36.** The consecration of Aaron and his sons.
(b) **9.1–24.** The installation of Aaron and his sons.
(c) **10.1–7.** Nadab and Abihu: the terrible fate of the layman who acts as priest.
(d) **10.8–11.** No intoxicants for officiating priests.
(e) **10.12–20.** The proper disposal of the priest's share.

THIRD SECTION. CHAPTERS **11–16** RITUAL UNCLEANNESS AND PURIFICATION RITES

(All this section is from the Priestly tradition.)

(a) **11.1–47.** Clean and unclean creatures.
(b) **12.1–8.** Purification of women after childbirth.
(c) **13.1–59.** The tests for leprosy.
(d) **14.1–57.** Purification rites.
(e) **15.1–33.** Unclean discharges ('issues').
(f) **16.1–34.** The Day of Atonement.

FOURTH SECTION. CHAPTERS **17–26** THE HOLINESS CODE

(This section is from the Holiness Code, but with interpolations by the editors of the Priestly tradition.)

(a) **17.1–9.** All slaughter is sacrifice.
(b) **17.10–16.** Prohibition against eating blood.
(c) **18.1–20.27.** Social laws.
(d) **21.1–22.33.** Sacred persons and sacred things.
(e) **23.1–44.** The sacred calendar.
(f) **24.1–4.** The lamps of the Tabernacle.
(g) **24.5–9.** The bread of the Presence.
(h) **24.10–23.** Laws against blasphemy and assault.

(i) **25.1–55.** The sacred calendar (continued), with laws concerning the redemption of property.
(j) **26.1–46.** Concluding exhortation.

FIFTH SECTION. CHAPTER **27** THE COMMUTATION OF VOWS AND TITHES

(All this section is from the Priestly tradition.)

(a) **27.1–29.** Vows.
(b) **27.30–34.** Tithes.

NUMBERS

The Book of Numbers is best considered as consisting of three sections, all of which are mainly from the Priestly tradition, but with earlier traditions interwoven. These sections can be summarized as follows:

FIRST SECTION. CHAPTERS **1.1–10.10** WHAT HAPPENED AT SINAI

(a) **1.1–54.** The first census.
(b) **2.1–34.** The disposition of the tribes in camp.
(c) **3.1–4.** The descendants of Aaron.
(d) **3.5–13.** The Levites are to serve the Aaronites.
(e) **3.14–51.** The census of the Levites.
(f) **4.1–49.** The duties and numbers of adult Levites.
(g) **5.1–6.27.** Miscellaneous regulations, containing especially (5.11–31) the ordeal of jealousy, (6.1–21) the Nazirite regulations, and (6.22–27) the Aaronic blessing.
(h) **7.1–89.** The offerings of the leaders of the tribes.
(i) **8.1–4.** The lighting of the lamps.
(j) **8.5–26.** The purification of the Levites.
(k) **9.1–14.** The supplementary Passover.
(l) **9.15–23.** The fiery cloud.
(m) **10.1–10.** The silver trumpets.

SECOND SECTION. CHAPTERS **10.11–20.13** WHAT HAPPENED IN THE WILDERNESS

(a) **10.11–28.** The Israelites break camp.
(b) **10.29–32.** Hobab returns home.

(c) **10.33–36.** The people set out.
(d) **11.1–3.** The place called Taberah.
(e) **11.4–35.** The quails and the manna.
(f) **12.1–16.** Moses is unique.
(g) **13.1–14.45.** The spies.
(h) **15.1–41.** Rules concerning sacrifices, and other matters.
(i) **16.1–50.** The rebellions of Korah and of Dathan and Abiram.
(j) **17.1–13.** The story of Aaron's rod.
(k) **18.1–32.** The priests and Levites: their duties and privileges.
(l) **19.1–22.** The red heifer: contact with the dead.
(m) **20.1–13.** The final events at Kadesh.

THIRD SECTION. CHAPTERS **20.14–36.13** WHAT HAPPENED FROM KADESH TO THE PLAINS OF MOAB

(a) **20.14–21.** The people are refused transit facilities through Edom.
(b) **20.22–29.** The death of Aaron.
(c) **21.1–3.** The fight with a king of the Negeb.
(d) **21.4–9.** The 'brazen' serpent.
(e) **21.10–20.** The journey from Mount Hor to the Plains of Moab.
(f) **21.21–35.** The victories over Sihon and Og, the two Amorite kings.
(g) **22.1–24.25.** Balak and Balaam.
(h) **25.1–5.** The affair of Baal-peor.
(i) **25.6–18.** The zeal of Phinehas.
(j) **26.1–65.** The second census.
(k) **27.1–11.** The daughters of Zelophehad.
(l) **27.12–23.** Joshua is chosen as Moses' successor.
(m) **28.1–29.40.** The list of offerings.
(n) **30.1–16.** The validity of vows, especially women's vows.
(o) **31.1–54.** The Holy War against Midian.
(p) **32.1–42.** Reuben, Gad and half Manasseh settle east of the Jordan.
(q) **33.1–49.** The itinerary from Egypt to the Plains of Moab.
(r) **33.50–56.** The final instructions before the crossing.
(s) **34.1–29.** The ideal boundaries of Canaan.
(t) **35.1–8.** The cities of the Levites.
(u) **35.9–34.** The cities of refuge and the law of homicide.
(v) **36.1–13.** The daughters of Zelophehad.

3. THE SOURCES OF THE BOOKS

The great majority of Old Testament scholars do not accept as authentic the tradition that Moses wrote the whole of the Pentateuch. They prefer to say that Moses was the 'father' of Israelite law, and that traditionally all the law was ascribed to him, just as David was the 'father' of Hebrew psalmody and Solomon the 'father' of Hebrew wisdom. The Pentateuch is recognized as being the work of more than one author or, more accurately, of more than one group of authors. It comes from more than one period of Hebrew history, and portrays widely differing conceptions of God and of theology and history. It is a compilation from at least five different sources, traditions which have solidified at dates differing by many centuries. Details of the steps by which these conclusions have been reached can be found in such smaller volumes as H. H. Rowley, *The Growth of the Old Testament* (1950), and G. W. Anderson, *A Critical Introduction to the Old Testament* (1959), and in two surveys, the article, 'Introduction to the Old Testament' by H. H. Rowley in *A Companion to the Bible* (2nd ed., edited by H. H. Rowley, 1963) and the article, 'Pentateuchal Criticism' by C. R. North in *The Old Testament and Modern Study* (edited by H. H. Rowley, Oxford Paperbacks, 1961). Full details are to be found in the larger 'Introductions': those by R. H. Pfeiffer (2nd ed., 1952), Bentzen (2nd ed., 1952), A. Weiser (5th German ed., 1966: English tr. of 4th ed., 1961), and O. Eissfeldt (3rd German ed., 1966; English tr., 1965).

Thirty years ago the orthodox modern scholar accepted the theory that the study of the origin and development of the Pentateuch involved the study of literary documents used by the various editors. Of these there were held to be five. The earliest is the Jehovist (Yahwist) document, designated by the letter J. It is of southern origin and was written about 850 B.C. Next, there is the Elohist document, designated by the letter E. It is of northern origin and was written down about 750 B.C. These two documents were combined into JE about 700 B.C. The third document is the central core of the Book of Deuteronomy (substantially most of Dt. 4.44–26.19), designated by the letter D, and held to be the scroll found by the priest Hilkiah during the renovations of the Temple by king Josiah, *c.* 621 B.C. This was enlarged into the present book of Deuteronomy during the Exile, *c.* 550 B.C. The fourth document is the Priestly Code, designated by the letter P, associated with Ezra's reforms, and including in its final form the Code of Holiness (Lev. 17–26), designated by the letter H. Finally all was embodied by the P-editors into the present Pentateuch, after the time of Ezra, but sufficiently early for the Samaritans to take a copy with them and use it as an authoritative document when they broke away from the Jerusalem Temple and priesthood (? *c.* 350 B.C.). Ezek. 40–48 is regarded as being in between D and P and not far distant in date or in ideals from H.

Various attempts have been made to deal with inconsistencies within the four major sources themselves. J has been divided into J^1 and J^2, since, apart from other divergencies, parts of J do not seem to involve knowledge of the Flood story. Eissfeldt proposed a *Laienquelle*, a Lay Source (L), at the other end of the scale from P with its priestly emphasis and concerns. Morgenstern posits an early ninth-century Kenite source (K). Some scholars have found as many as nine different strata in P. Thus the analyses have grown more and more elaborate, until some scholars have thought to abandon the method of literary criticism, and have held that the idea of four/five main sources is unsound. The position taken by some Scandinavian scholars is that such literary analysis is based on Western ideas of a consistency which was unknown in the ancient Near East. Notable among these scholars of the Uppsala school is Ivan Engnell, who writes in terms of two great collections of traditions, the one consisting of Genesis–Numbers and the other of Deuteronomy–2 Kings. The first group, a Tetrateuch, is the 'P-work'. It contains many traditions comprising narratives and laws. The laws were written down at an early stage, but the narratives consist of oral traditions, committed to writing at a late stage. These P-editors had their own traditional material which is roughly the P-material of the literary critics, but they added other material which cannot now be assigned to any particular times or localities. The Danish scholar, J. Pedersen, had seen the core of all the traditions in the Passover legend, Exod. 1–15, originally a liturgy used in the annual celebration of the deliverance by Yahweh of the people from the Egyptian bondage, that theme which is dominant in so much of Hebrew religion. Engnell adopted this theory of Pedersen's as the core of his P-work. Similarly, says Engnell, there was a D-work, compiled in much the same way as the other, mostly transmitted by oral tradition, and both works, as we now have them, belong as written documents to the fifth to fourth century B.C., the times of Nehemiah and Ezra.

Two German scholars have made important contributions to the solution of the problem of the origins of the Pentateuch, but both have started with the literary scheme of J, E, D and P. Martin Noth has pointed out that there is practically nothing of D in the Tetrateuch (Genesis–Numbers), and that there is virtually nothing of P in Deuteronomy–2 Kings. Thus we have two great literary works, Genesis–Numbers which consists of a framework of P with the JE-material woven into it, and Deuteronomy–2 Kings which consists of D-material, some of it based on JE-material, but definitely nothing of P, apart from a few verses in the last chapter of Deuteronomy. The P-work belongs to the post-exilic period, the time of the establishment of Judaism with its rigorous rules of Habdalah (Separation) and the Temple and its sacrifices as the central feature of the religion; the D-work belongs to the latter part of the Babylonian exile when some hope appeared of a restoration of nation and cult in Palestine.

Gerhard von Rad starts with two great cultic centres, Gilgal and Shechem. The most basic element is the ancient Credo of Dt. 26.5–10. Yahweh rescued Israel out of slavery in Egypt and brought them into 'this land, a land flowing with milk and honey'. This is the central theme not only of the Pentateuch but of the whole of Hebrew religion, and it was part of the liturgy of the Feast of Weeks as celebrated at Gilgal. The J-tradition was concerned with the events at Sinai and the core of this belonged to the autumnal feast at Shechem. This feast involved the annual renewal of the covenant. The J-editor added the stories of the patriarchs and the even earlier stories of the beginnings of things.

Modern scholarship suggests therefore a combined literary and oral origin and development. We have two great traditions: the P-tradition consisting of Genesis–Numbers, and the D-tradition consisting of Deuteronomy–2 Kings. The D-history reached its final form *c.* 550 B.C., soon after Evil Merodach of Babylon released the captive Jehoiachin on parole, granted him special favours and gave some hope of better things to come, 2 Kg. 25.27–30. The P-history reached its final form in the post-exilic period *c.* 400 B.C., the precise date depending on the date of Ezra's reforms and the extent to which it is believed that Ezra based his reforms on the P-regulations. Shechem was certainly the ancient cultic centre of the tribes, and even as late as the time of Rehoboam the king of Israel had to go there to be confirmed in his kingship (1 Kg. 12.1, 'to make him king'). It is probable that much of the E-material comes from Shechem, and that the ancient traditions were collected at the various shrines with Shechem the chief of the 'all-Israel' shrines. Thus the E-material is not 'northern' so much as 'old Israel', and this probably explains why the name used in it for 'God' is Elohim, the ordinary Hebrew word for 'God'. Possibly Gilgal was the centre at which most of the J-material gathered, though a good deal is to be said for Hebron, which was to the South what Shechem was to the North. We have to envisage the people making pilgrimages to the various shrines and there hearing the story of that shrine, how it came to be an Israelite shrine and how on later occasions also God was heard there and Israelites received blessings there. In course of time the traditions are collected, with the major shrines such as Shechem and Gilgal or Hebron or Bethel making the largest contributions. At some date these oral traditions were written down, but it is a mistake to suppose that written traditions are necessarily more accurately transmitted than oral traditions. Even in Britain the guides at local places of historic interest repeat their story year after year with extraordinary accuracy. In *A Pattern of Islands* (John Murray, 1952), Arthur Grimble writes of Nei Tearia 'renowned for her authority as a teller of stories': how she told him the myth of man's expulsion from the Happy Land of Matang. He says that fifteen years later, when he was again in her particular island of the Gilbert Group, he took the script of her earlier narrative for checking, and she repeated the story word for word. When this was pointed out, she replied: 'Sir, and shall it be otherwise? Each *karaki* [history] has its own body from the generations of old. These are the words of our grandfathers' fathers, and thus we pass them on to our children's children.' (Chapter i, p. 60 in the Reprint Society edition.)

The combination of J and E into JE must be assigned to some period of attempted unification of north and south, possibly the time of Hezekiah. The D-material is generally associated with Josiah's reform so far as the central portion is concerned (Dt. 4.44–8.20, 10.12–11.25, Chs. 12–26, 28.1–4, 43–46, 29.1) with the rest added *c.* 550 B.C. The P-material consists of priestly material belonging to many periods and places, different ages and different shrines, all brought together by priestly editors and written down in the post-exilic period, though some may have been written at earlier dates. The largest single element embodied in the P-material is the Code of Holiness (Lev. 17–26), though this itself is a collection of material of different origins. See L. E. Elliott-Binns, 'Some Problems of the Holiness Code', *ZAW* 67, 1955, 26–40.

The whole of Leviticus is composed of material from P and H. Chapters 1–16 and 27 are entirely P. Chapters 17–22 and 26 are undiluted H, but chapters 23–25 of the original Code of Holiness have been edited by the P-editors. The larger part of Numbers is composed of P-material (1.1–10.28, 16.35–19.22, 25.6–36.13). The rest is from JE with elements from P but the story of Balaam is true JE material. Num. 21.33–35 is regarded as a later insertion; it is virtually Dt. 3.1–3 with the first person changed to the third person. By far the oldest parts of the book are the short poetic fragments, including the oracles attributed to Balaam, though Mowinckel ('Der Ursprung der Bil-'am Sage', *ZAW* 48, 1930, 233–71) thinks that the oracles in Num. 24 are from the time of Mesha of Moab (ninth century), whilst Rudolph and Weiser think of the times of Saul and David. Albright ('The Oracles of Balaam', *JBL* 63, 1944, 207–33) holds that they have affinities with Ugarit, and he identifies the home of Balaam with the land of *Amau* in north Syria (*BASOR*, no. 118, 1950, f. n.). See also Eissfeldt ('Sinai-Erzählung und Bileamsprüche', *HUCA* 32, 1961, 179–90) and Mauchline ('The Balaam-Balak Songs and Saga', *Studia Semitica et Orientalia*, 1945, 73–94). Such fragments as Num. 10.35f., 21.14f,. 21.17f., 21.27–30 are certainly ancient, and the blessing of the Aaronic priests (Num. 6.24–27) may well have a long and independent history.

4. THE HISTORY OF THE PRIESTHOOD

There are three formal descriptions of priests in the Old Testament: that of P, 'the priests the sons of Aaron'; that of D, 'the priests, the Levites'; that of Ezek. 40–48, 'the priests the Levites, the sons of Zadok' (44.15). The three statements are: Levites are priests, Levites descended from Zadok are priests, men (Levites) descended from Aaron are priests.

In the earliest days the patriarchs were priests, each head of a 'father's house' being priest in his own house. The patriarchs built altars and themselves offered sacrifices on them: Noah (Gen. 8.20), Abram (Gen. 12.8, 22.9), Isaac (Gen. 26.25), Jacob (Gen. 35.7). Indeed, the picture we get is of the patriarchs moving from place to place throughout Palestine, building an altar at each temporary settlement, and there offering sacrifice and calling 'upon the name of the Lord'. Melchizedek was 'priest of God Most High' (Gen. 14.18), and Jethro, Moses' father-in-law, was priest of Midian and 'offered a burnt offering and sacrifices to God' (Exod. 18.1, 12). If a close and unique relationship with God, seeing God face to face, being time and again the sole intermediary between God and the people and between the people and God, creating the whole institutional and sacrificial religion of Israel—if all these things are the functions of a priest, then Moses was the greatest priest of all time (Exod. 19.14; Ps. 99.6). Indeed, in Exod. 19.24 Moses is to bring Aaron with him up the mountain, but must 'not let the priests and the people break through to come up to the Lord'.

Kings offered sacrifices: David (2 Sam. 24.25), Solomon (1 Kg. 3.15), Ahaz (2 Kg. 16.13), and Adonijah also as part of his claim to succeed his father David as king (1 Kg. 1.9). David's sons were priests (2 Sam. 8.18), presumably as deputies for their father. Zabud son of Nathan 'was priest and king's friend'; see the list of Solomon's officials (1 Kg. 4.1–6). Possibly this Nathan was Solomon's full brother (1 Chr. 3.5), but he may have been a son of Nathan the prophet to whom Solomon was primarily indebted for the fact that he ever became king (1 Kg. 1.11–27), though the name is a common one. According to 2 Sam. 20.26, Ira the Jairite 'was also David's priest', but AV (and RVm) found this so difficult that they rendered it 'a chief ruler (minister)', perhaps influenced by 1 Chr. 18.17 and 2 Sam. 8.18.

Each head of a family, then, was his own priest in the earliest days, but he could install one of his sons as priest. This is what Micah the Ephraimite did (Jg. 17.5), and presumably this is how David could appoint his sons as priests. But Moses in the days of the Wandering was priest *par excellence*, and so in later days was the king, though there came a time when the king's right to burn incense was disputed by the Aaronite priests (so, at least, 2 Chr. 26.18, which represents not what was thought in king Uzziah's time, but what was believed by the Chronicler). But even in the time of Micah the Ephraimite, it was better to have a Levite as priest, so that when the Levite from 'Bethlehem in Judah, of the family of Judah' came to him as a homeless wanderer, Micah made him 'a father and a priest' (Jg. 17.7, 10).

The relation of the tribe of Levi and the priesthood is complicated and much debated. A full discussion can be seen in G. B. Gray, *Sacrifice in the Old Testament* (1925), pp. 242–47; also *AI*, pp. 367–71. At one time Levi was a secular tribe like the rest (Gen. 34 and 49), but in Dt. 33.8–11 Levi, though listed among the sons of Israel, has ceased to be a secular tribe and is now a priestly caste. One probability is that Simeon and Levi were both divided and scattered (Gen. 49.7), so that both became attached to Judah. For Simeon, see Jg. 1.1–3; Jos. 15.26–32, 42, and 19.1–8; for Levi, see Jg. 17.7, 19.1. Possibly Levi would tend to develop priestly functions because Moses was a Levite, but there is evidence that in the Minaean colony of El-'Olā the word *lawi'a* denoted some kind of cultic official (Gray, op. cit., pp. 242–44). Possibly the development of a secular Levi into a priestly Levi was assisted by the association of the name with the root *l-w-h* (attach), dating from a time when the custom was developing, as in Jg. 17.10, 19, of preferring a Levite to anyone else. Certainly Samuel the Ephraimite (1 Sam. 1.1) became a Levite (1 Chr. 6.28) and the same transformation took place in the case of Obed-edom (1 Chr. 16.4f.), who actually was a Philistine from Gath (2 Sam. 6.10).

The family of Eli were priests in Egypt and also of the Ark in Shiloh (1 Sam. 2.27–36), but disaster overtook them, first when the Philistines captured the Ark at Aphek and Hophni and Phinehas were killed (1 Sam. 4.10f.), and later when Doeg, at Saul's command, massacred the priests at Nob and all their families, Abiathar only escaping (1 Sam. 22.11–23). The presumption is that the priests at Nob were refugees from Shiloh, generally understood to have been destroyed by the Philistines after the battle of Aphek. Later we find Zadok and Abiathar installed as priests in Jerusalem in the time of David. Zadok, generally thought to belong to the ancient Jebusite priesthood of Jerusalem, was continued in his office by David when he captured the city; see H. H. Rowley, 'Zadok and Nehushtan', *JBL* 58, (1939), 113–41. In the *coup d'état* through which Solomon became king, Zadok supported the successful claimant, but Abiathar supported Adonijah and was exiled to Anathoth. Jeremiah was perhaps one of his descendants (Jer. 1.1). All the Jerusalem priests, therefore, from Solomon to the destruction of the Temple in 587 B.C. were Zadokites. After the exile, according to Num. 25.13 P, God made 'the covenant of a perpetual priesthood' with 'Phinehas the son of Eleazar, son of Aaron the priest'. This Eleazar is the elder of the two surviving sons of Aaron, and it was from him that the Zadokites claimed descent in the Chronicler's time (1 Chr. 24.3). Further, although the priesthood of the P-tradition is always called 'the priests the sons of Aaron', yet two thirds of these post-exilic priests were Zadokites who claimed descent through Eleazar, and one third were 'Aaronites' who claimed descent through Ithamar, the younger of the two surviving sons of Aaron (1 Chr. 24.4). The Chronicler claims that this division and these proportions went back to the time of David (1 Chr. 24.3), but this doubtless is part of his general attitude whereby he reads back what is, or indeed what ought to be, into the incidents of former days. In the Qumran (Dead Sea) Scrolls, in 1 QS iii, there is a reference to 'the sons of Zadok, the priests, who keep the covenant and who seek his will', and there are also other similar references in the Scrolls, CD vi, and often in 1QSa; and in 1QSb. Zech. 3.1–9 gives an account of the struggle in which the Zadokite Joshua was involved to secure the Zadokite tenure of the high priesthood in the Second Temple, but he and his descendants were confirmed in their 'right of access' (verse 7), and there is every reason to agree that the Zadokites held the high-priesthood until the death of Onias III (de Vaux, *AI*, p. 401).

Before the Reformation of Josiah the situation was: Levite priests in the south, non-Levite priests in the north, but descendants of Gershom son of Moses at Dan in the far north (Jg. 18.30), and possibly the sons of Aaron at Bethel. This last is the suggestion of R. H. Kennett ('The Origin of the Aaronite Priesthood', *JTS* 6, 1905, 161–86), who supposed that the Aaronites moved into Jerusalem during the Exile, when the Zadokites had been deported, and were too firmly entrenched afterwards to be evicted. The suggestion that they came from Bethel depends largely on the fact that the sacred cry for the Golden Calf (Exod. 32.4) is precisely that for the bull at Bethel (1 Kg. 12.28), and Aaron was the priest of the Golden Calf (Exod. 32.1–6, 22–25). Further, the name of Aaron is not in the original J-tradition, and in the E-tradition his only contact with the Sacred Tent is for reproof (Num. 12.1–13). When Josiah sought to reform and centralize the worship he eliminated the non-Levitical priests of the North and apparently sought to bring all the local Levitical priests of the South to Jerusalem. At least, this is what Deuteronomy assumes with its equation of Levites and priests; see also Mal. 2.4, 3.3. But Josiah was unable to establish the Levites as full sacrificing priests in company with the Zadokites (2 Kg. 23.9), and Ezek. 44 is strongly against any Levites other than the sons of Zadok performing priestly duties. According to Ezek. 44.4–14 these other Levites were responsible for all the idolatries at the provincial shrines, and this is why they were relegated to menial tasks. This is the position in the P-traditions (Lev. 8; Num. 18.2–7), though without such wholesale condemnation. The distinction is equally clear in the Chronicler's writings, but he does nevertheless seek to give the Levites an honourable place in the administration of sacred duties.

5. THE TEMPLE SACRIFICES

According to P, there were five main Temple Sacrifices: the *'ôlāh* (Lev. 1.3, the whole-offering), the *minḥāh* (Lev. 2.1, the grain-offering), the *zeḇaḥ šᵉlāmîm* (Lev. 3.1, sacrifice of peace-offering), the *ḥaṭṭā'ṯ* (Lev. 4.3, the sin-offering), and the *'āšām* (Lev. 5.14, 6.6 (Heb 5.25), the guilt-offering). These English equivalents are the traditional English renderings as in AV and RV, except that AV has 'burnt sacrifice' for the first, and for the second AV has 'meat-offering', which in early seventeenth-century English meant 'food-offering', and RV has 'meal offering'.

The word *'ôlāh* means 'that which is made to go up', either to go up on to the altar or that which is to go up, ascend to God. This offering (*ḳorbān*, lit. that which is brought near) consisted of a ritually clean and in all respects perfect animal, a bull from the herd, a ram or he-goat from the flock, or a bird (Lev. 1). The blood was poured out round the sides of the altar. The whole of the body of the animal was cut into joints, the legs and entrails washed clean, and the whole of the animal apart from the hide was burnt on the altar. It was properly a 'whole-offering', since the essential point was that the whole of the animal was offered up to God. In so far as it was burnt, this sacrifice was an *'iššeh* (fire-offering), a term applied to everything that was burnt in the altar fire.

The word *zeḇaḥ* means 'slaughter'. The meaning of the word *šᵉlāmîm* is usually given as 'peace-offerings', but there is considerable difference of opinion. Some maintain that this sacrifice was intended to create an alliance between the god and mutually between the people who ate the flesh of the animal. Some think of it as a communion sacrifice partaken of by the god and the worshipper. Others think of the idea of fulfilment and think of it as a joyous occasion in thankfulness for blessings received. In Ugarit the word *šlmm* is used of gifts sent as pledges of peace, but the singular form *šlm* is some liquid poured out on the ground (oil, or possibly blood) to secure fertility. See de Vaux, *SOTS*, pp. 46f., and R. Schmid, *Das Bundesopfer in Israel* (1964). The Hebrew *zeḇaḥ* originally meant 'slaughter' and referred to the slaughter of any beast for food. The animal was slaughtered on a *mizbēaḥ*, lit 'a place of slaughter', which in early times could be a suitable stone (1 Sam. 14.33), but later was a formal altar. The blood was poured out on the ground, as in the Ugarit *šlm*, and the worshippers ate the flesh. There were sacred meals at the shrines, where the blood was poured on the altar, the intestinal fat was burnt on the altar, the priest had a share of the flesh, and the worshippers ate the rest of the flesh. When the worship was centralized at Jerusalem, a clear distinction had to be made between slaughter for food and slaughter for the sacred meal. The share of the priest varied through the centuries, but in P the right thigh was a *t^e^rûmāh* (EVV, heave-offering) and the breast was a *t^e^nûpāh* (EVV, wave-offering). The former was the perquisite of the officiating priest, and the latter the perquisite of the whole priesthood. Both words mean 'that which is lifted off'; see note on Lev. 7.14. It is unlikely that the *zeḇaḥ* was thought of as a communion meal of the god and his worshippers, since the god received no more and no less than was the case of any other sacrifice—apart, that is, from the whole-offering, of which he received the whole. See de Vaux, *SOTS*, pp. 237–42. The more likely explanation is that the flesh of the slaughtered animal was regarded as holy food, and the worshipper was 'eating the god'. Probably this led to the interpretation of the word *š^e^lāmîm* as meaning the good health and well-being of those who ate the sacred food, but the word in its singular form may well have referred originally to the essential 'life' of the animal contained in the blood and the fat (Lev. 17.11, 7.22–27), which is God's food (Lev. 3.16).

The word *minḥāh* means 'tribute, gift', that which is given by the inferior to the superior. In P, *minḥāh* is the term given to all edible offerings which are not the flesh of animals. Mostly, it is composed of cereals—hence the frequent rendering 'cereal-offering', 'grain-offering', but it did include first-fruits of every kind. Usually most of the *minḥāh* went to the priests, and a token (*'azkārāh*, usually translated 'memorial') was burnt on the altar. This token shows that originally the whole of the *minḥāh* was a tribute-gift to God, and indeed the grain which formed part of the Daily Offering (*tāmîḏ*, Num. 28.1–8) was part of the *'ôlāh* (whole-offering) and all of the *minḥāh* was part of the *'iššeh* (fire-offering). The early significance of the *minḥāh* is uncertain, but it seems probable that originally the *'ôlāh* was the herdsman's whole-offering to God, and the *minḥāh* was the agriculturalist's whole-offering to God, and that both were combined in the *tāmîḏ*, the regular daily offering of the Second Temple, which from Exod. 29.38–46 P may well be regarded as being the centre and core of the whole sacrificial system.

The word *ḥaṭṭā'ṯ* means 'sin, sin-offering'. This offering consisted of a living creature, usually an animal but it could be a bird and even in cases of real poverty some fine flour (Lev. 5.11). If it was a living creature, bull or goat or ram, the fat (as was normal) was burnt on the altar, the blood was poured out at the foot of the altar, and the flesh was entirely disposed of. If the priests were involved personally, either individually or as members of the whole community, then the flesh was taken outside the camp and there destroyed, but if the priests were not involved, then they ate the whole of the flesh. The sin-offering was due in cases where the offence was unwitting and it was not realized until afterwards that anything was amiss.

The word *'āšām* means 'compensation, equivalent, substituted', and the root means 'guilty' in the sense of liable to pay. This so-called 'guilt-offering' was due in all cases where damage had been done and loss had been suffered. In most cases the loss could be estimated, and the offender had to make full restoration plus 20 per cent, and he also had to bring an animal as an offering. The blood of this was poured on the altar, not at the base as for a sin-offering, and the priests ate the flesh of the animal. It could be that the offence was unwitting, and it is this aspect which has caused confusion (Lev. 4.1–5.13, see notes); but the essential element is that damage has been done and usually that damage can be assessed.

The Passover sacrifice was not a Temple sacrifice. It was essentially a home festival, though in later times the lamb was slaughtered in the Temple and the blood passed up to the altar.

The word *ḳorbān* is used in two senses. In its wider sense it means an 'offering', any gift or animal that it 'brought near' (the verb is *ḳārab̲*) to the Temple or to the altar. But there is a narrower meaning, which is that it is a gift for the maintenance of the Temple and its service. In this respect, the *ḳorbān* differs from the *ḳōd̲eš* (plural *ḳod̲āšîm*, usually translated 'holy things'). These holy gifts are for the maintenance of the Temple personnel, and the 'most holy things' *ḳōd̲eš ḳod̲āšîm* are for the absolute and exclusive use of the priests. There are two types of these; the *t'rûmāh* (the so-called 'heave-offering') which was for the individual officiating priest, and the *t'nûp̄āh* (the so-called 'wave-offering') which was for the whole priesthood.

In post-exilic times incense (*ḳ'ṭōret̲*) was offered. The word primarily means 'that which goes up as smoke' and before the exile it meant 'sacrifice'. Apparently incense was introduced into the Temple cult after the return from Babylonia. M. Haran ('The uses of incense in the ancient Israelite ritual', *VT* 10, 1960, 123f.) is of the opinion that the practice of burning incense in censers came into Canaan from Egypt long before the Israelite settlement, and was absorbed into Israelite worship at an early date. Nevertheless, the certain references to the burning of incense are in the P-tradition and in such comparatively late passages as 2 Chr. 26.16, and there does not seem to be any unquestionable evidence to show that incense was used in Yahweh worship before the exile.

There were various other offerings in the fully developed priestly tradition: the drink-offering (*nesek̠*), firstlings and first-fruits, special ordination sacrifices, and so forth. For further details of these, see the notes.

6. THE PRIESTLY TRADITIONS (P)

The amount of non-P material in Leviticus and Numbers is comparatively small, and is found in Numbers in the earlier traditions of the journey to Kadesh and round Edom to the east of the Jordan, opposite Jericho, with the long sojourn at Kadesh; and in the Balaam stories, which also embody poems from other sources, perhaps more ancient. Within the P-material in Leviticus there is the Holiness Code, chapters 17–26 (H, but with occasional editorial insertions by the P-editors).

The P-tradition as a whole is concerned with the history of the world from the beginning up to the time when the children of Israel were poised for the attack on Canaan across the river Jordan. All history is written from 'a point of view', and it is impossible for any history whatever to be written without a bias of some kind. The writer is bound to interpret what he writes. Even if he is of the opinion that there is no discernible plan in the series of events he describes, then his history must be written from that point of view. In the P-tradition this 'point of view' is more obvious than in most histories; religious and sacred. Indeed, as in the case of the writings of the Chronicler and in Ezek. 40–48, it sometimes verges on what in modern times is called Propaganda. The zeal of their house has eaten them up. The writing down of P-traditions belongs to the period when post-exilic Judaism was being firmly established with its strict

Habdālāh rules. *Habdālāh* is the technical word for that principle of separation which is the essence of post-exilic Judaism. This concerns the strict maintenance of the distinctions between what is ritually clean *ṭāhôr* and what is ritually unclean *ṭāmē'*, between what is holy *ḳōdeš* and what is non-holy, 'common', *ḥôl*. These distinctions involve a clear distinction between Israelites and non-Israelites, between the people of the covenant which is sealed by circumcision and the uncircumcised non-Israelites, a clear distinction also between the Temple personnel and the common people, and a clear distinction within the Temple personnel between priest and Levite. Further, as in the case of the Chronicler, and perhaps to an even greater extent, the priestly editors read back the institutions they knew and the theories they accepted into the whole story from beginning to end. In this they differ from the writers of Ezek. 40–48, who project their ideas and ideals into the future. P and Chronicles project their ideas and ideals into the past. This projection into the past involves, among other things, the beliefs that the system of sacrifices, the constitution of the priesthood and the Levites, and the detailed plans of the Second Temple go back to Sinai. It was Moses accompanied by Aaron who instituted all the institutions of Judaism.

For full details as to the P-traditions in Genesis and Exodus, see the commentaries on those books. Here it must suffice to point out that the P-editors began their four-volume history (as it is now) with their account of Creation by Habdalah, the principle of separation, making a division between things, and this they did in Gen. 1.1–2.4a. All was formless and empty, but God separated (the verb is *hibdîl*) between things, light from darkness, the waters above the firmament from the waters below the firmament, seas and dry land, day and night. All vegetation, both plants and shrubs and trees, was distinct, every species and each species with its own distinctive seed. The heavenly luminaries were to be signs (omens) to fix the sacred seasons and to regulate the calendar, which for P means the sacred calendar. And finally God hallows the sabbath, which was the day on which he came to the end (*šābaṯ*) of his work and rested (the later meaning of *šābaṯ*). The Flood was due to the break-up of the separation between the waters (7.11, 8.2a to 'closed', with 1.6f.). The P-traditions are notable for the genealogies throughout, since race and succession are of primary importance where any theory of exclusiveness is concerned. After the Flood, man is permitted to eat flesh for the first time (1.29 and 9.4), but there must be no blood in the flesh, since the blood is the life. The disposal of the blood of slaughtered animals becomes of considerable concern to the P-editors, and with it the disposal of the intestinal fat. God makes a covenant with Noah (9.8) and his posterity and the rainbow in the sky is the sign that there shall never again be a flood (to hold up the firmament and prevent another break through). God makes a covenant with Abram and his descendants. Abraham is Abram's covenant-name and circumcision is the sign of the covenant. In Exodus the P-editors have interwoven the older JE-traditions with their own P-traditions. One significant element is that Aaron is the partner of Moses. The P-tradition comes to its own in the Passover regulations (Exod. 12.1–20, 43–51), and Exod. 25–31 with its sequel, chapters 35–40, are entirely P, instructions with regard to the Tabernacle and its contents, the vestments of the priests and the placing of the holy vessels, and, in 35–40, the detailed fulfilment of the instructions. This Tabernacle is P's 'temple in the desert' and is part of P's projection into the Mosaic past of the institutions of his day. As Josephus said (*Ant. Iud.* III, vi, 1) it was a portable Temple which they could carry round with them, *metapheromenos kai sumperinostōn naos*. In Leviticus the detail of Israel's ecclesiatical (Temple) institutions is continued with details of the sacrifices (chapters 1–7), details of the hallowing and installation of the Aaronic priesthood (chapters 8–10), the laws dealing with ritual uncleanness and its removal, culminating in the rites of the Day of Atonement, as it is elsewhere (Lev. 23.27, etc., the plural is used, i.e. 'full atonement') called. The concluding chapter, 27, deals with the commutation of tithes and vows, which take the form of payments made to priests and Levites.

How far the P-elements inserted in the Holiness Code are actually idealistic proposals for the future, working out the ideas of separation and holiness to the last degree, is difficult to say. An example is the jubilee legislation, Lev. 25.8–13, 15f., 23, 26–34, 40b–42, 44–46, 48–52, 54. It may well have happened that the seventh year was a fallow year for the land (H-tradition), but it is scarcely likely that two successive fallow years (49th and 50th) is a practical proposition in a land next door to the desert and subject to bad 'rains'. In the Book of Numbers, this idealistic element is more pronounced: the astonishing high numbers of the tribes (1 and 26). The number of Hebrews who went out from Egypt must have been, according to P's reckoning, of the order of two million. It is small wonder that the food was short, and that it required bread from heaven to feed them in the desert (Exod. 16.3f.) or that Moses was driven to desperation because there was not enough water (Exod. 17.4)! Next, there are all the proposals concerning the distribution of the tribes in camp and on the march, taking care that the Tent of Meeting is in the middle of the camp, with a screen of Levites, and the secular tribes on the circumference (Num. 2). We then find a section dealing with the numbers and the duties of the Levites, with a new explanation for the choice of the Levites as semi-sacred persons: they are given to God as a ransom for Israel's first-born, and the priests, to whom the Levites are given as servants, receive an extra payment to make up for the difference in numbers. In chapter 7 the leaders of the tribes bring their offerings with which to start the sacrificial system, and they each bring one object and one animal necessary for all the main offerings and rites (7.12–17, which is repeated almost without any variation at all in the succeeding paragraphs), having already contributed the six wagons and twelve oxen needed for the transport of the sacred objects (7.3–8). This is the kind of material that occurs throughout P, ending with the strange story of the daughters of Zelophehad, which apparently is a story told to account for some of the tribe of Manasseh being west as well as east of the Jordan (see pp. 309f.). Much of P consists of reading the present back into the distant past. Some of P consists of hopes for the future, especially in the realms of P's special interests, the working out of the habdalah laws, especially in respect of the exclusiveness of the priests whose position seems to become more and more exalted as the years pass by and their perquisites to increase. Possibly even the anointing of all priests, and not the High Priest only, is a hope of P rather than a reality.

7. THE HOLINESS CODE (H)

The Holiness Code is found in Lev. 17–26. It is not easy to distinguish in great detail the verses which belong to H from those which belong to P, and modern scholars rightly hesitate to push such analysis too far, not only in separating H from P, but also J from E. It seems likely, however, that the Holiness Code did not contain any regulations for the festivals on the 1st and the 10th of the seventh month, possibly because the changes in the observance of rites consequent upon the change in the ecclesiastical year had not been properly worked out at the time when the Holiness Code attained its present form. Certainly the ecclesiastical calendar of Lev. 23 contains more than one stratum of instructions, and the different layers of traditions which are to be detected throughout P are at least as evident in this chapter as elsewhere. The climax of P's hopes comes in the ideal allocation of Canaan in Num. 34. Much of this territory never belonged to the Israelites, certainly not in David's time, and not at any other time, though the nearest they ever came to it was in the days of Israel's Indian summer in the time of the Hasmonaeans at the end of the second century B.C.

The Holiness Code is best regarded as one of Israel's legislative codes, similar in broad outline to the Book of the Covenant (Exod. 20.22–23.33) or the ancient code which contains the Ten Words (commandments: Exod. 20.1–17), but with the great difference that H is essentially of priestly origin. Like the Book of the Covenant, it begins with sacrificial regulations but it ends with an exhortation urging obedience to the laws. H has much to say about prohibited sexual relations, much about ritual uncleanness due to contact with the dead, the extra precautions which must be taken to secure an absolutely ritually clean and physically perfect priesthood. It anticipates (or parallels) the Deuteronomic legislation in demanding reasonable treatment for the daily wage-earner (19.9–14) and for the resident alien, whilst the instructions concerning the seventh year, the Year of Release, are designed to mitigate the worst evils of slavery. L. E. Elliott-Binns ('Some Problems of the Holiness Code', *ZAW* 67, 1955, 26–40) is of the opinion that H anticipates D on the grounds that it does not envisage a single sanctuary, is earlier than Ezekiel, and has affinities also with Jeremiah. He thinks it dates from the latter years of the monarchy but before the time of king Josiah. But the most distinctive element in the Holiness Code, and that which gives it its modern name, is the way in which very many sections conclude with 'I am the LORD' (19.12) or 'I am the LORD your God' (19.4) or 'I am the LORD who sanctifies (lit. makes holy)' (22.9). It is likely that here we have traces of a liturgy in which each section concluded with a response which in its full form was 'I am the LORD your God (or 'I am the LORD who sanctifies . . .'), who brought you out of the land of Egypt. . . .', 22.32f. and 19.36. Perhaps there was another variation: 20.24, 'I am the LORD your God, who has separated you from the peoples', which links up with the idea of 'holy', which in H and P tends to change from meaning 'separated to God' to 'separated from the peoples'. It must be pointed out that the association with the escape from Egypt brings all these regulations into the centre of the great theme of Israel's history, the *Heilsgeschichte*, the divine history of that Israel which is a people saved by the LORD who, to quote Martin Luther's hymn,

'Who shall at last set Israel free
From all their sin and sorrow.'

8. THE ITINERARY

There are two traditions concerning the route by which the Israelites journeyed from Egypt to the plains of Moab. According to the JE-tradition, they went roughly due east to Kadesh-barnea and settled in that area for most of the forty years. According to the P-tradition they wandered around the Sinai peninsula and did not arrive at Kadesh until near the end of their time in the desert. This double tradition involves a double tradition concerning the site of Mount Sinai. According to JE, it was apparently near Kadesh-barnea, some thirty miles south-west of the Dead Sea and twenty-five miles south-south-west of Beersheba. According to P, it must have been well to the south, some twenty-five miles from the southern tip of the Sinai peninsula. There is also a double tradition, not wholly in line with those as to the route, concerning the name of the sacred mountain. J has Sinai and so also P and the Song of Deborah (Jg. 5.4). E has

Horeb, and so also D and the Elijah traditions (1 Kg. 19.8). The place where Aaron died also is involved in a double tradition. According to Dt. 10.6, supposed to be a D adoption of the E-tradition, Aaron died at Moserah, after the people finally left Kadesh, but according to the P-tradition it was at 'Mount Hor, on the border of the land of Edom' (Num. 20.23), which is in the same area as Moserah and may involve a different name rather than a different site. Maps giving the probable route are found in most commentaries, and the route indicated is usually a conflation of the two traditions. It is more satisfactory to admit frankly the existence of the two traditions. They are irreconcilable and any attempt at conflation leads only to greater confusion and uncertainty. This much is certain: the Israelites did not follow the coast route, the regular caravan-route down to Egypt, the famous 'Way of the land of the Philistines' (Exod. 13.17f.), but took a more southerly route through the wilderness towards the *Yam-sûp̱* (traditionally identified with the Red Sea, but latterly interpreted as the Sea of Reeds; but see N. H. Snaith, 'Yam-suph, Red Sea, Sea of Reeds', *VT* 15, 1965, 395–8.). The difference between the two traditions is involved in the answer to the question: how far to the south (towards the *Yam sûp̱*) did they go? The 'route further south' of Exod. 13.18 could well be the *dereḵ Šûr* (Gen. 16.7) along which Hagar wandered, and later (Gen. 20.1) Abraham, when he settled in Gerar 'between Kadesh and Shur'. This route is roughly twenty miles to the south of the coast-line and skirting the northern edge of the 1,000-foot plateau of the Wilderness of Paran (see Grollenberg, *Atlas of the Bible*, map 9, p. 44). If the P-interpretation is followed, then the Israelites virtually followed the coast-line of first the Gulf of Suez and then the Gulf of 'Aqaba up to Ezion-geber, which is identified with *Tell el-Kheleifeh*, not far from the modern Israeli port of Elath.

The children of Israel set out from Rameses to Succoth and on to Etham (Exod. 12.37, 13.20). Some authorities consider these verses to belong to the J- or E-tradition, and others to the P-tradition. Such precision involves that type of jig-saw literary analysis which, as much as anything else, has led scholars to prefer a less rigid documentary theory. The probability is that both the JE- and the P-traditions envisage a journey out of Egypt along the modern

Wady Ṭumîlât to somewhere near the modern *Isma'îlîya*, near to the northern end of Lake *Timsâḥ*. Then the Israelites turned back (Exod. 14.2; Num. 33.5–8) and came down to the west of the line of the modern Suez Canal, with the result that the pursuing Egyptian army trapped them, possibly west of the Bitter Lakes, but certainly somewhere between *Isma'îlîya* and *Suez*. It was then that God rescued them by opening a way through 'the sea'. It must be remembered that *yam* (sea) can describe any stretch of water, and *yam* is used of the Sea of Galilee, the Dead Sea, whilst the Mediterranean is usually 'the Great Sea'. It is not stated either in the JE-tradition or in the P-tradition that the Israelites passed through the *yam-sûp* (? Red Sea, ? Sea of Reeds), though this is said in the Exodus Song of Moses (Exod. 15.4), and indeed according to the P-tradition the people did not arrive at the *yam-sûp̱* (? Gulf of Suez) until they had travelled for three days in the Wilderness of Etham, camped at Marah, then at Elim and next by the *yam-sûp̱*. Then the P-tradition (Num. 33.5–49) takes them down to Mount Sinai, siting Rephidim near to Mount Sinai, and afterwards up to Ezion-geber (verse 36), thence to Kadesh and Mount Hor, which are on the edge of the Edomite country. Later they set out from Mount Hor in the direction of the Gulf of 'Aqaba in order to avoid the Edomite country, and after some twenty miles struck east, crossed the Arabah and came up north on its eastern side almost as far as the Dead Sea. They then had to make a detour round the Moabite country and finally came to the river Jordan to the north of the Dead Sea.

What happened according to the JE-tradition after the crossing of 'the sea' is not known. Presumably the P-editors did not preserve those elements of the earlier tradition. In Exod. 17.8 we find Israel fighting with Amalek at Rephidim. Either these Amalekites were where David found them (1 Sam. 30.18) and where Num. 13.29 says they were—in the Negeb, or else we have to invent some story to account for them being in the far south of the Sinai peninsula. We conclude therefore that according to the JE-tradition Rephidim was near Kadesh and that the Israelites journeyed directly there after they passed through 'the sea'. Further, according to the earlier tradition it was from Kadesh that the spies went to explore the Negeb and the country round Hebron, and it was at Kadesh that

Caleb supported Moses and urged the people to attack (Num. 13.22–24, 26b–31); but according to P they went out from the Wilderness of Zin and explored the whole country as far north as Hamath on the Orontes, and both Joshua and Caleb supported Moses and Aaron (Num. 13.21, 26, 14.5–7) on their return to the Wilderness of Paran.

For further details, see the notes below; also the larger commentaries, especially Gray, *Numbers* (*ICC*), and S. R. Driver, *Exodus* (Cambridge Bible), pp. 186–91, for a long discussion of the identification of the 'southern' Mount Sinai, particularly the identification with the *Jebel Mûsā*. The JE-tradition favours the mountains of Seir, on the borders of Edom. This explains such passages as Dt. 33.2; Jg. 5.4–5; Hab. 3.3, 7, all of which must enshrine very ancient traditions.

THE THIRD BOOK OF MOSES
COMMONLY CALLED

LEVITICUS

THE THIRD BOOK OF MOSES
COMMONLY CALLED

LEVITICUS

FIRST SECTION **1.1–7.38** THE LAWS OF SACRIFICE

A. THE MANUAL FOR THE PEOPLE **1.1–6.7**

(a) THE RITUAL OF THE WHOLE-OFFERING **1.1–17**

1. This verse connects the manuals of sacrifice with the situation at the end of Exod. 40, where the cloud covered the Tent of Meeting so that Moses was not able to enter. He therefore stands in the opening.

the tent of meeting: AV 'the tabernacle of the congregation', following V *tabernaculum*, whereby much confusion has been caused, but the equation is in P itself (Num. 9.15). The writers of P sought to read back the details of the Second Temple into the ancient traditions of the wilderness, where the Tent of Meeting and the Ark which it sheltered were a long way outside the camp (Exod. 33.7, E). According to the E-tradition, Joshua remained permanently within the tent (Exod. 33.11), but under the P-regulations he would not have been allowed anywhere near it, since he was not even a Levite. According to P, there was a Tabernacle in the middle of the camp. This was a portable Sanctuary: Josephus, *Ant. Iud.* III, vi, 1, 'portable and going-round-together-with Temple' (*metapheromenos kai sumperinostōn naos*). This Tabernacle (Hebrew *miškān*, dwelling-place) was made of double curtains looped together and completely enclosed. Inside there were two sections separated by a Veil. Within the inner section there was the Ark, and in the outer chamber there stood the seven-branched lampstand, a table for the shewbread, and probably the altar of incense. The altar of burnt-offering stood in front of the Tabernacle in the outer court. The innermost section is called the Most Holy Place (lit. Holy of Holies). The outer section is the Holy Place. All this is based on the Second Temple. In Solomon's Temple the outer court was part of the royal complex of buildings, and the Temple itself was in two sections, the House and the *Dᵉḇîr*, a dark inner room in the shape of a cube. The altar was outside in the main courtyard. RV and RSV have rightly taken pains to try and obviate the confusion which AV, thanks to V, increased by translating *'ōhel* (Tent) by 'tabernacle' (*miškān*) 199 times; but no translation can make the matter completely clear, since there is confusion not only in the P-tradition but also in the description of Solomon's Temple in 1 Kg. 8. (See further, *AI*, pp. 249f.)

The idea that God must dwell in a tent is ancient, not only among the Hebrews (2 Sam. 7.6) but also in ancient Ugarit, where the gods had tents for their habitations (*Keret* III, iii, 18; the words used are *àhlhm* and *mšknthm*).

2. offering: Hebrew *ḳorbān*, strictly 'that which is brought near'. It is an ancient technical term for an offering in Accadian as well as in Hebrew, but not found in the Ugarit tablets. The term is found only in Ezekiel and in P. This does not necessarily make it a later term, since there is much early material in P. EVV have 'oblation', which is due to V *oblatio*, an exact Latin equivalent. In this section the word is used of any type of offering. For the narrower use of the term, see note on 2.2; cf. also Num. 7.13, 31.50, and Mk 7.11. LXX here has the general term 'gifts'.

cattle: this means the sacrifice must be of domesticated animals and 'not from wild beasts' (*Jerusalem Targum*).

flock: this regularly includes both sheep and goats, as still in the Near East. The Passover 'lamb' could be either a sheep or a goat (Exod. 12.5). It had to be a yearling *śeh* (animal from the flock), not necessarily a *keḇeś* (male lamb).

3. burnt offering: this is Coverdale's *burntofferynge*: essentially it was a whole-offering (V *holocaustum*, virtually transcribing from LXX) and so DV 'holocaust'. The hide was the perquisite of the priest (7.8); the blood was thrown on the altar, but the whole of the rest, including both head and entrails, was burnt completely on the altar (see p. 15).

door: better 'opening', since there was no door to the Tent of Meeting. V has *ostium* which can mean 'entrance' in general as well as 'door' (so DV) in particular. In the Second Temple all that had to be done 'before the Lord' by non-priests was done in the Upper Gate, the so-called Gate of Nicanor. (Some authorities assume that the Gate of Nicanor was the Beautiful Gate, made of Corinthian bronze.)

that he may be accepted: lit. 'for his (its) acceptance'. It is not easy to decide for whom or what the pronoun stands—worshipper, offering, or God. In any case, the meaning is that God shall accept both sacrifice and worshipper so that there shall be *rāṣôn* (goodwill, acceptance) between God and man.

4. lay his hand upon: he thereby signifies that it is he who is presenting the animal as a sacrifice wholly to God. This rite of laying on of the hands has different meanings on different occasions, transferring holiness or sin. The corresponding noun *sᵉmîḵāh* is the technical Rabbinic term for Ordination (cf. J. Newman, *Semikah*, 1950), but here the root has nothing to do with ordination. The term belongs to P. *Jerusalem Targum* says the hand must be laid on 'with firmness'.

to make atonement for him: the original meaning of the root *k-p-r* is not known, since it is not found except in cultic or semi-technical contexts. Probably it means 'cover over'; cf. Gen. 32.20 (Heb 21), 'appease', lit. cover his face so that he cannot see the wrong. In the P-tradition the normal meaning is: performed an expiatory rite over him, for him (cf. 5.10). The English word goes back to the thirteenth-century rhyming chroniclers and was 'to make an at-onement', i.e. to reconcile (cf. Milton, 'the king and parliament will soon be atoned'). Tyndale used the noun, but the verb is a back-formation (denominative) from the noun and is not found in AV. LXX thinks of propitiation, V of expiation, and S has 'de-sin'.

5. he shall kill: originally the worshipper slaughtered the animal, and Hebrew preserves this tradition. Later all animals for public sacrifices were slaughtered by the priests. The Rabbis said that the offerer was responsible for five actions: laying on of hands, slaying, skinning, cutting up and washing the entrails. The word here used, *šāḥaṭ*, is P's technical term for slaughtering an animal (thirty-eight times in the Pentateuch and thirteen elsewhere), but it can be used generally of killing. Strictly it means killing with a heavy, smashing blow: 1 Kg. 10.16 of 'beaten, hammered gold'.

bull: EVV have 'bullock', correct at the time of AV when it meant 'bull calf, young bull'. The word is wrong in modern English, since now it refers to a castrated animal and all sacrificed animals had to be entire and perfect in every respect.

throw: the 'sprinkle' of EVV is definitely wrong. In any case, this is not a cleansing rite. *zāraḳ* means 'throw, toss' (Arabic *mazrâḳ* is a javelin). The priest caught the blood in a silver cone-shaped vessel as it flowed from the severed arteries and kept it stirred lest it should coagulate. He then threw it against the north-east corner of the altar so as to cover the north and east sides, and then against the opposite corner so as to cover the other two sides. According to *b. Zeb.*, 53b, the blood was thrown above a red line which ran all round the altar half-way down, whereas the blood of the sin-offering was thrown below the line. All blood is *taboo* for man, since the blood is the life. Only the god can deal with it. Clean blood goes above the line, and sin-blood below. This latter must go to the god, but not as an offering.

6. he shall flay: Heb has preserved the ancient law whereby the offerer did the flaying as well as the killing. Sam, LXX, and V have the plural, following ancient custom, and so also for the other processes.

cut into pieces: properly, 'cut up and divide by the joints' (Jg. 19.29), and so LXX *melizō* (dismember, de-limb). See Ugarit tablets (*Baal* V, ii, 36), where the virgin Anat distributes the limbs of the victims at the banquet of the gods. The sacrificed animals were food for the gods.

7. the sons of Aaron the priest: here is evidence of editing. V omits, five Hebrew MSS, Sam, LXX, and three T MSS have 'priests'. S has 'the priests the sons of Aaron', as in verses 5, 8, 11, etc.

put fire: some think this is an earlier stage of development than that of 6.13

where the fire is not allowed to go out. V and DV say that first they made a pile of wood on the altar and then set light to it. It is hard to believe that the ever-burning fire was an innovation. Doubtless (verse 8) the fire smouldered for most of the time and wood was added when an animal had to be burned. The wood-pile (*ma'ᵃrāḵāh*) had to be laid with great care, since no one log was allowed to project beyond the rest (*Tam.*, ii, 3).

8. the fat: this is the intestinal fat and (V and DV) 'all things that cleave to the liver'. The fat was different from the flesh, and it was *taboo* equally with the blood (7.25). Both contained the life-stuff and therefore both the blood and the fat went to the altar whatever the sacrifice.

9. its legs: better 'hind legs'. V and DV have 'feet', following LXX. The root means 'bend, bow down' (cf. Arabic). The noun therefore refers to legs with a bend in them. Cf. 11.21, where the word is used of the legs of the leaping orthoptera, which have a considerable bend in their hind legs. The washing removes the filth of excretion.

burn: Hebrew *ḳ-ṭ-r* is a technical term at all periods for sending up smoke in ritual worship, as against *ś-r-p*, which is 'secular' burning. In pre-exilic writings the noun *ḳᵉṭōreṯ* refers to the smoke of sacrifices, but in P and in Chronicles it means 'incense', the burning of which seems to have been introduced towards or after the exile, due to Mesopotamian influence and encouraged by the frequently accepted theory which develops in all religions whereby the fuller and the richer the worship the better.

a pleasing odour: lit. 'a fire-offering of odour of soothing', but RSV has followed LXX and V. The phrase is a survival from the time when it was said that the gods ate the food (3.11) sent up to them in the form of smoke. They enjoyed the savoury smell of the roasting flesh (Gen. 8.21 J). Cf. the Babylonian flood legend, the so-called Gilgamesh epic (*DOTT*, p. 23), with its description of the gods gathering round like flies over the sacrifice so as to smell the goodly savour. These crudities of earlier days have passed, but the idea of appeasing God or of pleasing him to ensure his good favour still remains to this day. This survival accounts for verse 4, where even the whole-offering has the object of 'making atonement', an idea normally concerned with the sin-offering. The extension to all sacrifices is seen in Ezek. 45.15, 17; but see Mic. 6.6.

A Whole-offering from the Flock 10–13

11. on the north side of the altar: this was where the 'most holy' sacrifices were slaughtered (6.25 (Heb 18), 7.2, 14.13)—whole-offerings, sin-offerings if a priest was not involved, compensation-offerings (guilt-offerings), all of them victims which never afterwards left the holy place, being either burned on the altar or eaten by the priests.

A Whole-offering of Birds 14–17

A concession for the poor. Cf. 5.7, where this is expressly stated. Even in the rigidity of the legalistic Temple system of sacrifices there was this care and concern for the poor (cf. Lk. 2.24).

14. young pigeons: it is not essential to insist on 'young', since the Hebrew idiom can mean 'belonging to the class of': e.g. 'son of might' means 'belonging to the class of mighty men': also the Aramaic *bar-nāšā'* (lit. son of man) can mean a typical human being, an ordinary man, except where it is used as a title for the Heavenly Man who is the judge at the End of Days. Nevertheless Jewish tradition (Sifra, Talmud *b. Hull.*, 22b, Jerusalem Targum) insists that the doves were adult and the pigeons not adult. The pigeons were bred by the high-priestly family on the mount of Olives, where there were four shops (*jer. Taan.*, iv, 8). There was also the market in the Court of the Gentiles, known as 'the bazaars of the sons of Annas'.

15. wring off its head: The Hebrew *mālaḵ* means 'nip, wrench off' since the head had to be burned on the altar. Contrast V and DV here, and all in 5.8, which is a sin-offering. The blood had to be squeezed out (LXX) to the last drop. According to Rashi, no instrument was to be used. The priest had to use his finger nail, nip close by the nape, through the neck-bone, and then cut through the wind-pipe and the gullet.

16. its crop with the feathers: RSV returns to AV, following LXX and V. The *mur'āh* is the crop, alimentary canal (cf. Arabic root, 'be digestible'). RV has 'with the filth thereof', which goes back as far as Sifra and T. Rashi says that *nôṣāh* means anything loathsome (*b. Zeb.*, 65b). Cf. Arabic *waṣaya* (be polluted) and Hebrew *ṣô'āh* (excrement). The word *nôṣāh* (plumage) is in fairly common use, but it is likely there was this other word also and we should read 'filth, *faeces*' or some word describing the contents of the crop.

east side: not actually in front of the altar, which would be between the altar and the worshippers, but east of the *keḇeš*, the ramp which led up to the altar on the south side (*Midd.*, iii, 3; *Zeb.*, v, 3). The width of this ramp was less than that of the altar so that there was a space on each side. The ashes and unburnt fat were deposited here when the altar fire was raked out just before dawn, and later were cast into the Kidron valley below.

ashes: the word is *dešen* (fatness), in general use for rich food and even for spiritual blessing (Isa. 55.2; Ps. 36.8), but also for the refuse from the altar, which contained considerable quantities of unconsumed fat since all the fat of all slaughtered animals in Temple rites was placed on the altar.

(b) THE RITUAL OF THE GRAIN-OFFERING **2.1–16**

This chapter is concerned with the *minḥāh*, AV 'meat offering' after Coverdale, and RV 'meal offering'. In modern English 'meat' means butcher's meat, but the older general meaning 'food' still survives in some popular expressions. At Ugarit quantities of bread corn were placed on the altar (*Keret* I, iii, 58), but in Israel, except for the daily offering, only a token was placed on the altar (see p. 16).

1. fine flour: this translation is due to LXX *semidalis* and V *simila* (finest wheaten flour). It was sifted (*Kel.*, xv, 3) but not ground fine. In the Talmud *siltā'* (Aramaic equivalent) is used of kindling chips.

oil: strictly the word means 'fatness, richness, fertility' (Isa. 5.1, where 'very fertile' is lit. 'a horn, a son of oil'), but commonly it is olive oil, the oil in common use.

frankincense: from the Old French *franc encens*. The English 'frank', used now mostly of uninhibited speech, was used of trees and plants which grew freely ('franked' letters) and richly. Hence 'frankincense' means 'rich incense'. The Hebrew name is *lᵉḇônāh*, allegedly because of its whiteness, but the Greeks used an aromatic gum called *libanōtos* in their rituals, which they obtained from the *libanos*-tree. According to *OED*, frankincense is an aromatic gum from trees of the genus *Boswellia*.

2. memorial portion: from LXX 'its memorial', V *memoriale*, whence the somewhat obscure English rendering. The word means 'token' (G. R. Driver, *JSS*, I, 1956, 97–105), the rest being a perquisite of the Aaronite priesthood. They stored their share within the Temple buildings (Neh. 13.12).

3. a most holy part: RSV is wrong in introducing the word 'part'. As S has seen, Hebrew is making a statement that the grain-offering is 'most holy', better 'a holy gift of holy gifts' (*ḳōḏeš ḳᵒḏāšîm*), which means it could be eaten only by the male descendants of Aaron (6.16f. (Heb 9f.)). A 'holy gift' could be eaten by the families of the priests. Gifts to the Temple were either *ḳoḏāšîm* (holy gifts), which were for the maintenance of the priesthood, or *ḳorbānîm* (offerings), which were for the maintenance of the Temple. This is the narrow use of the word *ḳorbān*, and not the general use as in 1.2. The reference in Mk 7.11 is to a gift willed at death to the maintenance of the Temple and therefore not available even for family needs.

The Baked Grain-offering 4–10

4. baked in the oven: the major LXX MSS have 'baked from frankincense', an error through haplography, *ek libanou* for *ek klibanou*. Cf. Codex Ambrosianus. The oven (*tannûr*) was a portable stove or fire pot, a breakable (11.35) large earthen jar still used in the Near East. In more settled communities the oven was a pot-shaped hole sunk in the ground. It was heated by burning dried grass inside (Mt. 6.30; Lk. 12.28) and the sides became black with smoke (Lam. 5.10, 'black as an oven', Hebrew *k-m-r* II). Cf. the 'smoking fire pot' of Gen. 15.17.

unleavened cakes: the *ḥallāh* was a perforated cake, but the perforations were probably to aid the baking process. T calls them *gᵉrîṣîm* (slices), either twisted or in layers. Women were prohibited from baking their bread in this shape on holy days (*Bets.*, ii, 6), possibly because such cakes baked on holy days were for Temple use. The 'unleavened' is because of the general association in early religions of yeast with fermentation, which rendered such materials *taboo* to gods though not to men (*HDB*, iii, p. 90; article 'Leaven'). At Ugarit honey was offered to the gods in a vessel of gold (*Keret* I, iv, 2), but this was *nbt* (Hebrew *nôpeṯ*), flowing honey from the comb.

mixed with oil: EVV 'mingled'. The word *b^e lûlāh* is P's word for mixing the sacrificial cakes and flour with oil. The Arabic verb involves mixing with water, so that Hebrew *b^e lîl* (Job 6.5, etc.) probably means 'fresh (moist) fodder' rather than 'mixed fodder'. V (*conspersus*) thinks of the oil as applied after baking, but LXX (*phurō*, of mixing something dry with something wet) and the Rabbis say it means mixed with the dough. But T (Onkelos) refers to cakes soaked in oil and so S (*pîl*), probably after baking (*Zeb.*, xiv, 3).
wafers spread with oil: these were thin round cakes (Arabic *ruḳâḳaṭ*), though 'wafers' (EVV) has become the traditional rendering. V has 'loaves' (*panes*) and so DV. They were smeared (primary meaning of *māšaḥ*, anoint). Rabbinic opinion varies. Either they were smeared repeatedly until all the oil was gone, or (Sifra; *b. Men.*, 75a) they were marked in the form of a cross (Greek *chi*), though some dispute this, understandably since the adoption by the Christian of an ancient sign would render it unacceptable to many orthodox Jews.

5. griddle: this was a flat pan or iron plate (Ezek. 4.3). What was cooked on it was solid (*Men.*, v, 8). The pan (verse 7) was of considerable depth, and T speaks of sponge-cakes, the contents being so soft that 'when one pressed his finger upon a pancake of this description, the oil with which it is saturated moves in it'.

10. a most holy part: see note on verse 3.

12. an offering of first-fruits: *Rē'šîṯ* is here used as a general inclusive term, as in 2 Chr. 31.5. No first-fruits went to the altar, not even a token, unless they were grain. Strictly, *rē'šîṯ* consisted of all first-fruits except the *bikkûrîm* (see note on verse 14).

13. season . . . with salt: salt was essential, so that the writer of Ezek. 47.1–12 had to moderate his zeal for unlimited fertility and leave the swamps and marshes (verse 11) to provide salt. Salt was used sacrificially by the nations of antiquity, since whole-burnt-offerings were the food of the gods (Ezek. 43.24), and the gods needed salt with their food as much as men. See *HDB*, iv, article 'Salt'. Also 'to eat a man's salt' establishes a bond between host and guest. This is probably why covenants were sealed with a sacred communal meal (Hebrew *zeḇaḥ*, usually translated 'sacrifice': see pp. 15f.). We thus have 'a covenant of salt' (Num. 18.19; 2 Chr. 13.5) which binds the two parties in an irrevocable covenant. If people have salt in themselves, they will be at peace with one another (Mk 9.50). The remission of the tax on salt was a concession to Jewish religious scruples (Josephus, *Ant. Iud.* XII, iii, 3; 1 Mac. 10.29, 11.35). There is a Jewish tradition that at Creation 'the waters below the firmament' were disappointed at having no place in heaven, and this is why they were offered on the altar at the Feast of Tabernacles in the form of salt and water: salt with the offerings and water at the house of water-pouring ceremony.

14. first fruits: the word here is *bikkûrîm*, which here involves grain only. Technically, it included the first-fruits of wheat, barley, the vine, figs, pomegranates, olives, and honey. 'Honey' (*d^e ḇaš*, Arabic *dibs*) included both tree honey (wild bee-honey) and date-honey, but Rashi held that it included the sweet juice of any fruit; cf. modern Hebrew *'āsîs*, whilst Maimonides expressly states that bee-honey was not included, thus taking *bikkûrîm* to refer to agricultural products only.

crushed new grain from fresh ears: this was fresh grain, first roasted and then pounded (LXX *erikta*) rather like the grits served in ordinary homes at every meal south of the Mason-Dixon line. Cf. Virgil, *Aen.* ii, 133 and xii, 173, of sacrificial roasted barley meal mixed with salt. The Hebrew *'āḇîḇ* is 'new grain' perhaps still green, or just ripening (Exod. 9.31). The tender (LXX *apalon*) fresh ears were *karmel* (fresh, fertile growth), the Carmel range being so called because of its luxuriant growth in early times and the last part of the country to suffer from drought (Am. 9.3, 1.2).

(c) THE RITUAL OF THE SHARED-OFFERING (RSV PEACE OFFERING) **3.1–17**

This was a sacred meal eaten by the people, apart from those two pieces which were the perquisite of the priests (see pp. 17, 78f.). The rendering **peace offering** is due to V *pacificorum*. LXX has 'salvation', good health, prosperity, and well-being, and this is not far from the true meaning. The worshippers ate the holy food and were strengthened in both body and soul. The animal could be a female, since it did not go to the altar, where only male animals could be offered (Josephus, *Ant. Iud.* III, ix, 1). Further, nothing is said about the age of the animal, nor about acceptance by God, nor about atonement. It was a sacred meal which the worshippers ate.

2. kill it at the door of the tent of meeting: i.e. in the opening, but not where the whole-offerings were slaughtered (1.5). Thus the flesh of the shared-offering, apart from the shoulder and the leg, never entered the holy area, since neither God nor priest received it. What went within, never came out. There was one exception: the two lambs which were offered as shared-offerings at the Feast of Weeks (23.19). These were the perquisite of the priests, and were therefore brought within to be slaughtered to the north of the altar.

3. the fat covering the entrails: the parts of the entrails listed in this verse and the next are those parts of the shared-offering which were a fire-offering, i.e. which was burnt on the altar. This is the *omentum*, the membrane which encloses the intestines and in the case of a healthy animal has large pieces of fat clinging to it.

4. the appendage of the liver: the Talmud (*b. Tam.*, 31a) calls this 'the finger of the liver' because in a sheep it reaches upwards on the right like a finger, with the top end level with the kidney. It is the *lobus caudatus*, the caudate lobe, and it can easily be separated from the rest of the liver when the kidneys and their fat have been removed. The renderings of AV and RV are due to V *reticulum jecoris*, the small omentum, the caul (membrane), which covers the liver. This particular part of the liver was of great importance in hepatoscopy, the science which deals with divination by the examination of the livers of animals newly slain. The absence of the right lobe of the liver was a warning of the utmost seriousness: in Rome, Cicero, *de Divin.*, ii, 13; in Greece, Xenophon, *Hellenica* III, iv, 15; in

Babylonia, Diod. Sic., ii, 12. At Gezer a tablet of hard-baked red clay was found (Macalister, *Gezer*, ii, pp. 453f.), the shape of a beast's liver and covered with lines, a diagram similar to a palmist's guide (see S. A. Cook, *RAPLA*, p. 103, and plate xxiii, fig. 2). The liver was sacred as one of the vital organs containing much blood. It was a place where the god signifies his will and intentions.

9. the fat tail entire: this is the broad tail of a species of sheep bred then as now in Palestine. It can contain as many as ten pounds of fat and is esteemed a great delicacy. The sheep are specially fattened and it is said that the tail becomes so heavy towards the middle of October that the sheep cannot stand. The fat-tail is then carried on a little cart attached to the sheep (see picture in *JEn*, xi, p. 50). According to *HDB*, iv, p. 487, this fat is rendered, mixed with small pieces of meat, and stored by the Lebanon peasants for the winter. It is uncertain whether this 'rump' (so AV) was ever eaten by the Israelites, since the only references to it are dealing with sacrificial animals wherein the fat was *taboo* and had to be burned on the altar. The Talmud (*Aboda Zara*, 25a) says that 'the leg and the rump' were offered to Saul by Samuel (1 Sam. 9.24, reading *'ālep* for *'ayin*, with different vowels). This may have been the original reading, altered to bring the verse into line with later laws. We know that there were changes during the centuries in the perquisites of the priests and different pieces of the animals may have been burnt on the altar at different periods. All this, however, is speculation.

11. food: as RVm points out, the Hebrew is *leḥem*, usually translated 'bread'. In Semitic languages the word refers to the regular food of the country. Thus in Arabic it is 'flesh', and in seashore areas it can mean 'fish'. In Jg. 13.16 it refers to a goat kid; in 1 Sam. 14.24 it is honey. It is P's frequent word for what is burnt on the altar and is therefore God's food. The English word 'meat' still survives in some parts of the country with the general meaning of 'food'. Cf. also the word 'corn', which in England means wheat, but in the U.S.A. means maize.

17. The blood *taboo* and the fat *taboo* are both plainly and clearly stated. The blood *taboo* applies also to animals killed for food, and so also the fat, except that the fat of animals slaughtered for food could be used for various purposes other than food. Cooking was done in oil, not in animal fat.

(d) THE RITUAL OF THE SIN-OFFERING 4.1–5.13

For details as to the differences between the sin-offering and the compensation-offering see 'The Sin-offering and the Guilt-offering', *VT* 15, 1965, 73–80 (see also *SOTS*, pp. 98–102). The sin-offering was due for unwitting (*bišᵉgāgāh*) offences, the compensation-offering for offences where damage has been done and loss incurred, which in most cases can be assessed. There are six major differences: (1) the 'owner' placed his hand on the head of the sin-offering, transferring the sin; (2) the blood was used in de-sinning rites; (3) the blood was thrown down at the base of the altar, except for a small quantity used in the de-sinning rite; (4) the animal of the compensation-offering was always slaughtered to the north side of the altar; (5) the compensation-offering was always eaten by the priests; (6) the compensation-offering was always a male and a goat. There were two types of sin-offering, depending on whether or not a priest was involved. If the priests were involved, either as priests or as part of the whole community, the animal was slaughtered 'at the door of the tent of meeting' (4.4, 14f.) and none of the flesh was taken within the Holy Place: it was all destroyed by fire 'outside the camp'. If the priests were not involved, the animal was brought inside the Holy Place, slaughtered at the north side of the altar (4.29, 33), and the flesh eaten by the priests. The two offerings, the *ḥaṭṭā'ṯ* (sin-offering) and the *'āšām* (compensation-offering), are quite distinct, and ought never to be discussed as if belonging to the same class.

2. unwittingly: so RV, with 'through error' in the margin. AV has 'through ignorance', following V. LXX has *akousiōs*, involuntarily, not a free agent. There are included not only instances where a man himself makes a mistake in ignorance, but also cases where a man is placed by others in a position where he must break a rule: e.g. a devout Jew of modern times involved by a breakdown of transport on the Eve of the Sabbath so far from home that he must break the Sabbath rule concerning making a journey. It is the exact opposite of a sin of intention.

The Sin-offering of the Anointed Priest **3–12**

In 6.22 (Heb 15) 'the anointed priest' certainly means the High Priest of post-exilic times, the ruler of the theocratic community, the successor of Aaron. Rashi understands the High Priest to be intended here. In 8.10f. it is Aaron who is anointed but not his sons, though all are consecrated by being sprinkled with the blood of the ordination ram (8.23f.). There is no evidence that the chief priest of pre-exilic times was anointed, and the anointing of all priests (if it ever took place at all) seems to be later than P. Our conclusion is that the post-exilic High Priest was anointed because he was ruler rather than because he was priest. The consecration of a priest in P was by 'filling his hands', i.e. by placing the offering in his hands when he offered sacrifice for the first time (cf. the phrase 'celebrating his first mass').

3. bringing guilt: much confusion has been caused by the assumption that moral guilt is intended. The High Priest (or possibly any priest) has made an unintentional mistake in some ritual matter, and since the ceremony has been on behalf of the people, the people are involved in whatever blame there is. It would be better to translate 'thus involving the people', but everything depends on the importance that is attached to the precise observance of ritual details.

a young bull: not 'bullock' (see note on 1.5). The Hebrew here has *par ben-bāḵār*, and the additional *par* is what the Americans call a steer: young beef cattle of any age. The Sifra says the combined phrase means a three-year-old.

4. The priest lays his hand on the head of the young bull, partly because he was the original offender, but mostly because he is representative of the whole people who are all involved in his mistake. By laying on his hand he transfers the sin, so that the animal becomes the *ḥaṭṭā'ṯ* (lit. the sin). There is nothing in the ancient versions about an 'offering', and it would appear that the ancient translators went to some trouble to avoid the word. The sin-offering is in no sense an offering to God.

6. seven times: seven is the magic number, i.e. the number which is both sacred and effective. Its origin, certainly so far as the Near East is concerned, is in the Mesopotamian cults of the seven stars, the sun, the moon, and the five planets known to antiquity. This is the origin of the seven-day week, which has nothing to do with the phases of the moon. It is the origin of the seven days of birth (circumcision took place on the eighth day, the first day of the child's new life, Gen. 17.12), the seven days of marriage (Gen. 29.27), and the seven days of mourning (Gen. 50.10). All these are 'passage times' when a person moved from one house of life to another, dangerous occasions when the demons were most active (see van Gennep, *Les Rites de passage*. See also *JNYF*, pp. 110–16, where it is shown that the Sabbath has to do with the seven-day week in a secondary rather than in a direct way). The number 'seven' occurs in numerous ways: seven times round the walls of Jericho, the seven archangels, seven sprinklings, etc.

in front of the veil: EVV have 'before', but Heb says actually on the front of the veil (see *AI*, p. 419). Perhaps this is what V intended by *contra*, though DV translates this 'before'. In Exod. 29.12 a cleansing rite is described whereby blood is smeared with the finger on the horns of the altar. The difference is sometimes said to be due to a development of the de-sinning rite, but this is not necessarily so. Many of the altar and Temple rites have different origins, so that the significance of the rite may or may not be different.

the veil of the sanctuary: better 'the holy (sacred) veil'. According to Exod. 26.33 this veil was designed to make a separation between the Holy Place (court of the priests) and the Most Holy Place (Holy of Holies), though there is confusion concerning the 'holy place', as though sometimes it is part of the Holy of Holies itself. The veil was torn from top to bottom at the Crucifixion (Mt. 27.51). Some Rabbis held that there was a double veil, and that the High Priest entered at the southern end of the first veil, walked along what was virtually a corridor between the two veils, turned left-about at the northern end, and so past the second veil. Rabbi Josiah said there was only one veil, and this is assumed by de Vaux (*AI*, pp. 314, 325), but A. Parrot (*The Temple of Jerusalem*, 1957, p. 95) favours the idea of the double curtain (for more evidence see *HDB*, iv, pp. 847f.).

7. the horns of the altar: these are the most sacred parts of the altar. In the Second Temple they appear to have been right-angled tetrahedra fitted at the four corners (illustration in *HDB*, iv, p. 658), but these were doubtless stylized. Earlier altars had much larger and more obviously shaped horns. In Solomon's time to grasp the horns of the altar was to find sanctuary (1 Kg. 2.28), but in later times no non-priest was allowed anywhere near. Perhaps this is why 'cities of refuge' were invented. It was on these horns that blood was smeared in some cleansing rites. Some say the horns represent the horns of the victims offered (cf. Roman altars); others, that they represent pillars (*maṣṣēḇāh*) and are emblems of the god; de Vaux (*AI*, p. 414) favours the idea that the extremities emphasize the holiness of the altar, just as the extremities of the body of the priest are smeared with blood (Exod. 29.20; Lev. 8.23). Possibly the extremities are smeared over as including the whole. Another possible explanation is that they are a survival of the cult of the High-god of Canaan, the Bull-El of the Ugarit tablets, the bull being the emblem of fertility and strength (Dt. 33.17). There is no need to assume that such a survival involves the survival of the original pagan ideas. The survival of untutored and even pagan forms and symbols is a common feature of religious rites in all religions, including Christianity. Man is never so conservative as in the continuance of customs, especially if they are religious. We do what our fathers did, but find different reasons for doing it.

It is strange from the modern point of view that blood from a sin-offering could be put on the horns of the altar, when the surplus had to be thrown down at the base of the altar as being sin-blood and therefore not proper to be flung on the sides of the altar. Our difficulty arises from the fact that *taboo* and its equivalent in Hebrew in early times (*ḳōḏeš*, holiness) belong to a time when our modern categories of personal and non-personal did not exist, a wholly animistic way of thinking, neither did later ideas of what is ethically right and what is ethically wrong. The Hebrew *ḳōḏeš*, like the primitive *mana*, was that mysterious otherness which can be 'dangerous and deadly as well as beneficent and life-giving'. Thus the Hebrew verb *ḥāṭā'* means 'to sin', but in the intensive (*pi'el*) form it can mean 'to de-sin'. The same blood can be potent either way. In this realm, as in that of *taboo*, one man's meat can actually be another man's poison.

the altar of fragrant incense: lit. altar of incense of *sammîm*. The word may well be a loan-word in Hebrew, signifying any kind of fragrant spice, drug, or poison. There is considerable uncertainty as to whether this altar ever existed. Compare Exod. 30.6 and 40.5 for variant statements as to the relative positions of the Ark, the veil, and this altar. If the veil was between the Ark and the altar, then was this altar in front of the whole inner building or were there two veils after all, rather than even a double-veil? If the veil was between 'the holy place' and 'the holy of holies', does this mean a veil inside the sacred inner building, which, in this case, was divided into two sections, or was the veil between 'the holy of holies' and the court where we know the altar of burnt-offering was situated (sometimes, but not always, 'the holy place' of P)? The difficulties are unresolved, but they arise from the different ground-plans of the two Temples, Solomon's and the Second Temple. They are further complicated by the details in the Mishnah, especially the tractate *Middoth*, where we are involved with the changes which Herod the Great made. The fact of the three different Temples does not in itself cause complications, but the way in which persistent attempts were made to identify the same plan in all three. 1 Kg. 8 has been freely glossed by scribes who knew only the Second Temple, and in the Mishnah scribes have sought to explain the already hopelessly complicated 1 Kg. 8 with their own traditions of the layout of Herod's Temple. As an example of complete confusion, see 1 Kg. 8.6, 7. P's attempt to create a portable Temple for the wilderness has only increased the confusion.

pour out: the verb is *šāpak̬*, ordinary pouring, and not *zārak̬*, used in 1.5, 11, 3.2, etc., to denote the ritual tossing of the blood against the two opposite corners (see note on 1.5).

8. The fat from the sin-offering which was burnt on the altar was exactly the same as that taken from the shared-offering (so-called peace-offering), as verse 10 makes quite clear. If the fact that God received this fat is taken as evidence that God shared the so-called peace-offering with the worshippers, then it must also be said that he ate part of the sin-offering—which makes nonsense on any basis of thought.

11. All of the slaughtered animal except the blood and the fat was taken 'outside the camp' and burnt 'in a clean place'. The symbolism is that the sin was disposed of entirely. It no longer existed. It was destroyed with the carcase of the animal to which it had been transferred. It was no longer in between the priest and God. The priest could not eat a sin-offering in which he was involved, because it would still be 'there'. The idea of the transference of sin still survived in England in the sin-eater, who as late as the last century functioned in some parts of the country and formally took upon himself the sins of the deceased.

12. a clean place: this is to ensure that the sin-offering does not go to the city refuse heap with all sorts of unclean material, both ceremonially unclean and generally nasty. The carcase was still 'holy' (*k̬ōḏeš*), even though it was 'sin', and had to receive proper bestowal. Further, since the sin had to be completely destroyed, there could be no remnant of ceremonial uncleanness where it had been deposited.

13–21. This section deals with a sin-offering brought on behalf of the whole people. The ritual is as before except that the elders of the congregation lay their hands on the beast's head. The carcase is destroyed as before because the priest as a member of the community is involved.

13. congregation, assembly: RSV has followed RV and tried to maintain the equations 'congregation' for Hebrew *'ēḏāh* (LXX *synagōgē*) and 'assembly' for *k̬āhāl* (LXX *ekklēsia*). For LXX, both terms denoted Israel as a religious community, but later Jewry thought of the synagogue as the Israel that is and the *ecclesia* as the ideal Israel. It is said that the Christians ultimately chose the word *ecclesia* because they regarded themselves as the ideal Israel, though perhaps the real reason was that they had to make a distinction between themselves and the existing Jewish synagogues. In modern times the word 'church' is used indiscriminately with every kind of meaning, with the result that there is no small amount of confusion.

20. make atonement for them: V (and DV) have 'and the priest praying for them, the Lord will be merciful to them'. Plainly, V saw here no atonement theories, and interpreted *kipper* as meaning 'prayer', but not as involving ritually effective propitiatory action.

22–26. Here the offender is not a priest, and the ritual is different. There is no sprinkling seven times, and the blood is smeared on the horns of the altar of burnt-offering, not on P's altar of incense. The animal is a male goat, not so valuable as when a priest is involved, but more valuable than the female lamb which was the animal necessary for the common people. In this case and the following the priests dispose of the sin by eating it in the Holy Place. This time the animal is killed within the Holy Place, where the whole-offering is killed. This is because the priest can dispose of the sin by eating it, since he is not involved.

27–35. Here the offender is any ordinary individual, not a priest, not one of the ruling classes. He must bring, subject to concessions given in 5.7–13, either a she-goat or an ewe lamb. Otherwise the ritual is as for 'a ruler'.

27. the common people: the Hebrew is *'am hā'āreṣ*. Here the phrase means 'the ordinary layman', not a priest and not a ruler. In Ezek. 45.22 it means the people as distinct from the prince; in Hag. 2.4, the people as distinct from the priests; here, the people as distinct from both priest and rulers; in Ezr. 4.4, the allegedly mixed population. Ultimately the phrase means 'the country people and so 'illiterate and unrefined' (cf. Ac. 4.13), until at last it means those who did not observe the rules of Levitical cleanness, 'the publicans and sinners' of the Gospels. In the Talmud (*b. Sabb.*, 63b, etc.) they are contrasted with 'the wise disciple' (cf. Sir. 38.24–39.11).

5.1–6. This whole section deals with four particular instances where a sin-offering is due, and it has been interpolated into the details of the ordinary man's sin-offering before the concessions are dealt with. Thus 5.7 is the continuation of 4.35. The whole section is composed of one sentence, the four cases being introduced by 'or' and the apodosis beginning at 5.5b. It is mainly in this section that we have the confusion, both in Heb and in subsequent translations and comments, between the sin-offering and the compensation-offering (see pp. 16f.). In the first case, a man keeps silent when he is put on oath (Jg. 17.2; Jos. 7.19; Jn 9.24; and even Jesus, Mt. 26.63, who all keep silence until they are put on oath). The other three cases are all instances where **it is hidden from him** (verses 2, 3, 4). V and DV interpret this as meaning 'and having forgotten it', making the fault one of lack of awareness afterwards, and not at the time. Probably the phrase means not paying proper attention at the time, in which case we have four cases of partially culpable unwittingness; but they all come under the head of sin-offerings because no damage has been done.

1. shall bear his iniquity: the Hebrew phrase *nāśā' 'āwôn* is used regularly in H, P and Ezekiel to mean 'bear the responsibility' of sin or guilt. Sometimes it means 'pay the penalty' (Gen. 4.13; Isa. 53.12), but mostly 'take away', though never this in H, P and Ezekiel.

5. confess: this involves public confession before the whole religious community, as is still required from (say) an erring husband in religious communities in remote villages in Texas. Cf. LXX *exagoreuō*. V and DV for the whole verse have 'let him do penance for his sin'.

6. guilt offering: this is the word (*'āšām*) which has caused most of the confusion. We are not dealing with a 'guilt'-offering, as is said later in the verse. This is a non-technical use of *'āšām*, and the meaning is 'as his penalty'. This and the previous phrase 'it is hidden from him' show that we are dealing with a different stratum of the P-traditions.

A Concession for the Poor Man **7–10**

This section follows properly on 4.35. The concession is the same as for the man who is too poor to bring the proper whole-offering (1.14–17). But here there are two birds to be brought, one for a whole-offering, presumably as an acknowledgement of the concession which God has graciously laid down for his benefit.

7. guilt offering: LXX has its normal equivalent for 'sin-offering'. It is clear that *'āšām* here means 'what he is required to bring', since it involves a sin-offering and a whole-offering. We have another non-technical use of the word.

9. on the side of the altar: the procedure for dealing with the blood of birds differs from that followed in the case of animals. This is because of the small quantity, too little to be caught in a bowl or to be flung at the corners of the altar or thrown down at the base. It was drained out against the side.

10. ordinance: the Hebrew *mišpāṭ* means 'judgment, verdict' but essentially 'judgment following precedent'. Here the meaning is, according to normal procedure, according to the normal rites for whole-offerings and no further details are necessary.

The Concession for Extreme Poverty **11–13**

The 'scribes and Pharisees' may have bound unbearable burdens on men's shoulders (Mt. 23.4; Lk. 11.46), but the Law itself went to great lengths on behalf of the poor. If the poor man could not afford two pigeons, then seven pints of flour was sufficient. This sin-offering is now also a *minḥāh* (P's grain-offering) and therefore all except a token goes to the priest.

(e) THE RITUAL OF THE COMPENSATION-(RSV GUILT)OFFERING **5.14–6.7** (Heb 5.14–26)

All cases here are concerned with a breach of faith against God. The Hebrew word is *ma'al*. The Arabic equivalent means 'perfidy, fraud', and so also in modern Hebrew. In each case loss of property is a result of the fraud, and compensation has to be paid: an *'āšām* (compensation-offering: guilt-offering) to God and an *'āšām* (compensation-payment) to the one who has sustained a loss—if, that is, the loss can be estimated.

Holy Things for The Lord **14–16**

These are the *ḳodāšîm*, the offerings of the people which were the perquisite of the priests (see p. 34, and Num. 18.8–32); even the priests' clothes are *ḳodāšîm* (Exod. 28.36–38). Thus if a man unwittingly appropriated to his own use that which was properly a holy-gift (e.g. first-fruits), then the priests suffered material loss which could be assessed. The penalty was a ram from his flock, satisfactory in value to the priest; all the flesh went to the priest, none to the altar. In addition, there was to be full restitution plus a 20 per cent fine, all of which went to the priests, since they had suffered loss. V and DV give a figure as the exact value of the ram: two shekels, but this figure (5s according to 1914 standards) gives no indication of the value according to present-day standards.

15. the shekel of the sanctuary: this is the ancient native silver shekel of 224 grains, the old Phoenician shekel, fifteen of which equalled the ancient gold shekel of 253 grains. The former British silver half-crown was 218 grains and the gold sovereign is 123·274 grains. The 'holy shekel' was therefore slightly heavier than the British half-crown before so much nickel was used. There was also a later shekel, the light shekel, which weighed 112·25 grains, and a light gold shekel 126·5 grains. Since none but the holy currency was accepted in the Temple, there were money changers in the Court of the Gentiles (Mk 11.15; Jn 2.14). See *HDB*, article 'Money', iii, pp. 422, 419.

The Unknown Fault **17–19**

In this case the man may have committed a fraud, but he is not sure, and he never can be sure. Nobody knows what the loss is, if indeed there is any loss. The devout man brings his *'āšām* (compensation-offering) in case he has defrauded anybody, but no compensation-payment. In the last days of the Temple this was known as the *'āšām tālûy* (suspended 'guilt'-offering), and the scrupulously pious brought this every day. Like Job (1.5) he wished to guard against the slightest unwitting offence.

Breaches of Trust involving Close Associates **6.1–7** (Heb 5.20–26)

These cases are the nearest to deliberate sin found in the Levitical Code. It is best to place the hyphen before 'swearing falsely' (verse 3), as LXX virtually has done by not reading 'or' at the beginning of verse 5. If this is done, we are dealing not with civil misdeeds in general, but with those which have been brought well within the specifically religious sphere through the false swearing of an oath in the Holy Name.

2. neighbour: the word *'āmîṯ* is rare in Hebrew, twice here, nine times in H, and elsewhere only Zech. 13.7, where the meaning is 'close associate' and importantly so. The Accadian equivalent means 'family connexion', and in modern Hebrew it is 'associate'.

2. deposit or security: V treats the two items as one, and so also DV: 'the thing delivered into his keeping, which was committed to his trust'. The second is represented in LXX by *koinōnia*, whence AV 'fellowship', but Rashi explains the Hebrew *t^e śûmeṯ yāḏ* as putting money into the other's hand in a partnership. So also T. In the Talmud the phrase is used in business contexts (*b. Erub.*, 71b). It is best to think in terms of a business deal or partnership.

3. found what was lost: this is the English 'stealing by finding'. He says nothing about it even when he is put on oath.

5. on the day of his guilt offering: that is, on the day when he brings his guilt-offering, but AVm and RV follow LXX with 'in the day of his being found guilty', which is better. V has 'being convicted of the offence'.

7. and thereby become guilty: better, 'and thereby incur liability', since the distinguishing feature of the guilt-offering is that the offender is liable to pay full restitution plus 20 per cent. He is guilty over a sin-offering offence, but he must pay up for a guilt-offering offence.

B. The Manual for the Priests 6.8 (Heb 6.1)–7.38

(a) the ritual of the whole-offering 6.8–13 (Heb. 6.1–6)

These two chapters (6 and 7 in Heb) describe what the priests must do with the various offerings. The previous chapters have dealt with the types of offerings and, where necessary, the reasons for the different types.

9. hearth: the form *môḳᵉḏāh* occurs only here. RSV follows RV and assumes it means 'place of burning'. But it may mean 'burning mass' (cf. AVm, RVm (firewood), and LXX; cf. the masculine form of the same noun, Isa. 33.14; Ps. 102.3 (Heb 4)). V and DV take the word as a verb (it shall be burnt) and thus have no reference to an altar-hearth. The reference is to the *tāmîḏ*, the regular (continual) whole-offering (verse 13). LXX makes certain by adding 'it shall not go out', as in verses 12 and 13.

10. breeches: the Hebrew root means 'gather together', the point being that not only did these garments reach from the loins to the thighs (Exod. 28.42) but that they were gathered at the bottoms. Hence LXX 'ankle-bands' and V *feminalibus* (with thigh bandages). It was to ensure that the priest's private parts were securely covered, not so much lest they should be exposed to the people but lest they should be exposed before the altar. Hence *bāśār* (body, AV and RV 'flesh') is a euphemism.
he shall take up the ashes: the reference is to the unconsumed fat (see note on 1.16). T thinks of 'separating the fat' (cf. the common English 'clearing the ashes', which involves separating the unconsumed remains with the intention of using them again). This was understood by the ancient Jewish commentators, who connected *hērîm* (take up) with the *tᵉrûmāh*, the so-called 'heave-offering' (see 7.14). They thus took the verse to refer to the *tᵉrûmāṯ haddešen* (the heave-offering of ashes, *b. Yoma*, 22a) whereby each day a handful of ashes was laid aside for the next day, thus ensuring a continuity of sacrifice.
beside the altar: in 1.16 the place is further defined: east, beside the altar (i.e. east of the ramp but south of the altar). The tradition is that the fire-pan removed the ashes from the centre of the burning wood pile, where the flesh of the sacrifices was most likely to be burnt to ashes. The removal was a daily duty, and the final removal from the heap beside the altar took place when the heap became too big.

11. to a clean place: see note on 4.12. V and DV make it 'a very clean place', but add that when outside the camp the ashes are to 'be consumed to dust', *favilla*, strictly 'hot glowing ashes', but more generally 'any dust after a fire'.

12. The wood for the altar-fire was brought into the Temple nine times a year, the last time being the Feast of Wood-Offering on the 15th Ab, roughly the first fortnight of August. On this occasion everybody helped, but on the other eight occasions only those families' descendants of those chosen by lot by Nehemiah (Neh. 10.34, 13.31; *Taan.*, iv, 5). 'Everybody' included 'all whose tribal descent was in doubt' and also 'the pestle-smugglers and fig-preservers'. Five of the nine occasions were in the month Ab, the best time for cutting wood. The wood was sorted for woodworm and rot, and the sound wood was stored in a special room on the S. side (*Midd.*, v, 4). T (Pal) says the wood on the altar was replenished four times a day.

13. The ever-burning fire is an ancient religious custom found in many religions (J. G. Fraser, *The Magic Art*, ii, pp. 253–65). According to R. K. Yerkes (*Sacrifice in Greek and Roman Religions and Early Judaism*, 1953, p. 138), the origin is to be found in the mundane necessity of keeping a fire burning in days when kindling a fire was not easy, and he holds that the 'symbolic explanation' came later. Most assume a religious explanation from the beginning (cf. the Roman Vestal fire, but see note on 24.4).

(b) THE RITUAL OF THE GRAIN-OFFERING **6.14–18** (Heb 7–11)

15. memorial portion: better 'token' (see note on 2.2). Except for the grain-offering described in verses 19–23, nothing but flesh and fat and tokens of anything else were placed on the altar.

burn: always the Hebrew for burning on the altar is *hiḵṭîr*, from the root *ḵ-ṭ-r*, send up in smoke. The word for 'secular' burning is *ś-r-p*, which is used of the disposal of those sin-offerings which were burnt outside the camp.

16. in a holy place: this is defined as being **in the court of the tent of meeting,** which in the Second Temple meant the Court of the Priests. The extent of this court is uncertain, as a comparison of various suggested plans of the Temple buildings shows. Both this court and the Court of Israel were within the Upper Gate, but where the division was is disputed. Probably the confusion is due to changes made in the time of Herod the Great.

18. touches: holiness, like uncleanness, is contagious. There is nothing ethical about this kind of holiness and this kind of ritual uncleanness. Both are relics of ancient, primitive *taboo* (cf. article 'Holiness' in *ERE*, vi, p. 732; and *DIOT*, pp. 36–42).

decreed for ever: lit. a perpetual decree. But instead of *ḥôḵ* (decree) Sam has *ḥēleḵ* (portion, share), thus saying that this offering is a perpetual, inalienable perquisite of the priests.

(c) THE RITUAL OF THE DAILY GRAIN-OFFERING **6.19–23** (Heb 12–16)

It is not entirely clear what this grain-offering is, whether it is the *minḥaṯ haḥᵃḇittîm* (the grain-offering of baked pieces), i.e. pieces baked on the griddle (*maḥaḇaṯ*, verse 21), or whether it is the *minḥaṯ haḥinnûk* (the grain-offering of initiation) which the priest offered on the day of his initiation. The confusion arises from the phrase 'on the day when he is anointed' (verse 20), which many think is a mistaken gloss from 8.26 and 9.4. Probably this is right. There was a daily cereal-offering, provided by the High Priest (Josephus, *Ant. Iud.* III, x, 7). Thus the phrase here, 'Aaron and his sons', means Aaron the High Priest and his successor (cf. verse 22). This cereal-offering was different from all others in that the whole of it was burnt on the altar. The rite is of the utmost importance, since it is a survival of the days when the *minḥāh* (grain-offering) was truly the *minḥāh* (tribute) of the agriculturalist, just as the flesh whole-offering (*'ôlāh*) was the gift of the pastoral nomad. This particular grain-offering consisted of one tenth of an ephah (about 7 pints) of flour, baked on a griddle. One half was offered in the morning and the other half in the evening. This is doubtless the origin of such phrases as 'the time of the offering of the oblation' (*minḥāh*) (1 Kg. 18.29, 36) and the later term *minḥaṯ 'ereḇ* (evening offering, sacrifice). The Talmud (*b. Men.*, 50b) gives minute instructions as to what is to be done if the High Priest dies during the day: a whole new cereal-offering is to be provided, one half substituted for the half already offered and the new evening half to be offered in the ordinary way.

There was a grain-offering offered by every priest on his first day, and probably this is the reason for the confusion. In this case 'Aaron and his sons' means every priest. The whole section is not found in LXX (Cod. A).

21. well mixed: the Hebrew *rāḇaḵ* means 'mix, stir', but the Talmudic *rᵉḇîḵāh* is a dough, made of flour mixed with hot water and oil. This is why (verse 22) V and DV say that the offering must be hot when it is offered, and Rashi says it is to be 'scalded to saturation with hot oil'; hence RV 'soaked'.

baked pieces: Hebrew tradition is that the offering was broken in pieces. The Mishnah (*Men.*, vi, 4) says that the pieces were the size of olives, and that *minḥāhs* were always so broken when no handful tokens were taken. But the Hebrew word involved (*tupînê*) is difficult and uncertain. G. R. Driver suggests *tô'pennāh* (root *'-p-h*, bake) 'thou shalt bake it'; Merx, *tᵉputtennāh* (root *p-t-t*, break) 'thou shalt break it in pieces'. LXX has *helikta* (rolls, twists: root *p-n-h*, turn), and Rashi has something of this when he says it means many times baked (? turned again and again; cf. Hos. 7.8), with the grain first scalded to saturation and then fried in a pan (so *b. Men.*, 75b and the Sifra).

23. No priest could eat his own offering, even if it was a grain-offering, which normally went to the priest.

(d) THE RITUAL OF THE SIN-OFFERING **6.24–30** (Heb 17–23)

The truly important element of this rite was to get rid of the sin, represented by the animal, whether actually or symbolically contained. If the priest was not involved in the sin he ate the flesh, being a sort of sin-eater. If the priest was involved, either personally or as a member of the whole people, he could not eat it, so it had to be taken outside to a clean place and destroyed by fire.

27f. Holiness is contagious, especially the holiness of the sin-offering. 'Holy' here means *taboo* and has nothing to do with what is ethically right or wrong. An odd spatter of blood on a garment makes that garment 'holy' (*taboo*). The 'holiness' can soak into an earthen bowl, which must therefore be destroyed. A bronze vessel can be scoured and then rinsed. The Hebrew word translated 'scoured' is *šāṭap* and the *šeṭep* is the sudden spate of waters caused by a tropical downpour, the 'flash flood' which sweeps everything before it (Isa. 28.18; Mt. 7.27).

30. This is a complicated way of saying that a priest cannot eat the flesh of any sin-offering in which he himself is involved (4.7 and 16).

(e) THE RITUAL OF THE COMPENSATION-OFFERING (RSV GUILT OFFERING) **7.1–10**

This section ends with a digression (7–10) concerning the priest's perquisites. For the differences between the sin-offering and the compensation-offering see note on 4.1–5.13, and the article there cited.

The Perquisites of the Priests **7–10**

The common feature of the sin-offering and the guilt-offering is that the priest who performs the ceremony receives the flesh. Also, the priest receives the hide of the whole-offering. He also receives all cooked cereals, but all uncooked cereals, wet or dry, belong to the priests as a whole.

(f) THE RITUAL OF THE SHARED-OFFERING (RSV PEACE OFFERING) **7.11–36**

There are three types of these offerings, the flesh of which provided a sacred feast: thanksgiving (LXX *ainesis*, praise), vow (LXX *euchē*, which actually means 'vow' rather than 'prayer'), and freewill. For a discussion concerning this sacrifice, see p. 15.

12. The thanksgiving sacrifice differed from the other two in that it had to be accompanied by wafers and cakes. For the shape of these so-called wafers and these cakes; see note on 2.4. There were three types of unleavened cakes: perforated cakes (*ḥallôṯ*) mixed with oil, thin round cakes (*rᵉḳîḳîm*) traditionally but erroneously called 'wafers', and perforated cakes (*ḥallôṯ*) made from a dough consisting of hot water and oil (cf. 6.21). The man also had to bring *ḥallôṯ* of leavened bread. The Mishnah says (*Men.*, vii, 1) that the total quantity of flour required was seventy pints for the unleavened cakes and seventy for the leavened.

14. an offering to the Lord: EVV have 'heave offering'; the Heb is *tᵉrûmāh*, the usual explanation of which is that it was moved up and down by the priest as a ritual action, just as the *tᵉnûpāh* (EVV 'wave-offering') has been explained as an offering that was waved to and fro, either forwards and back again or from side to side, though it has never been explained how the whole of the Levites could be 'waved' (Num. 8.11, etc.). For *tᵉrûmāh* V and DV always thought of first-fruits. They were only partly right, because whilst first-fruits were a *tᵉrûmāh*, not every *tᵉrûmāh* was a first-fruit. LXX has *aphairema* (that which is taken away), which is almost correct. The *tᵉrûmāh* was a 'reserved portion', that which was 'lifted off' (root *rûm*) from the rest. For *tᵉnûpāh* V has *elevatio* and often *separatio* for *tᵉrûmāh*. According to G. R. Driver (*JSS* 1, 1956, 97–105), the *tᵉnûpāh* was 'a special contribution and has nothing to do with waving in any direction whatever'. We would derive the word from *nûp* II (be high, overtop; cf. *nôp*, elevation, Ps. 48.2); see *ET* 74, 1962–63, 127. Both words, *t^erûmāh* and *t^enûpāh*, mean that which is lifted high. The distinction is that the *t^erûmāh* was the perquisite of the individual officiating priest, whilst the *t^enûpāh* was for the use and service of the whole priesthood. This is why all the Levites were a *t^enûpāh* (Num. 8.11).

15. LXX precedes this verse with the statement that the pieces of flesh (*ta krea*) of the thanksgiving-offering 'shall be his', i.e. the officiating priest's. Actually the right thigh was his share, whilst the priesthood received the breast. The rest of the flesh could be eaten anywhere in the city by any man and cooked in any fashion (*Zeb.*, v, 7). The flesh of the thanksgiving-offering had to be eaten the same day, but that of the other two types, the vow and the freewill, could be eaten on the second day also. There is a complete prohibition concerning the third day. The permission to eat the flesh on the second day is surprising, since in really hot countries no meat may be left 'to hang'.

18. an abomination: the word is *piggûl*, which *RS*², p. 343, says is flesh with the blood, but this cannot be right, since presumably the blood had been drawn off when the animal was slaughtered (3.2, 7.14). The corresponding Arabic root means 'be thick and soft, flaccid'. The word refers to meat gone bad, soft and flabby and becoming putrescent. The Masoretes altered the vowels to those of the word *šiḳḳûṣ*, that which is thoroughly abominable and detestable to God, usually because of its association with false gods and idols. Compare *Sikkûṯ* (for *Sakkut*) and *Kiyyûn* (for *Kewan*), idolatrous names in Am. 5.26; also *gillûlîm*, a Hebrew name for 'false-gods, idols', commonly supposed to be derived from *g-l-l* II (roll, and so 'logs of wood'), but more likely to be allied to the Arabic *jalla*, be great in majesty, especially of God, but given the 'abominable' vowels to declare that such majesty is filthy and detestable.

A Digression on Food Taboos 19–21

The flesh that is eaten at these sacred meals must be ritually clean, just as the eater must be ritually clean.

Prohibitions against eating Fat and Blood 22–27

No fat of any animal whatever is to be eaten. The fat of sacrificed animals must be burnt on the altar (1.8, 12; 3.3–5; 9–10, 14–15; 4.8–10, 11, 19, 26, 31, 35, 7.3–5). The fat of an animal that dies a natural death or is mangled by wild beasts cannot be eaten, but it may be used for general domestic purposes. The fat, equally with the blood, is regarded as containing the life, and both are therefore *taboo* to men.

The Priests' Shares from the Shared-offerings 28–36

The fat of the animal is an *'iššeh* (fire-offering), because it is burnt on the altar. The breast is a *t^enûpāh*: it goes to the priesthood. The right leg is a *t^erûmāh*: it goes to the officiating priest (see note on 7.14). Gradually through the centuries the share of the priests increased: that is, the share of the offering which was destined for the sacred meal. In the time of Eli at Shiloh the priest's servant plunged a three-pronged fork into the pot in which the flesh was being boiled, and the priest received what came up on the fork. One of the crimes of Eli's sons was that they wanted more. According to Dt. 18.3, the priest received 'the shoulder and the two cheeks and the stomach'. In P, it is the breast and the hind quarter.

32. thigh: following RV, but RVm follows AV with 'shoulder', and so also DV, after LXX and V 'upper arm', that is, the shoulder joint of the animal. Rashi says that the *šôḳ* is the middle of the three limbs of an animal's leg and his commentators assumes that he means the hind leg. It is what we would call the hind quarter.

35. portion: following RVm. Elsewhere *mišḥāh* means 'ointment, anointing' (8.2, etc.; twenty-one times and all in P), and so LXX, V, and DV here. AV inserts 'portion'. The Accadian verb means 'to measure' and the noun 'measurement'. This is the justification of the rendering 'portion'. The complication is caused by the use of the verb *māšaḥ*, meaning 'anointing', in verse 36, a verse which bears every mark of being an addition. It represents a different attitude. In verse 35 the share of the priests is regarded as being taken from 'the fire-offerings', which include everything which crosses the holy line. In verse 36 the share of the priests is taken out of the flesh of the animal which is for the people. Read, therefore, 'portion'. The word has nothing to do with anointing.
consecrated: this word is not found in MT, but may be due to the traditional translation of *mišḥāh* as 'anointing-portion'. EVV are here correct.

(g) SUMMARY 7.37–38

These two verses form the closing summary of the whole section which deals with the Temple sacrifices.
consecration: the Hebrew is *millû'îm* from the transitive verb *millē'*, to fill. The regular Hebrew phrase for the installation of a priest is 'fill the hand' (8.33). The use of such terms as 'consecration' is unfortunate, since it imports later ecclesiastical ideas into the original.
the wilderness of Sinai: the site of Sinai is uncertain (see pp. 23–26). The tradition which identifies Mount Sinai with the *Jebel Mûsā* is as early as the fourth century A.D. It has also been argued that it is the *Jebel Serbal*, twenty miles to the north-west. Many modern scholars think it is in the neighbourhood of Kadesh. For details, see J. Bright, *A History of Israel*, 1960, pp. 113–15; *DB*, p. 923; and for a full discussion of the earlier ideas, S. R. Driver, *Exodus* (Camb. Bible, 1911), pp. 177–91.

SECOND SECTION 8.1–10.20 THE PRIESTHOOD

(a) THE CONSECRATION OF AARON AND HIS SONS 8.1–36

For details of the changes in personnel in the priesthood during the centuries, see pp. 11–14. This chapter tells how the instructions of Exodus 28 were carried out, that chapter in which, according to the P-traditions, Aaron and his sons were chosen at Sinai to be the only true priests. Primarily this present chapter deals with the anointing and the robing in special garments of Aaron. It is he that has the anointing-oil poured on his head. The ceremonies in which 'his sons' participated are: being bathed in water, being clothed in their own clothing, which differs from that of Aaron, and all the ceremonies connected with the sacrifices.

2–4. The whole congregation assemble at the opening of the tent, Moses, Aaron and his sons, and all the people.

2. the garments: this is correct. LXX has 'his' and V 'theirs'. It is best not to define them, since both sets of clothes are included.
the anointing oil: this was specially compounded (Exod. 30.23–24): two parts liquid myrrh, two parts cassia, one part each of cinnamon and aromatic cane, with olive oil added. The proportions worked out at about 1 pint of olive oil to 54 lbs. of dry spices.
the bull: it was a *par*, young bull (see 4.3). The Arabic *purâr* (same root) stands for the young of any domesticated animal. The Sifra says it was a young bull in order to atone for the incident of the Golden Calf (see also Rashi on Lev. 9.1). The P-tradition plays down the connection between Aaron and the Golden Calf and makes him almost co-equal with Moses from the beginning, but the Targums and early Jewish tradition do not let him off so easily.
basket: the *sal* was an open plaited basket (cf. Gen. 40.16). Details as to the contents are given in verse 26, following Exod. 29.2, but according to custom there were ten cakes each of the three types (cf. note on 7.12).

Aaron is invested **5–9**
The traditional date is 23 Adar, which varies between the end of February and the middle of March.

6. brought: the same word is used here as in 1.3, where it is translated 'offer', as V and DV here. Lit. it is 'brought near', but 'present' is suitable in all cases.

7. the coat: this is the High Priest's tunic, the *k^{e}ṯōneṯ* or *kuttōneṯ*, which both men and women wore next to the skin. In Accadian and Arabic the word means 'linen, cloth'. The Greek *chitōn* (in earlier times for men only, the woman's shift being the *peplos*) is a loan-word. V has *subucula* (undershirt), and DV 'strait linen garment'. The High Priest's tunic was embroidered (Exod. 28.4, 39) and of the finest (? Egyptian) linen thread (Exod. 39.27).
the girdle: this was a long embroidered sash (Exod. 28.39). It was forty-eight feet long (Talmud) and wound round and round the waist. It is quite distinct from the 'skilfully woven band of the ephod'.
the robe: Rashi (on Exod. 28.4) says the *m^{e}'īl* was a kind of shirt, but not worn next the skin. It is the 'robe of the ephod' of Exod. 28.31, all of blue, a large spread of cloth with a hole for the head and the edge of the hole oversewn to prevent

tearing and fraying. Josephus says (*Bell. Iud.* V, v, 7; *Ant. Iud.* III, vii, 4) that it reached down to the feet, like the outer flowing robe of the modern Arab.
ephod: LXX has *epōmis* (shoulder strap) and V has *humerale* (cape, covering for the shoulder). Details are given in Exod. 28.6–7, 39.2–4, but these descriptions do not make it plain whether the ephod was a sort of waistcoat with shoulder-straps or a pair of short trousers (drawers) with braces.

There were apparently three (or four) types of ephod. First, there was the *'ēpôḏ baḏ* (the linen ephod), drawers made of white linen, which the priest wore to cover his private parts. The boy Samuel wore such an ephod (1 Sam. 2.18), and so did David (2 Sam. 6.14, 20), where it is plain from what Michal said that the garment was decidedly scanty. A second type is the ephod which Abiathar carried in his hand when he escaped from the massacre at Nob of the ex-Shiloh priests (presumably) of the House of Eli (1 Sam. 23.6). It must have been reasonably light, since Abiathar was the only survivor. Abiathar used this ephod whenever David sought divine guidance in the old freebooting days (1 Sam. 23.9), etc. ('Bring the ephod here'). It was a special ephod, used in divination in connexion with the casting of the sacred lot. Possibly it was an embroidered garment, put on by the priest on special occasions. A third type is the High Priest's ephod, mentioned here and described in Exod. 28.6–7, 39.2–4. It had shoulder-straps attached to it and it was fastened with 'a skilfully woven band'. Most modern scholars think of the ephod as worn above the waist with the band acting as a belt at the lower edge, a sort of waistcoat reaching as high as the armpits and having shoulder-straps. Rashi (on Exod. 28.4, 6) says he found no tradition anywhere as to shape and form, but he himself thinks in terms of the Old French *pourceint*, a kind of apron which ladies of rank tied on when they rode horseback, tied round the waist and fastened behind. If, as one may reasonably assume, there is a connexion at all between the linen ephod and this divination ephod, it is that the linen ephod was extremely scanty, whilst the other was a much more elaborate affair. The High Priest's ephod, in this case, is an elaborate consciously devised archaism with pouches for the sacred lot (Urim and Thummim), designed for tradition and splendour, the original methods of divination having long since been outgrown. Possibly there was a fourth type, since some think that Gideon's ephod was an image (Jg. 8.27), and so also Micah's ephod (Jg. 17.5). This is by no means certain, since Gideon could have made the ephod from the purple garments and not from the gold, and it says of Micah that he made an image of the silver, and the reference to an ephod and teraphim occurs in the next verse. On the other hand, the cognate noun *'ᵃpûḏāh* is used in Isa. 30.22 of the sheathing of idols, made of wood and overlaid with gold (cf. Dt. 7.25; Isa. 40.19). The best solution appears to be: the root *'-p-d* refers to that which fits closely like a sheath and can be used either of closely fitting garments for a priest (or possibly in Arabic of an ambassador) or of closely fitting envelopes for idols made of wood. The ephod was worn below rather than above the waist, in the form of short drawers or closely fitting split skirts, but the divination ephod was high-waisted. See the long note in S. R. Driver, *Exodus* (Camb. Bible), pp. 312f., where he refers to Perrot and Chipez, *Egyptian Art*, i, pp. 247, 302, and two figures portrayed there 'wearing vestlike garments, reaching from the breasts nearly to the knees, with a band round the waist and shoulder straps'. Cf. Rev. 1.13, 'clothed with a long robe and a golden girdle round his breast'.

skilfully woven band: AV has 'curious girdle': 'curious' meant 'skilful' as late as the latter half of the eighteenth century. RV has 'cunningly woven'. These renderings, together with RSV, depend on taking *ḥēšeḇ* to be the Hebrew root *ḥ-š-b* (think, devise), but the ancient authorities do not recognize this root here. The Targum on Exod. 28.4 says it was a girdle, and it knows nothing of anything cunning or skilful. It has the word *hemyāynā'* (Persian *hemyan*), girdle, belt. LXX has *poiēsēs* (work), whilst V telescopes the two verses, but has *balteus* for *'aḇnēṭ* (RSV 'girdle', but it was actually a sash) and *cingulum* for *ḥēšeḇ*: two different Latin words, but both meaning 'belt, girdle'. Read therefore 'belt'.

binding: this is the verb *'-p-d*, fastened it closely. It is thus most likely that the ephod was something that fitted closely.

The end of this verse is the half-way mark of the Pentateuch according to verses.

8. breastpiece: AV and RV have 'breastplate'. LXX has *logion* (announcement, oracle), whilst V has the extraordinary *rationale* (DV 'the rational'), which looks like an attempt to translate the Greek *logion* as an adjective. Rashi (on Exod. 28.4) says the Hebrew *ḥōšen* means an ornament worn in front of the heart. It was some sort of pouch, mostly a receptacle for Urim and Thummim.

the Urim and the Thummim: the reference is to the sacred lot (Exod. 28.30). Whatever these were, they were kept in a pouch, in ancient times in the ephod, and they were thrown. There were three possible answers: Yes, No, No answer. In 1 Sam. 28.6 God gave Saul 'no answer' whether by dreams or prophets or by Urim. When these 'dice' (?) were cast, God was called upon to give either Urim or Thummim (1 Sam. 14.41). The Targums do not help. LXX and V have 'teaching and truth'; Sym has 'lights and perfections'. This last is quoted by Rashi and it is in the Talmud (*b. Yoma*, 73b), and it connects the words with the roots *'ôr* (be light) and *t-m-m* (be perfect). There are many ancient explanations. The Talmud says that the Holy Name was inscribed between the two folds of the breastplate and that through the inscription the statements were clear (lights) and the promises true (perfects). Josephus (*Ant. Iud.* III, viii, 9) says that the twelve gems gave the oracular decision by shining. Philo (*Vita Mos.*, iii) suggests that they were two small images like the oracle images of Egypt. This might explain why the ephod is mentioned so often in association with the teraphim and other idols. Possibly Urim and Thummim were two flat discs, like the small discs with the faces of gods stamped on them placed in crevices and suchlike in Hindu homes, but with one surface (say) yellow and the other (say) black. In this way both could fall yellow, or both black, or they could fall one yellow and one black. This would provide the three different answers. Possibly the words are derived from the roots *'-r-r* (curse) and *t-m-m* (perfect), so that Urim means No and Thummim means Yes. See *DB*, pp. 1019f., and *AI*, pp. 352f.

9. turban: LXX *mitra*, whence DV 'mitre'. The Greek *mitra* was eastern in origin and was worn by women and effeminate young men, or as a nightcap, but it was also the name of the headdress of the priest of Herakles at Cos (Plutarch, ii, 304C) and of the headgear of the god Bacchus (Propertius, IV, ii, 21). V has *cidaris*, which, like the Talmud *keṯer* a loan-word from Persian, was the headdress of Persian kings or what was known as 'the high tiara' (Curtius, III, iii, 19), mainly a dark blue band picked out with white. In Est. 1.11; 2.17, etc., the *keṯer* is the royal crown of Persia. The inference is that this headdress is post-exilic and belongs to the time when the High Priest was both priest and ruler. It was a turban, as the Hebrew *miṣnepeṯ* implies, being wound round the head (Lev. 16.4), though it may have been wound permanently round a skull-cap and put on entire, like turbans worn in India by non-Sikhs.
the golden plate: the Hebrew *ṣîṣ* means 'flower'. There is a strong ancient tradition that it was a golden plate, so EVV following V *lamina*. Rashi (on Exod. 28.36) says it was a kind of gold plate, two fingers in breadth, reaching from ear to ear, whilst the Talmud (*b. Zeb.*, 19a) says that the High Priest's hair was visible between the plate and the turban. The plate was suspended over the forehead by three strings. Perhaps there was a change in the tradition because the LXX *petalon* means 'leaf', though it can also mean a leaf of metal, and so a lamina.
the holy crown: or 'sacred diadem'. The Hebrew *nēzer* means 'consecration, diadem, crown'. In old Israel all sacred persons wore unshorn hair. Hair is usually *taboo* and all sacred persons must preserve it from defilement, either by letting it grow long (Hebrew fashion, e.g. Nazirites) or by keeping the head shaved (Egyptian, Buddhists, Roman priests; cf. the modern tonsure, as a token baldness). Kings wore a circlet round their heads to keep the long-flowing hair (cf. Jg. 5.2, the charismatic leaders who let their hair go unbound, Hebrew *p-r-'* III) under some sort of control. This is why kings wear crowns. LXX, V, and DV take the two words as defining 'plate' and have 'consecrated with sanctification'. Josephus (*Ant. Iud.* III, vii, 6) says the High Priest's mitre was made like the headdress of the other priests, but with another above it, and round this a polished golden crown of three rows, one above the other, with a cup of gold at the top, like a flower with open pointed petals. In saying that the priests had the same headdress (i.e. apart from the triple crown) Josephus may well be right for his own time. There seems to have been a tendency for customs and privileges gradually to extend to lower grades. At one time only the High Priest was anointed (Lev. 8.12), but Exod. 28.41. apparently says (or proposes) that all priests were anointed. Until the time of Herod Agrippa II (king of Chalkis in A.D. 48, but was given much wider territory by Nero) only the priests were allowed to wear white robes, but in his days this privilege was extended to the Levites. He was given general supervision of the Temple, and it is quite possible that when the Levites began to wear the white robes, the priests adopted a more ornate headdress.

11. seven times: see note on 4.6.
the laver and its base: according to P, there was one bronze laver, and it stood

'between the tent of meeting and the altar' (Exod. 30.18). According to 1 Kg. 7.27–39 there were ten lavers set on wheeled bronze stands (cf. lavers found at Larnaka and Enkomi, A. Parrot, *The Temple of Jerusalem*, 1957, pp. 48f.). The ten lavers were in groups of five, one group to the right of the Temple and the other to the left. It is evident that there was a change in the arrangements (cf. the alteration of the position of the altar in the Established Church in the time of Archbishop Laud).

12. poured . . . anointed: priests were not anointed during the time of the monarchy (*AI*, pp. 105, 114, 347) or afterwards, certainly at first; only the High Priest, as here. In Dan. 9.25 the anointed one is the prince, so we may judge that the High Priest was anointed because he was ruler rather than because he was priest. The tradition is (*b. Ker.*, 5b) that a drop of oil was placed on his head, then a drop between his eyebrows, and these were joined with the finger in the form of a cross (the Greek *chi*). Cf. the cross which was smeared on the baked cereal offering (2.4). Some have seen evidence here that the cross had a religious significance before the Christian era, but the explanation is probably much more simple. In Ezek. 9.3–4 the angel scribe puts 'a mark' on the foreheads of those who are to be preserved. The Hebrew is *tāw*, which is the last consonant in the alphabet and which in the old script was a cross. This is why we must cross our letter *t*, since both our script and the Hebrew script go back to a Phoenician original. What more natural mark would anybody put on anything than a straight cross? Apparently the rest of the oil was poured over his head so that it ran down over his beard and his robes (Ps. 133.2).

13. caps: the Hebrew is *miḡbā'ôṯ* (round caps, skull-caps). Josephus says (*Ant. Iud.* III, vii, 3) that the ordinary priest's headdress was a *pilos* (felt cap shaped like half an egg) and not a *petasos* (hat). AV has 'bonnets'. They were caps in the Middle English sense, without a brim; cf. the friar's cap. The priest's skull-cap was made of fine linen (Exod. 39.28). DV follows V with 'mitres', perhaps because Josephus also said (*Ant. Iud.* III, vii, 6) that all priests had their headdresses made in the same way.

14–17. This section follows the instructions of Exod. 29.10–14. It was slaughtered outside the opening of the tent of meeting (Exod. 29.11), because it was for the priest and priests could not eat their own sin. The animal therefore never came within the Holy Place, but was destroyed by fire outside the camp.

18–21. Again following instructions, and a normal burnt-offering.

22–36. The ram of ordination. This section follows the instructions of Exod. 29.19–26, but verse 30 (Exod. 29.21) is interpolated.

22. ordination: AV and RV have 'consecration', following V and DV. The Hebrew is *millû'îm* (cf. 7.37). It is better to avoid the word 'ordination', since it introduces other ideas into the context, and in any case there was no laying on of hands except on the head of the sin-offering.

23. tip of . . . ear: Frazer (*Folklore of the Old Testament*, iii, pp. 165–269) gives many instances of the mutilation of the ear and fingers in magical rites to avoid the influence of evil powers, it being (he says) important that these outlying parts of the body should be specially guarded against contamination. See note on 4.6; if the extremities are consecrated, then the whole is consecrated. The notion is virtually world-wide that the right is good and the left is bad. In some parts of the world to wave dismissal with the left hand is an insult, and to eat with the left hand is a filthy habit. The blood of the ordination ram is not sin-blood, and therefore the remainder is thrown over the altar and not at the foot of it.

26. the right thigh: the right thigh of this offering is a *t^e^nûp̱āh* (so-called wave-offering), and so also the breast. The ritual of the ordination ram is unique. Apparently it was slaughtered at the opening of the Tent of Meeting, where the *zeḇaḥ* (shared-offering) was slaughtered, and was eaten there by the priests. Normally what the priests ate was eaten within the Holy Place, and if they ate the whole of the offering, as in the cases of the people's sin-offering and of the compensation-offering, then the animal was slain in the Holy Place. This variation is correct, since Aaron and his sons were not yet priests, and they would have to eat as laymen, outside the Holy Place (but see note on verse 31). But usually the right thigh was a *t^e^rûmāh* (RSV offering, EVV heave-offering) and as such was the perquisite of the officiating priest. Possibly, since this is an ordination ceremony, God is regarded as the officiant, and therefore he receives the priest's portion, but this does not explain why the thigh is called a *t^e^nûp̱āh*. The breast is also a *t^e^nûp̱āh*, which is normal, but this goes to Moses, presumably because he represents the whole priesthood. Rashi (on Exod. 29.22) noticed the anomalies and offers a complicated explanation based on the idea that both *millû'îm* (RSV ordination) and *š^e^lāmîm* (RSV peace-offerings) can mean 'full, perfect', but his explanation is far from satisfactory. The fact is that this ceremony does not fit into the general pattern, and this is acknowledged by the parenthesis 'for it is a ram of ordination' in Exod. 29.22.

31. The flesh is eaten by the priests-to-be at the opening of the Tent of Meeting. They are not priests enough to eat it within the Holy Place, and not laymen enough to eat it anywhere outside. They are on the border, and must eat the flesh on the border.

33. seven days: see note on 4.6. The whole interval is a passage time, passing from 'the house of laity' to the 'house of priests'.

34. make atonement: i.e. perform a ritual cleansing ceremony. The High Priest is separated for seven days before the Day of Atonement, and the priest concerned with the rite of the Red Heifer also.

(b) THE INSTALLATION OF AARON AND HIS SONS 9.1–24

Aaron and his sons commence their duties, this being the eighth day and thus the first day of their priesthood. He offers sacrifices for the first time: sin-offering first and then whole-offering, but no shared-offering, which was essentially a layman's sacrifice, and no compensation-offering, since no damage had been done to anybody.

2. a bull calf: LXX has 'a tender little calf from the oxen'. Rashi says that '*ēḡel ben bāḳār* (the phrase used here) means a bull-calf in its second year, whilst '*ēḡel* alone means a calf in its first year. He is here dependent on Mic. 6.6 (calves a year old) and Lev. 9.3, the only other places where this word is used of a sacrificial animal. The Jerusalem Targum makes the most of the calf for the sin-offering and the ram for the whole-offering. The calf is 'that Satan may not accuse thee concerning the calf thou madest at Horeb'. The Targum never allows Aaron to forget. The bull is 'as a memorial for thee of the righteousness of Isaac whom his father bound as a ram on the mount of worship'. There is a marked trend in Jewish theology whereby the Binding of Isaac tends to occupy a place similar to that of the Crucifixion in Christian theology.

3. calf: once again the Jerusalem Targum improves the occasion. The male goat is a reminder of the goat which Joseph's brethren killed (Gen. 37.31), the calf is because the Israelites worshipped the Golden Calf (Exod. 32.4), and the lamb because Abraham bound Isaac like a lamb (Gen. 22.7).

unto the people of Israel: LXX and Sam have 'elders' assimilating to verse 1.

4. will appear: all translators read the participle, strictly 'is about to appear', but Hebrew has the perfect 'has appeared'. The Targums have the usual reverent circumlocutions: Onkelos, 'the *yᵉḳārā'* (honour, dignity) of the Lord will be revealed'; Jerusalem, 'the glory of the Shekinah of the Lord'. The beginning of this tendency is to be seen in Ezek. 1.28.

6. the glory of the LORD: more accurately 'that the glory of the Lord may be revealed to you'. The root *k-b-d* means 'be heavy, weighty', and so 'honoured', but the noun *kāḇôḏ* is used almost wholly of the external appearance of wealth and prosperity, on the analogy of the eastern prince and the resplendent way in which he shows his greatness. Thus the 'Glory of the Lord' is the shining splendour with which he is encompassed in a theophany. The Targums naturally refer to the Shekinah (lit. the Presence), the luminous cloud which shrouds the presence of God. The shepherds of Bethlehem were surrounded by this glory (Lk. 2.9); it was the luminous cloud at the Transfiguration (Mk 9.2–8). It is mentioned in P's descriptions of theophanies in Exodus, often in the Psalms, and on all great occasions in 1 Kings in the history of the Temple (8.10f., etc.). The regular LXX equivalent is *doxa*, and thence in the New Testament. In classical Greek this word means 'opinion' and 'repute' in the sense of the good opinion which others may have of a man. Thus it could mean 'glory' in the sense of credit and reputation, but in the New Testament it means 'glory' in the Old Testament sense of splendour (cf. the Latin *gloria*). Further, see *BDB*, pp. 458f., and article 'Glory' in *HDB*, ii, pp. 183–6, and that in *DB*, pp. 331f.

7. make atonement for: once again V and DV have 'pray for', but, as elsewhere in P, the root *k-p-r* involves propitiatory rites for errors that are largely ritual. Elsewhere the reference is to sins in which sacrificial rites may or may not be involved (cf. the parallel phrase 'cover the face' (Gen. 32.21)).

8–11 This ritual is normal for a sin-offering in which a priest is involved (see 4.1–12).

12–14. The usual routine of the whole-offering is followed (Lev. 1.3–9), except that the priests act as assistants to Aaron the High Priest, who here is 'celebrating his first sacrifice'.

15. offered it for sin, following EVV: this rendering is unfortunate, since it suggests that the sin-offering was offered to God. This is not the case, since nothing of it (except, as usual, the blood and the fat) went anywhere near the altar. Translate 'performed the de-sinning rite'.

16–17. He inaugurates the daily whole-offering, the *tāmîḏ*, which consisted of the animal and grain-offering, the whole of which in this instance was burnt on the altar. But see note on 6.19–23 (Heb 12–16).

16. offered it according to the ordinance: better 'according to custom (tradition)', LXX 'as is proper'. He did not burn the sacrifice then and there (verse 24), so we should read 'prepared'. Cf. Gen. 18.7, where the same verb (*'āśāh*) is used of dressing a calf ready for eating.

17. filled the hand: this is not the handful of 2.2. The phrase belongs to the special installation rites (*millû'îm*: filling full, Exod. 28.41, etc.; Lev. 8.33), where 'filling the hand' (root *m-l-'*) means 'make his first sacrifice' and so 'institute to priestly office'. Here the whole of the *minḥāh* (grain-offering) is burnt on the altar. The priest is offering his first *tāmîḏ* (cf. note on 6.19–23 (Heb 12–16)).

18–21. The High Priest deals with the *zeḇaḥ š^{e}lāmîm* (RSV sacrifice of peace-offerings) of the people. The variation from the normal procedure is that both the breast and the right thigh are wave-offerings, i.e. a *t^{e}nûpāh* (special contribution; see 7.28–36). In this case all the priests were participating, so both breast and thigh go to all the priests; thus in this particular instance, the thigh also is a *t^{e}nûpāh* (for all the priests).

The Final Blessing **22–24**

It is only to be expected that Jewish tradition should be strong in saying that Aaron uttered the Aaronite priestly blessing of Num. 6.24–26. The tradition is that the second blessing (verse 23) consisted of the last verse of 'the Prayer of Moses' (Ps. 90.17).

24. fire came forth: it is sometimes said that there is a discrepancy here, since the whole-offering was already consumed (verses 13, 14). But there were two, and this is the whole-offering of the people. This sacrifice had been prepared (RSV offered) but not burnt. The supernatural kindling of such fire is a sign of God's special approval (Jg. 6.21; 1 Kg. 18.38) and acceptance. The other instances (1 Chr. 21.26; 2 Chr. 7.1) are occasions of the inauguration of fundamental elements in the Temple worship—David erecting the first altar on the sacred site, and Solomon offering the first whole-offering in the new Temple. Here we have the first whole-offering of the priesthood on behalf of the people.

they shouted: this is the *rinnāh*, the loud, ringing cry of the worshipper, sometimes in supplication (1 Kg. 8.28, cry), but mostly in joy and praise. The ancient versions have 'praise', except LXX which has 'were amazed', the only case where the Hebrew *rinnâh* is translated by *existēmi.*

fell on their faces: the root *n-p-l* is normally used of a sudden swift descent. Rebekah did not merely alight from her camel when she saw Isaac (Gen. 24.64), nor did she 'fall off'. She got down hurriedly. In Am. 3.5 the verb is used of the sudden swoop downwards of the bird when it sees the bait in the trap. The Jerusalem Targum says that 'they bowed in prayer on their faces', but the phrase denotes the speedy and full abasement in prayer which is proper before the mighty God.

(c) NADAB AND ABIHU 10.1–7

This story does two things. It stresses the terrible fate of the layman who tries to act as priest; it explains why the two elder sons of Aaron and their descendants had no place in the priesthood. In the one case, holiness is dangerous unless approached by the proper persons and according to the proper rules. In the second place, the post-exilic priesthood was composed of Zadokites who traced their descent from Eleazar through Phinehas and of Aaronites who traced their descent from Ithamar, the two younger sons of Aaron. The earlier J-tradition (Exod. 24.1, 9–11) is that the original sacred persons, next in the order after the unique Moses, were Aaron, these two elder sons, and the seventy elders (Exod. 24.9). These were allowed to see the vision of God, and God did not harm them. But later, these two elder sons of Aaron presumed on their status and sought 'to come near' (P's term for the approach of the priests to the altar), with disastrous results. Compare the story of King Uzziah (2 Chr. 26.16–21), who was struck with leprosy because he did what (to the Chronicler) only the priests might do. These are late stories told to establish the rights of the post-exilic Aaronic priesthood, descended, they claimed, from Eleazar and Ithamar. Originally both Nadab and Abihu and kings such as David and Solomon held sacred offices such as the post-exilic priests claimed themselves alone competent to hold.

1. censer: the Hebrew is *maḥtāh*, from the root *ḥ-t-h*, snatch away (Ps. 52.5 (Heb 7)), or pick up coals from the hearth (Isa. 30.14). The word stands for any utensil which can be used for carrying what is too hot to be held in the hand. It can be a snuffer (Exod. 25.38) or a fire shovel (Exod. 27.3). Here it is a censer.

incense: the Hebrew is *ḳᵉṭôreṯ*, from the root *ḳ-ṭ-r*, 'to smoke' as of a fire. Compare the cognate noun *ḳîṭôr* (Gen. 19.28 'thick smoke' and Ps. 148.8 'thick snowstorm'). The Ugarit *ḳṭr* means 'vapour, breath'. There is no certain evidence in pre-exilic Israel of the burning of aromatic spices in worship, so that before the exile *ḳᵉṭôreṯ* meant 'sacrifice' and the verb 'to send the sacrifice up in smoke' (see pp. 17f.). The burning of incense in post-exilic times is part of the general development of forms of worship familiar in all religious cults.

unholy fire: the Hebrew *zār* means 'strange, foreign', but in P it means not belonging to the tribe of Levi (Num. 1.51) and not belonging to a priestly family (Num. 16.40 (Heb 17.5), and Lev. 22.12, H). In Exod. 30.9 P it refers to incense not made up according to the 'holy' prescription. The fire offered by Nadab and Abihu was illicit and illegal, but the real point at issue is that it was 'lay fire' and not 'priest fire', since an accurate modern rendering of P's *zār* is 'layman'. Rashi offers the explanation that they entered the sanctuary when they were intoxicated. This is because the next section deals with the use of intoxicants by the priest. In later Hebrew there is a word *zār* which refers to idolatrous worship, but this may be another word meaning 'loathsome' (Num. 11.20; Job 19.17 (Arabic *ḏāra*, and not *zāra*)).

2. The holy fire flares out and devours the offenders. Here is the primitive element in religious thought which Rudolf Otto emphasizes (*The Idea of the Holy*), later ethicized into wrath against sin and latterly largely discounted altogether in modern times in liberal humanistic thinking. The idea of God as 'a devouring fire' is frequent in earlier contexts such as 2 Kg. 1.10 and survives in later priestly traditions, as here.

3. will show myself holy: or, 'I will vindicate my holiness among those who come near me, And I will exercise my glory in the presence of all the people.' The verse is a good synonymous couplet, and the original meaning is that God insists on being treated with holy reverence and this must be demonstrated before all. In this context it means that the priests ('those that come near' in P means priests) are the ones to come near, whilst the rest (P's *zār*) must keep their distance; otherwise the results will be disastrous.

Aaron held his peace: the Jerusalem Targum says that for this silence he received a good reward, the priesthood. The Talmud (*b. Zeb.*, 115b) says his reward was that the next time God spoke it was to him alone (verse 8) and not to Moses also. LXX has *katenuchthē* (was stupefied), reading the same root *d-m-m*, but in the strong sense found in Ethiopic. Cf. Exod. 15.16, 'was petrified'. This gives quite a different picture.

5. their coats: Hebrew has 'tunics', and so also the ancient versions.

6. Eleazar and Ithamar: henceforward the ancestors of all the post-exilic priesthood (1 Chr. 24.3) already must follow the rule for priests and not mourn their family dead.

hair . . . hang loose: Rashi (on Num. 6.5) says that *pera'* means overgrowth of hair. This is defined in the Sifra and in the Talmud (*b. San.*, 22b) as hair that has not been cut for thirty days. Taking off the head-covering (Hebrew *pᵉ'ēr*) is a sign of mourning in Ezek. 24.23, as also is tearing the clothes.

wrath: Hebrew has 'lest he (God) be angry with'. RSV has followed AV in seeking to depersonalize the Wrath of God. RV keeps the personal nuance. For a modern comment, see C. H. Dodd, *Romans* (Moffatt Commentary, 1922), pp. 20–24, where the author says, 'He [Paul] retains it [the phrase "the Wrath of God"], not to describe the attitude of God to man, but to describe an inevitable process of cause and effect in a moral universe.' See also A. T. Hanson, *The Wrath of the Lamb*, 1957, pp. 68–111.

7. do not go out . . .: in the Second Temple this meant: not outside the Upper

Gate. Cf. 21.12, where it is clear that the reference here to the anointing oil being on him does not refer to the seven days of installation (8.35), but to the fact that once anointed the priest is always anointed. Presumably the prohibition lasted for the normal seven days of mourning.

(d) NO INTOXICANTS FOR OFFICIATING PRIESTS **10.8–11**

The prohibition is not absolute, but is concerned only with the times when the priest is on duty. LXX adds 'or when you are approaching the altar'. Jewish tradition has always associated the prohibition with the Nadab-Abihu incident. The reasons given concern the necessity to be clear-headed and accurate in maintaining the distinctions between the holy (for the altar and the priests) and the common (for non-priests) and to be able to instruct the people accurately. The Rabbis noticed that God here speaks to Aaron alone, and that the three other instances (Num. 18.1, 8, 20) are all in a section which deals with the need to be sedulous in the matter of *ḳoḏāšîm*, the 'holy gifts' which were the perquisite of the priests (see note on 2.2).

8. strong drink: all English translations cling to this phrase, which *OED* says retains the Old English sense of 'strong' as 'powerful in operative effect'. Any intoxicant is meant (V and DV), but the word *šēḵār* occurs so often in conjunction with *yayin* (wine) that the former would seem to refer to intoxicants made from other ingredients.

10. distinguish: the Hebrew is the verb *hiḇdîl*, to make a *haḇdālāh* (separation), the technical word for those distinctions which are of the essence of Judaism. This principle concerns the distinction between holy and common, clean and unclean, Sabbath and other days, Jew and Gentile. The Candlestick (*mᵉnôrāh*) which the pious Jewish housewife lights at the onset of the Sabbath is the Habdalah light. The story of Creation in Genesis 1 is creation by Habdalah. The development of this principle belonged to the days when God's choice of Israel led to a greater emphasis on their separation from other peoples than on their separation to God.

the holy and the common: *ḳōḏeš* (holiness) represents an idea basic to all religion (see R. Otto, *The Idea of the Holy*, especially his use of the word 'numinous'). It involves the idea of separation to God, out of which there easily develops the idea of separation from man. In Hebrew *ḳōḏeš* is that which belongs to Yahweh alone and is for him and for his priests. The Sabbath is holy because it is God's day: the priest is holy because he belongs to God; and so forth. For Israel, *ḳōḏeš* is that which belongs to Yahweh, and *ḥērem* (the 'holy' word in other Semitic languages) is that which belongs to any other god. The word *ḥôl* (common) is everywhere the antithesis of both *ḳōḏeš* and *ḥērem*. Always, *ḥôl* is that which does not pertain to the gods. If what is 'common' is ritually clean (*ṭāhôr*), then it is free for man, but if it is ritually unclean (*ṭāmē'*) then it is *taboo* for man. In Ac. 10.14f. 'common' is used in the narrow sense of ritually unclean. The author was not a Jew and did not understand the distinction clearly. None of this had any ethical association whatever in early days, and it is hard to see what ethical content there ever was or is.

The ethical content of *ḳōḏeš* developed because of the teaching of the prophets and whatever non-ritualistic elements there were in the priestly teaching.

(e) THE PROPER DISPOSAL OF THE PRIEST'S SHARE **10.12–20**

12–15. This section concerns the priest's dues from the *minḥāh* (ordinary grain-offering) and the *zeḇaḥ šᵉlāmîm* (shared-offering). See 6.16–18 (Heb 9–11) and 7.30–36, but here there is an attempt to distinguish between what the priests only may eat and what their families may eat. The distinction is between what is 'most holy' and what is 'holy'. The grain-offerings from which a token has been taken and put on the altar are 'most holy' and therefore may be eaten only by the priests themselves. Those parts of the shared- (so-called 'peace'-) offerings which accrued to the officiating priest (the *tᵉrûmāh*, the so-called heave-offering) and to the priesthood (the *tᵉnûp̄āh*, the so-called wave-offering) were 'holy', but not 'most holy', and could be eaten by any member of the priest's family in any clean place. In later times this meant anywhere in Jerusalem. But there is some confusion. Instead of 'clean' in verse 14, LXX has 'holy', which is exactly wrong. 'Holy place' means within the Upper Gate; which was where the priests had to eat what belonged to them alone. Also in verse 15 the shoulder apparently is also called 'a wave-offering', which it is not. Some commentators omit the reference to the shoulder. V tries to get out of the difficulty by calling them both heave-offerings, which the breast is not. The explanation is that we have here not a general rule, but a special rule which applies only to the eighth-day 'sacrifice of peace-offerings for the people' in the installation ceremony (cf. 9.21).

16–20. This section deals with a complication which arose out of the second sin-offering which was brought on the eighth day (9.15). This was a male goat, and not the calf of the earlier sin-offering (9.8). Moses assumed (verse 17) that this second sin-offering was most holy and should be eaten by the priests within the sanctuary. The second sin-offering was regarded as being on behalf of the people not including the priests, for whom the first sin-offering sufficed. If the blood had not been brought into the inner sanctuary, then the priests should have eaten it; in verse 9 the altar mentioned will have been the incense altar. Many explanations have been offered. That given in the text by Aaron is: so many dreadful things have already happened today through men dealing with holy things who had no right so to do, that we thought it better to leave well alone, lest a worse thing befall. The Jerusalem Targum (and V) says it was because they were mourners for kinsmen not yet buried. Another explanation is that it was a new-month day (Num. 28.11, 15), and that special sin-offering was not eaten by the priests. The fact is that this eighth-day ritual of installation does not fit into the regular pattern of offerings, and the regular rules do not apply. The Talmud says that this sin-offering was not for the purpose of atonement (*b. Zeb.*, 101b), and Rashi also realized that it was not a usual sin-offering.

17. bear the iniquity: following EVV. It is better to follow RVm and render 'take away, bear away' (cf. LXX). The purpose, in spite of the Talmudic statement above, was to take away sin and get rid of it, either by consuming it within the Holy Place or, wherever a priest was involved, by destroying it outside the camp.

18. into the inner part of the sanctuary: this rendering of RSV is very strange, as though there was an inner sanctuary and an outer sanctuary. Hebrew says 'into the holy place within', i.e. within the Upper Gate of the Second Temple. The difficulty arises because sometimes 'holy place' seems to mean within the Upper Gate, and sometimes apparently it means the Holy of Holies. If the priests ought to have eaten the flesh 'in the sanctuary' (within the Upper Gate), then RSV means within the area beyond the veil, i.e. the Holy of Holies. But all this is part of the general confusion concerning this particular sin-offering.

THIRD SECTION **11.1–16.34** RITUAL UNCLEANNESS AND PURIFICATION RITES

(a) CLEAN AND UNCLEAN CREATURES **11.1–47**

Verses 1–23 deal with four types of creatures: animals (2–8), fish (9–12), birds (13–19), and swarming creatures (20–23). The distinction is between what may or may not be eaten. The rest of the chapter deals with ritual uncleanness caused by contact with unclean creatures, dead and alive. There is a parallel passage in Dt. 14.3–20, where clean animals are listed. The Leviticus lists include various kinds of locust (verses 22f.). It is difficult to see why some creatures are clean and edible and others neither. Possibly the reason is to be found in association with heathen cults. Sometimes it seems to be because of unpleasant habits. In the case of birds, they are apparently all birds of prey and possibly the reason is that they shed blood. It has been suggested that the origins are totemistic, but there are totemic systems where the totem is eaten. No one explanation fits all cases, and we can no more fit them all into one scheme than we can fit all the various sacrifices. These things 'just grow', and ritualistic assimilation does the rest.

Unclean Animals **2–8**

The word *b^e^hēmāh* (**beasts**) here means animals in general. Etymologically the word means 'dumb animals' (cf. Ethiopic *behema*). Often the word means domestic animals as against wild animals (*ḥayyāh*). LXX has this narrower meaning and reads *ktēnē* (flocks and herds).

3. The test is: clean animals fit to eat must have cloven feet and must also chew the cud. The rock badger and the hare do not chew the cud, but their habit of munching gives that appearance.

4. the camel has been domesticated among the Israelites from ancient times, if the J-tradition is sound in Gen. 12.16. Albright, however, is very sure that the Israelites were ass-nomads and not camel-nomads, and that the camel was not properly domesticated by the thirteenth century (*Archaeology and the Religion of Israel*, 1946, pp. 96–8).

5. rock badger: Hebrew *šāpān*. Most of the creatures mentioned in this chapter are hard to identify; the ancient versions add to the confusion. The chief characteristic of this animal is to shelter under rocks from birds of prey (Ps. 104.18; Prov. 30.26). LXX has *dasupous* (rough foot), a hare or (Pliny) a rabbit, though the rabbit is not found in Palestine. V has *choerogryllus* (? marmot, but see LXX in next note). The animal is *hyrax syriacus*, the rock badger.

6. the hare: Hebrew *'arneḇeṯ*. LXX has *choirogrullios*, which is used in Dt. 14.7 for *šāpān*. V has *lepus*, the hare, and there is general agreement about this.

7. the swine: the Hebrew has *ḥᵃzîr*, which is connected with the Arabic *ḫazara*, used of the eye being narrow. To the Jew all down the centuries the swine has been the most offensive abomination of all. The origin is in its association with heathen cults (Isa. 65.4, 66.3, 17). The swine is not filthy in its habits unless it is kept in close, filthy conditions. Just as throwing incense on the fire before the statue of the emperor was the prime test for the Christian, so eating swine's flesh was the test for the Jews; 2 Mac. 6.18f. and the persecution under Antiochus (Epiphanes) IV.

Water Creatures 9–12

If edible, they must have both fins and scales. This applies both to sea-fish (**anything in the seas**) and fresh-water fish (**in the rivers**).

swarming creatures: the Hebrew *šereṣ* is a collective noun. It includes all small creatures that go about in shoals and swarms, insects that fly in clouds, such as gnats and flies generally (cf. Ethiopic, germinate), and small creatures such as weasels, mice, and lizards that are low on the ground (cf. Aramaic, crawl).

an abomination: the word *šeḳeṣ* is something that is foul. In Accadian the corresponding *šiḳṣu* is an unpleasant illness to do with women after childbirth. In Hebrew the association with impurity is even more pronounced. It refers to creatures that are ritually unclean and fit for food, but there is something nasty about them. Cf. LXX *bdelugma*, and V *abominabile*, whence EVV. The word 'vermin' is a reasonably good rendering, and has the merit of expressing something of the revulsion involved; the difficulty is that all vermin are not *šeḳeṣ*, and all *šeḳeṣ* are not vermin. Somebody had to touch these creatures sometimes in spite of the prohibitions. Apparently some had to render themselves ceremonially unclean in order that others could remain ceremonially clean.

Unclean Birds 13–19

These are birds of prey, unclean because of their association with fresh blood, a *taboo* of the utmost importance in the Levitical system. See notes on chapters 12 (after childbirth) and 13 (so-called leprosy). It is difficult to identify the various species of birds. RSV mostly follows RV, except that rightly RV identifies various kinds of owl in verse 17.

13. the eagle: the *nešer*, the bald griffon-vulture of the desert, soaring high in the sky, noted for the wide spread of its wings and its care for its young (Exod. 19.4; Dt. 32.11).
vulture: AV 'ossifrage', that is, the *Lammergeyer*, the 'gier-eagle' (see *OED*), as RV.
osprey: the *'ozniyyāh* is said to be some kind of eagle, and most identify it with the sea-eagle, or better the fish-hawk.

14. kite: most scholars agree that the *dā'āh* is the kite, though AV follows LXX and has 'vulture'. The Hebrew word means 'darting swiftly' (cf. the verb in Dt. 28.49).
falcon: this concludes the main list of the family of *falconidae*; read: and every kind of falcon.

15. every raven: the Hebrew *'ōreḇ* means 'the black one'. It includes all kinds of crows (family *corvidae*), especially the raven (*corvus corax*), one of the famous Old Testament birds (Gen. 8.7; 1 Kg. 17.4; Ps. 147.9).

16. ostrich: this traditional identification is as old as LXX and the Targum. AV has 'owl', as is probably right, since all the birds mentioned in verses 16–18 seem to be owls (family *strigidae*) of one kind or another. The Hebrew *baṯ-ya'ᵃnāh* has been interpreted as 'daughter of greed' (cf. Aramaic), but 'daughter of the desert' is nearer the truth (*BDB*, p. 419a, Wetzstein, cf. Arabic *wa'nat*).
nighthawk: following T. The identification with some kind of owl is ancient, and probably right. Cf. LXX *glaux* and V *noctuus*, the night-owl, sacred to Athene-Minerva.
sea gull: the idea of the sea-mew (RV) or the sea gull is from LXX and V. Many guesses have been made, any kind of gull, and even the cuckoo (AV). It is probably some kind of owl.
hawk: the *nēṣ* is certainly some kind of a bird of prey. V has *accipiter*, a general name for birds of prey, but especially the common hawk and the sparrow-hawk.

17. owl: the Hebrew *kôs* is a general term for owls living in ruins (Ps. 102.6 (Heb. 7)). T has *ḳadyā'*, probably the little owl, and so AV and RV. The other ancient versions have various kinds of owl.
cormorant: following AV and RV. It is generally agreed that *šeleḵ* is a fish-eater, so if it is an owl it is the fisher owl. V has *mergulus*, some kind of diving bird, one that hurtles down from above, which is the etymological basis of the Hebrew word.
ibis: following LXX and V. T and S think of an owl, either the 'great owl' of EVV, or the tawny owl.

18. water hen: this goes back to LXX *porphyrion* (purple coot) or to V *cygnus* (swan), whence AV and RVm. But the word *tinšemeṯ* occurs, both here and in verse 30, in the list of swarming, creeping things. Hence T thinks of creatures that fly or grope in the dark, some kind of night-bird such as the owl or the mole. RV has 'horned owl'.
pelican: the *ḳā'āh* inhabits ruins (Isa. 34.11; Zeph. 2.14) and is thus unlikely to be a sea-bird. LXX and V have 'pelican', but DV has 'bittern'. The bird belongs

to the wilderness (Ps. 102.6 (Heb. 7)). The pelican is not a lonely bird, but a gregarious fish-eating water bird. It is best therefore to think in terms of some kind of owl.

vulture: the *rāḥām* is some kind of vulture (cf. Arabic). The gier-eagle of AV is from T. V has the purple coot.

19. Most versions are agreed about the stork and the bat. Otherwise the versions supply us with a bewildering variety: woodpecker, green plover, stone curlew, night-owl, etc.

All Winged Insects **20–24**

It is better to avoid the word 'insects' if we are going to use the phrase 'upon all fours'. These are all small creatures found in swarms. Those that crawl may be eaten if they have jointed legs.

legs: following EVV. The point is that they have jointed legs (Hebrew *keraʿîm*: the root means 'bow down, bend over'). The creatures must be saltatorial. They must have jointed legs if they are to leap, and the longer and thinner their legs the better they leap. V and DV go further with 'but has its hind legs longer', which gives an excellent picture.

22. the locust according to its kind: RVm says these creatures are four kinds of locusts or grasshoppers not certainly known. It is not surprising that the Versions are uncertain, since the locust, like insects generally, can take surprisingly different forms at different stages of its growth, and even one season's 'solitary locust' can be next season's swarming locusts. It is argued that John the Baptist's locusts (Mt. 3.4) were the fruit of the carob tree, but locusts are eaten to this day, fried in *samn* (clarified butter), after the legs, wings, and head have been removed. It depends on whether John did any cooking. The word *mîn* (kind) is used in modern Hebrew for 'species', but it is better here to avoid scientific terms.

locust: some derive the word *'arbāh* from the root *r-b-h* (be many), but others refer to the Accadian *aribu* (the locust swarm) and the root *'-r-b* (destroy, devastate). LXX has *brouchos*, a wingless locust. T has *gôḇā*, the locust swarm (Arabic *jabā'*, collect).

the bald locust: uncertain; Hebrew has *solʿām*, the destroyer.

cricket: following RV, but AV has 'beetle'. The Hebrew *ḥargôl* is some creature that runs swiftly to and fro. LXX is non-committal (*akris*), but V has *ophimachus* (serpent killer), which is what LXX has for the next word. This is the ichneumon which is the name both of a fly and of a small mongoose-like animal, whence V. Possibly the creature intended is the cicada, whose continuous 'chirping' is a sufficiently strident feature of hotter lands than Britain to ensure its place in any list of insects.

grasshopper: the *ḥāḡāḇ* is a creature that hides, conceals; some say it conceals the sun, others that it conceals the ground. Some swarms are reported to cover an area of 200 square miles or more. The desert locust breeds several times a year, and each locust lays up to 100 eggs at a time (W. Thesiger, *Arabian Sands*, 1959, p. 28).

Probably the best translation here is 'hopper', since there is a tradition that the creature intended is wingless.

Uncleanness by Contact **24–28**

This paragraph naturally follows verse 8. The 'these' of verse 24 means 'the following', viz. verses 26f. It is forbidden even to touch their dead bodies, though this is a type of secondary uncleanness, since nothing is said about a man washing himself.

26. parts the hoof: the word *parsāh* means 'a cleft', but came to mean any hoof, whether cleft or not (Isa. 5.28; Ezek. 26.11, of horses).

27. go on their paws: lit. 'walk on their palms'. The distinction is between animals which have a hollow in their hoofs and so do not walk on the middle portion of their feet, and those which walk on the whole of their feet, like dogs and cats.

animals: this means wild animals (*ḥayyôṯ*), as against domesticated animals (*bᵉhēmāh*) in the previous verse.

Small Earthbound Creatures **29–38**

These are creatures which breed freely and feed on living creatures (see note below on 'mouse'). The dividing-line between clean and unclean so far as these creatures are concerned seems to be whether they are carnivores or vegetarians. Thus only locusts are fit to eat among the saltatory insects. It is the shedding of blood that constitutes the division.

29. weasel: following LXX and V. Judging by the Arabic *ḥuld*, the Hebrew *ḥōleḏ* could be the common mole (family *Talpidae*) or any kind of rat including the mole-rat (family *Spalacidae*).

mouse: following LXX and V and Jewish tradition; but the Arabic *'akbar* is the male jerboa and this is what we should have here.

great lizard: the Hebrew *ṣāḇ* is some large lizard (cf. Arabic *ḍabb*) though not necessarily the great lizard. The versions vary from crocodile to toad and tortoise.

30. In all five cases RSV follows RV. Identification is doubtful, but, as RVm says, they are probably five types of lizard. The first three seem to be geckos. For the fourth, AV (snail) is following Rashi, who quotes the Old French *limace*.

32. The chance of any of these creatures falling on to any object or into any uncovered receptacle is understandable in a country where small lizards are a regular feature of the walls of rooms. Objects must be soaked and regarded as unusable until sunset. Earthenware pots must be destroyed because the uncleanness, like holiness, soaks into the pot itself (cf. 6.28 (Heb 21)).

sack: this is not necessarily a poke or a large bag. It is 'sacking'. The word is a loan-word from ancient Egypt. It was the coarse cloth which the slave wore as a loin-cloth, and later was a sign of mourning. Cf. Hebrew *śaḳ*, Greek *sakkos*, Latin *saccus*, French *sac*.

34. in it: the insertion of these two words, following RV 'therein', complicates matters. The reference is to food on to which water from the unclean pot is poured.

35. oven: this is the *tannûr*, the portable cooking vessel of 2.4.
stove: the word *kîrayim* is found only here in the Old Testament. The Mishnah (*S̲habb.*, iii, 1) says it was a cooking range (cf. AV, RV) with places for two pots; hence the dual form of the Hebrew word. Cf. the native Indian cooking arrangements with the modernized form which has been developed in the area round Hyderabad. LXX has *kythropodes*, used of small portable stoves with feet, also of small storage jars with narrow openings, such as those in which the Qumran scrolls were found, made narrow to minimize the risk of unclean objects falling into them. The Mishnah (*Kel.*, iii, 2) says the mouth was wide enough for a fig, a walnut, or an olive to fall through.

36. a spring or a cistern: the spring (*ma'yān, 'ayin*) is a natural spring of water, fresh ('living') water. The cistern (*bôr*) is a pit for water storage, often hewn out of the solid rock (Jer. 2.13), usually privately owned (2 Kg. 18.31), and sometimes as much as twenty feet square and deep, and, if the regulations are observed, covered (Exod. 21.33). The word was used of any well dug for water (Gen. 26.18), though the proper word for this (*bᵉ'ēr*) seems to be quite another word.

37. seed is not affected, unless it is being soaked in water, presumably preparatory to actual sowing. The permeating effect of water comes into consideration and the seed becomes unclean.

The Carcases of Clean Animals **39–40**

These are unclean if the animal died of itself, i.e. was not slaughtered. This is because the blood is still in it, another instance of the presence of blood being the decisive factor in uncleanness.

Earthbound Creatures that Swarm **41–45**

The Hebrew *šereṣ* means 'swarm, teem' and is a wider term than 'creep' (EVV), due to LXX, V, and the Aramaic meaning of the root. It includes snakes, small four-footed animals, and creatures like centipedes and millipedes.

42. The letter *wāw* in the word *gāḥôn* (belly) is written and printed much larger than the others. According to the Masoretes it is the middle consonant of the Pentateuch.

44–45. The emphasis on the holiness of God and that his people must be holy also is characteristic of H, with which some scholars associate these verses. 'Holy' here means ritually clean, though doubtless many read into it the idea of moral purity. What is more important is the reference to the rescue from Egypt, that central motive of Israel's history. All of it is the work of the great Saviour God who brought Israel out of Egypt. The Passover rite was linked with it (Exod. 12; Dt. 16.1), the three agricultural feasts of Canaan (Dt. 16.3, 12; Lev. 23.43), all rules of ritual uncleanness (as here), the return from Babylon (Isa. 51.10). All history must be written from a point of view, even if it is written negatively. Hebrew history is the history of the Acts of God the Saviour. D. Daube (*The Exodus Pattern in the Bible*, 1953) finds that this same theme is interwoven into the ancient laws and customs concerning the freeing of slaves. The Old Testament is indeed *Heilsgeschichte*, but the *Heils*, like the Hebrew *ḳāḏôš* (holy), belongs to God alone, and the outstanding example is the rescue from Egypt.

46–47. This is the colophon, the paragraph which rounds off the section. Verse 47 makes it wholly clear that the section deals with the application of the principle of Habdalah to living creatures, the distinctions which are essential to Judaism.

(b) THE PURIFICATION OF WOMEN AFTER CHILDBIRTH **12.1–8**

The essential factor is the discharge of blood. The woman is unclean so long as there is any discharge. Nothing immoral is involved. She is ritually unclean because all blood is *taboo*. In some parts of Britain today some will not allow a woman after childbirth to enter their house until she has been 'churched', a ceremony in which there is an attempt to give a truly religious content to an ancient superstition.

2. seven days: here again we have the seven days of birth (see 4.6).
her menstruation: lit., 'the shunning (*niddāh* is 'she that is shunned', root *n-d-d*) of her being unwell' (this English euphemism is the exact meaning of the Hebrew *dāwāh*).

3. Circumcision is an ancient rite established as a pre-marriage rite in Mesopotamia, Ugarit, and ancient Israel. The Hebrew *ḥāṯān* (daughter's husband) is etymologically 'the one who undergoes circumcision', and *ḥōṯēn* (wife's father) is the circumciser (cf. Arabic *ḫātin*, and Accadian *ḫatanu* (daughter's husband)). In early times the woman's father performed the rite of circumcision on the prospective bridegroom. At Ugarit, *ḫtn* means 'marriage' (*Nikkal and the Kathirat*, ii, 4) and the same three consonants occur in NK i, 25 of 'son-in-law'. The rite is so widespread throughout the world that no one can say how it spread and where was its origin. At first it fitted a man for marriage, but among the Hebrews it became associated with infancy, and marked the beginning of the life of a male infant (eighth day from birth). Perhaps Exod. 4.24–26 has to do with this transition. After the exile, circumcision became the initiation rite into the religious community of Israel, the people of God. It became the sign of the covenant (Gen. 17.1–27 P), and took place at the earliest possible moment, long before there could be any personal choice. The same change has taken place in Christian baptism, which at first was the outward sign that the believer was joined with the new Israel, but (possibly even in New Testament times) the rite became associated with infancy. The leaders of the Christian church at first tried to insist on circumcision as essential to entry into the new Israel, but St. Paul withstood this (Gal. 5.6; Ac. 1–21). For much of traditional Christianity, infant baptism is held to be as essential as circumcision is to the Jew.

4. The mother is *taboo* for another thirty-three days if the child is a boy, and twice both periods if the child is a girl. The generally accepted explanation is that in ancient time the delivery of an infant girl was regarded as much more dangerous for the mother. But such a statement does not mean what it appears to mean. The danger is because evil spirits are doubly active, and probably because the child is a future subject of menstruation. Certainly the reason is not a medical one.

6. a young pigeon: Hebrew idiom allows the phrase to mean 'a pigeon', one member of a type (see note on p. 33), but both LXX *nossos* and V *pullus* (whence English 'pullet') assume the phrase to mean 'young, nestling, chick'. The whole-offering is a gift to God, on the analogy that no man must come before the king without a gift; the sin-offering is to enable the priest to perform the cleansing rite.

7. This verse makes it plain that it is the flow of blood which makes the woman unclean.

8. This is the usual concession for the poor. In Lk. 2.24 the mother of Jesus avails herself of this concession, which applies to the ritual cleansing of the mother. There is no concession for the redemption of the first-born (Exod. 34.20; Num. 18.15).

(c) THE TESTS FOR LEPROSY 13.1–59

It is necessary to quote C. Creighton, article 'Leprosy', *EB*, col. 2765: 'It may be doubted if any one would ever have discovered true leprosy in these chapters but for the translation of *ṣāraʿaṯ* in LXX and V.' The unfortunate translation is *lepra*. This article gives a detailed description of the signs of true leprosy. See also the most recent article on the subject in *DB* by G. R. Driver with the help of R. G. Cochrane and H. Gordon. The technical name for modern leprosy is *elephantiasis graecorum*, a loathsome disease prevalent in Europe in the Middle Ages. It has been thought that leprosy is not now as widespread as formerly, but it is becoming apparent that it is at least as great a scourge as ever, all the more because the sufferer hides the symptoms as long as he can. It is said that in villages of south India the incidence of leprosy is nearly one hundred per cent. In ancient times the disease was associated with Egypt (Lucretius, vi, 1113f.), though Herodotus does not mention it. Possibly this is 'the disease of Egypt' (Dt. 28.60; the singular is correct). Naaman's leprosy was probably leucoderma. King Uzziah may have had either true leprosy or *lupus erythematosus*, a disease which shows itself first on the forehead. This may well be the only case of true leprosy in the Old Testament.

The Hebrew *ṣāraʿaṯ* seems to involve the idea of 'prostration, abject humbleness', and it is applied in this chapter to various skin diseases, of which the feature is either open sores or depressions in the skin which sooner rather than later may break out into open sores. It is this running sore with the naked blood that makes these skin diseases ritually unclean. Whether they are medically contagious or not is not the point at issue; what matters here is that they are ritually contagious. The resultant uncleanness is ritual, not medical. Medically they may or may not be contagious. The clearest example is 13.9–17. If there be 'quick raw flesh', then it is *ṣāraʿaṯ* and the man is unclean. But if the raw place heals and the man becomes white all over, it is not *ṣāraʿaṯ*, and the man is ritually clean, only to become ritually unclean again if the raw place appears. The 'leprous disease' of RSV is no real improvement on 'the plague of leprosy' of EVV. It was a defiling skin disease.

2. swelling: the Hebrew word *ś^e'ēṯ* is the Arabic *ši'atu* (colour, mark) (G. R. Driver, *DB*, p. 575b), and hence LXX 'a scar (*oulē*)' and continuing 'of a distinct (outshining) appearance (*sēmasias*, used by the first-century A.D. medical writer Aretaeus to mean the decisive appearance of a disease)'. The word cannot mean 'swelling' (see verse 3). T defies the other versions and has '*amḳā'* (deep spot). **or an eruption or a spot:** two marks or scars which may turn to a leprous disease, that is, may break out into open sores. Both Hebrew words suggest that the scar is showing signs of activity and is definitely inflamed (so LXX). Thus V has *pustula* (DV 'blister', but it is inflamed) and 'like something shining'. The priest has to decide whether it is a permanently open sore and spreading or only a *mispaḥaṯ* (passing eruption).

3. hair: we should read 'hairs' here (sing. of masc. form) and 'not a single hair' in verse 4 (sing. of fem. form). Rashi says that hair turned white is a symptom of uncleanness, but this in itself is not enough. There must be a depression in the skin, and the mark must be showing signs of activity, eating away the flesh or breaking out and becoming raw. If there is no sign of further activity after fourteen days, then the man is clear; by this time the scar will either have broken out or have become less inflamed. The Hebrew for this last is *kēhēh*, used in 1 Sam. 3.2 of an old man's sight becoming dim and in Isa. 42.4 of smouldering flax. If there are later developments, the man must come back again to the priest.

5. in his eyes: but see verse 55 which is literally 'has not changed its appearance '*ênō*)', which is what some would read here.

9–17. The previous verses have dealt with scars which are not *ṣāra'aṯ*, but may become so and thus cause ritual uncleanness. They may easily develop into open sores. Here we deal with places which are already *ṣāra'aṯ*.

10. swelling: better 'mark, scar' (cf. verse 2, and always).
quick raw flesh: in modern English, this is an ulcer. The word 'quick' was once used much more widely than today, and meant 'alive'. We use it now to mean 'lively, speedy'. The older meaning survives in special phrases: a quickset hedge, which is a hedge of live slips set in the ground to grow: 'cut to the quick', used of finger nails cut back into the flesh and so raw; whence its figurative meaning of badly hurt feelings.

12. breaks out: this does not mean break out in an open sore, but spread, cover over (so T). If the original white mark spreads and covers the whole body from head to foot, then the man is not unclean provided there is no raw place. He may be 'a leper, white as snow' (2 Kg. 5.27) like Gehazi, but, according to the priestly rules of Leviticus 13, he is not ritually unclean. The test is raw flesh (verse 15). Raw flesh is *ṣāra'aṯ*. In verse 15, V and DV have 'raw flesh if spotted with leprosy'. This extra detail introduced by V has been as responsible as any other one factor for the age-old misunderstanding of biblical 'leprosy' in general and of this chapter in particular. G. R. Driver (*DB*, p. 576a) thinks that 'white skin all over' means healing by desquamation, i.e. the scaly crust pealing off and leaving clear white skin beneath.

A Recurrence of Symptoms **18–23**

If a *š^e ḥîn* has healed, but later a white or reddish-white mark appears, then we have once more the situation of verses 2–8. A *š^e ḥîn* is an inflamed spot (Arabic *saḫuna*) and so Rashi. LXX and V have 'ulcer'; RSV has followed EVV with 'boil'.

23. scar: following RV, and T; cf. the verb in Dan. 10.21 of 'what is inscribed'. Rashi refers to the Old French *rétréçir* (contract) (cf. Ezek. 20.48 (Heb 21.4)), 'and every face shall become shrivelled', where the verb *ṣārab̲* means 'scorched', shrivelled with the heat. The Hebrew *ṣāreb̲et̲* (used here) is from this root, which certainly means 'blaze, burn, scorch', whence AV 'burning boil'. V has *cicatrix*, which is right. It is best to read 'puckered scar'.

24–28. deals with burns which turn septic and do not heal. This is a *ṣāra'at̲* and is ritually unclean. The test is: inflammation which causes the first suspicion, then hair white and a depression in the skin, and a breaking out.

28. scar: see verse 23. AV has 'inflammation' (cf. 'burning boil' above. LXX comes out clearly with the idea of a scar, *charaktēr*, something engraved, marked in).

29–37. This section deals with various skin diseases, perhaps impetigo, scurf, ringworm, shingles, etc.

30. itch: the Hebrew is *net̲eḳ*, lit. a tearing off, hence 'itch', something so irritating that the sufferer cannot keep his hands from scratching. In modern Hebrew the word means *tinea* (ringworm) or *herpes* (shingles). AV has 'dry scall' and RV 'scall', a scaly infection of the skin, especially in the hair of the head, though in old Norse and Teutonic *skalle* means 'bald', which the Hebrew might conceivably mean, in the sense of what is torn out. A dry scall might be *psoriasis*, red patches covered with whitish scales, and this can be very irritating and widespread. A moist scall might be *eczema*, which can be most unpleasant and irritating. Possibly 'scurfy patch' is the best rendering for the preliminary stage of all these affections, less definite than scurf, but carrying with it the possibility of developing into something much more troublesome. Shaving off the hair to the edge of the patch is a certain way of telling whether the trouble is spreading.

38–39. This is *vitiligo* (G. R. Driver, *DB*, p. 576a). LXX has *alphos* (dull white leprosy), non-contagious, probably what Gehazi had, but non-contagious, common in tropical and semi-tropical countries, appearing first in small spots, but any cure, except possibly in the first appearance of a single small spot, is unlikely, and ultimately it spreads all over the body. It is unsightly, but no danger to health. It is *bôhaḳ*, and the Arabs call it *bahaḳu*, for which RSV (verse 39) has 'tetter', following RV, but AV has 'freckled spot'.

Baldness due to Sores **40–44**

It may be ordinary baldness or what the Hebrews called *gibbēaḥ*, forehead baldness, baldness which starts from the front and not from the crown. In either case there is nothing to worry about and the man is ritually clean even if the baldness is complete and is due to *alopecia*. If, however, there is a reddish-white scar on his bald patch, then we are back again at verse 18, except that here the matter of the colour of the hair does not arise.

45–46. The unclean 'leper' must give everyone warning so that they do not touch him. This is not because his disease is contagious, though impetigo and ringworm can be very contagious. Most of the skin diseases mentioned are not contagious, but ritual uncleanness is very contagious indeed. The afflicted one must wear rags, let his hair go unkempt, symptoms of mourning (10.6). He must cover his upper lip, cry aloud 'Unclean, unclean', and stay permanently outside the city.

Leprosy in Garments **47–59**

This is a mould, a mildew, or a fungus which appears in clothes worn without being washed for a long time in a tropical or semi-tropical climate. It can be found in all sorts of clothes, whether made of linen or wool or skin. The treatment is similar to that of persons, one seven-day period of isolation and then a second. If the fungus has spread after the first seven days, then wash it and keep it for another seven to make sure. If the fungus spreads after the first seven days or after the second seven days, then the cloth must be destroyed.

48. warp or woof: following EVV. This goes back to LXX, but how could there be an infection in the warp of woven cloth without it being in the woof also? Or, if it was in the one or the other, how could the priest tear out the one without destroying the whole cloth? RVm realized this and suggested 'woven or knitted'. Probably it should be 'yarn or piece'. The Hebrew *šᵉṯî* can mean 'warp', i.e. the mass of threads which hang downwards in the loom. The Hebrew *'ēreḇ* is from the root *'-r-b* I (mix), and could mean either that which is mixed with the woof and so the warp, or it could refer to the resultant mixture. Thus *šᵉṯî* could mean 'threads' (i.e. yarn) and *'ēreḇ* 'woven material' (piece). LXX has *stēmōn* for the first and V has *stamen* (both 'thread') (cf. Ariadne's thread).

51. a malignant leprosy: the word 'malignant' is strange in this context. EVV have 'fretting', probably following T. Both LXX and V have 'persistent, incurable', which is good.

55. leprous spot: the Hebrew is *pᵉḥeṯeṯ*, that which is perforated, eaten out. The AV 'a fret inward' is due to V. Probably 'rot' is best, which suggests a near perforation.

on the back or on the front: the Hebrew uses the two words for baldness. It means 'wrong side or right side'.

(d) PURIFICATION RITES **14.1–57**

For the Cured Leper **1–32**

The writers are dealing with conditions that were curable, so that Levitical leprosy cannot have been what is known as leprosy in modern times, for which nothing approaching a cure was known until comparatively recently.

Some maintain that we have two distinct ceremonies, the first and older in verses 2–8a (to 'into the camp') and the second in verses 8b–32. The first consists of getting rid of the ritual uncleanness by releasing a bird, the man washing his clothes, shaving off all his hair, and then bathing himself, after which he may enter the camp. The second says that although he may enter the camp, he must 'dwell outside his tent' for a second seven days. Rashi says this means no marital intercourse. On the eighth day the shaving and bathing rites are repeated, and offerings are brought with which the priest performs a special cleansing rite.

2. brought to the priest: but the priest has to go 'out of the camp' (outside where men dwell), because the man cannot come in until he is cured and ritually cleansed, which latter only the priest can do.

4. living clean birds: the 'living' seems tautologous, so Rashi explains it as meaning 'capable of continuing to live', not suffering from some fatal disease. V and DV make it clear that 'clean' means 'fit to eat', by adding a note to that effect. 'Birds' is *ṣippᵒrîm* in Hebrew, which strictly means birds that cheep and twitter. The Talmud (*b. Arakh.*, 16b) says this is because the disease is a punishment for chattering slander. LXX has *ornithia* (small birds). V (with DV) has *passer* (sparrow), hence the New Testament translation of *strouthion* (Mt. 10.29; Lk. 12.6). **cedarwood and scarlet stuff and hyssop:** the scarlet thread was used to tie together the stick (*maḳḳāl*) of cedarwood and hyssop. Jewish tradition says that the cedarwood was used because the cedar is a high tree and the cause of leprosy is pride; also, that the 'worm' and the hyssop were used because the cure is humility (cf. 1 Kg. 4.33 (Heb 5.13)). Cedar was the most durable wood known to antiquity, and according to Pliny the cedar roof of the famous temple of Diana at Ephesus lasted for 400 years. But the reason for the use of cedar in this cleansing rite is probably its aromatic qualities. Trees with aromatic qualities were regularly used elsewhere in cleansing rites. The word *'erez* was used of various trees, not only for the cedar of Lebanon (*Pinus Cedrus*) but for other trees of the same family and for trees more or less resembling the true cedar, such as certain junipers, tamarisks, and cypresses, whilst the Arabic *'arz* is identified as the pine. The scarlet stuff (lit. scarlet stuff of the worm) is *šᵉnî tôlaʿaṯ*. The word *šānî* means 'scarlet *cloth*' (cf. Accadian *šinitu* (dyed cloth)), and *tôlaʿaṯ* is a worm, in this case *Coccus ilicis*, a grub which attaches itself to a certain kind of oak (*Quercus coccifera*). The dried body of the female yields a scarlet-crimson dye. The hyssop is the ordinary hyssop, a bushy little plant used in the Passover rite for sprinkling the blood on the doorposts and the lintel, but in the rite of the red heifer (Num. 19.6) all three, cedarwood, scarlet, and hyssop, are thrown into the fire to be burnt with the heifer and so form part of the cleansing dust. This suggests that all three had cleansing properties. Cf. Ps. 51.7 (Heb 9), 'Purge (lit. de-sin) me with hyssop, and I shall be clean.' The matter is complicated by Jn 19.29, according to which a hyssop-stalk could support a sponge and raise it high enough to reach the head of a cross.

A stalk of the caper-plant (*Capparis spinosa*) would suffice for this, and this plant is found in the crevices of city walls (1 Kg. 4.33). Probably 'hyssop' was a general name for various species of small plants. It may well have been a species of marjoram (*Origanum maru*), though parts of the caper-plant were used popularly as medicine and the plant is supposed to have healing and stimulating properties.

5. over running water: this means spring water and not water from a well or cistern. The Hebrew is *ḥayyîm* (living water), and there is no suggestion in Jewish tradition that the ceremony is to be performed over a running stream, the point being rather that the water must be fresh and clean, not having stood even for a short period. Indeed, according to the Talmud (*b. Soṭah*, 16b) about a quarter of a pint of water sufficed and this was placed first in the earthenware bowl.

7. seven times: once again the magic seven (see 4.7).

the open field: the *śāḏeh* is the open country round the walled town or village. Sometimes it includes the cultivated land of the villagers (Ru. 2.3) similar to the medieval system in England, but more often it was open range. It is Homer's *pedion*, the flat open country of his battlefields.

8. The man had to wait seven days outside his home. This is the regular 'passage time' (cf. 4.6), as though the man is being born again into the community of the people of God. The newborn child also had to wait for seven days. The shaving of all the hair is similar to the shaving of the Nazirite whose vow has been broken (Num. 6.9). All this has to do with the fact that hair is *taboo*, though whether it is *taboo*-good or *taboo*-bad is never certain. This is not surprising when it is realized that these customs are survivals of a time when such a distinction was not made in ritual matters, and there is always this tendency.

9. eyebrows: lit., 'the curves of his eyes'. The Latin is *supercilia*, whence 'supercilious' actually means 'lifting the eyebrows'.

10. three tenths of an ephah of fine flour: this is the normal amount for three lambs (Num. 15.4f.). The difference consists in the fact that one of the lambs was to be a sin-offering and another a compensation-offering, and normally there was no cereal-offering to accompany either of these. According to verse 21 a tenth of an ephah is brought with the compensation-offering, but (verse 31) this one tenth is used to accompany the burnt-offering, as is proper. Possibly the three tenths were brought because there were three lambs, but all used with the lamb which was the burnt-offering. Most likely of all, we are here dealing with an ancient rite which, like the priestly installation rites (Lev. 8 and 9), does not fit into the regular pattern. Thus there are here anomalies only on the supposition that the regular pattern of the main sacrifices applies to all—which it manifestly does not. AV has 'three tenth deals'. This word 'deal' was used as late as the middle of the eighteenth century to mean 'part, portion'. It still is used of sharing out cards in card games. It survives in the modern 'dole', and is still used for a plank as distinct from a batten.

one log of oil: about seven eighths of a pint. This amount bears no relation to the normal, which was a quarter of a hin, about three times as much (Num. 15.5).

12. The *'āšām* (compensation-offering) is also a *t^e^nûpāh* (wave-offering). This means that this particular compensation-offering was the perquisite of the officiating priest (see 7.30). The names of offerings such as sin-offering, compensation-offering, parts of the shared-offering describe why the offering was brought. But names like *t^e^nûpāh* and *t^e^rûmāh* are concerned with what happened afterwards. It is strange that a compensation-offering was brought at all, and also strange that it was a male lamb (*keḇeś*) and not a full-grown ram (*'ayil*). The same two anomalies are found in the case of the Nazirite whose vow had been broken by contact with a dead body (Num. 6.12). He also had to bring a sin-offering (pigeon) and a whole-offering (pigeon), but also a yearling male lamb as a compensation-offering. This last is strange, since normally it involves payment for damage done that can be assessed. Here, as in the case of the *'āšām tālûy* (suspended 'guilt'-offering, Lev. 5.17–19), any damage done cannot be assessed, so there is no compensation and no extra 20 per cent. Probably the reason for the compensation-offering is that the man's exclusion from the people of God involved loss to the people and to God, but unassessable, just as the Nazirite had caused loss, having lost so many days of the period of his vow.

15. some of the log of oil: presumably the rest of the oil was the perquisite of the priest, since he would not pour much of it into the palm of his left hand; it was a *t^e^nûpāh* (verse 12). For **log,** V has *sextarius*, which was roughly a pint, and thus a reasonably accurate Roman equivalent. DV has 'sextary', a term used as a dry measure in late Middle English, doubtless because of the important part which monks like the Cistercians played in the development of agriculture.

20. The whole of the *minḥāh* (grain-offering) was burnt on the altar, like the priest's offering of Lev. 6.19–23 (Heb 12–16). Normally the *minḥāh* which 'any one brings' mostly goes to the priests (Lev. 2.1–3), and only a handful to the altar. It is another example of the folly of trying to fit all the sacrifices into a rigid pattern.

The Concession for the Poor **21–32**

This involved very considerable reductions. The male lamb for the compensation-offering remains, and so also the pint of oil. But the other two lambs are reduced to two pigeons, and the flour to one tenth of an ephah.

A Leprous Disease in a House **33–53**

This may be the fungus of dry rot which sometimes forms a layer of greenish or reddish material between lath and plaster, or it may be a deposit of calcium nitrate which can form by the action of the gases of decaying matter on the lime of the plaster, sometimes called mural salt (see Creighton, *EB*, col. 2763, and Macalister, *HDB*, iii, p. 98). The term *lepraria* is sometimes used of these fungoid growths.

34. and I put: better 'if I put', making it the protasis of a hypothetical sentence. The Sifra says it means that God will deliberately put these fungoid growths in their homes, because the Amorites secreted their treasures of gold in the walls whilst the Israelites were in the desert. When the fungus appeared, the Israelites would pull down the walls and find the treasure.

35. some sort of disease: it is laid down in the Mishnah (*Neg.*, xii, 5) that, however educated a man may be and however certain he is what the trouble is, he must report the matter to the priest with this measure of uncertainty.

37. walls: strictly *ḳîr* is a flat vertical surface, our ‘blank wall’. It is mostly used of city walls, but also of the side of the incense altar (Exod. 30.3) and the flat surface of an up-ended tile (Ezek. 4.3). It can mean either the inner or outer surface of a wall, but it must be a flat vertical surface.

spots: the word *š*^{e}*ḳa‘*^{a}*rûrāh* means ‘depression, hollow’, the root being *ḳ-‘-r* (be deep). So T (hollows), LXX and V (*valliculas . . . deformes*, unsightly little hollows), and DV (little dints, disfigured).

41. the inside of the house: RSV apparently understands that all the plaster within the house is to be scraped off, but Jewish tradition (*Torath Kohanim* and Rashi) understand that it means the plaster round the plague spot, as though ‘the plague spot’ is to be understood after ‘round about’.

43. We gather from verse 48 that the priest inspects the house again after the seven-day period in any case. Thus verses 43–47 deal with the situation which arises if the trouble has recurred, and verses 48–53 describe the cleansing rites due if there is no further trouble.

54–57. A concluding summary of the whole chapter.

(e) UNCLEAN DISCHARGES (‘ISSUES’) 15.1–33

This chapter deals with the *zāḇ* and the *zāḇāh*, the man or the woman who suffer from a discharge from the genital organs. The discharge is not from his body (verse 2) but ‘from his flesh’, where *bāśār* (flesh) is a euphemism, as in 6.10 (Heb 3) and 16.4. This is why there is the particular emphasis on what the sufferer sits on or lies on. The Greek equivalent to *zāḇ* is *gonorrhuēs*, the spelling of which makes sufficiently clear the type of disease which may be involved.

3. Rashi says the verse means that the man is ritually unclean whether the discharge is clear in appearance or whether it is thick so that it closes up the opening of the *membrum virile*.

9. saddle: following EVV, and going back to LXX *episagma onou*, ass’s pack-saddle. The reference is to anything on which the man sits when he rides: saddle, cloth, seat in a chariot. Any contact whatever involves washing and remaining ritually unclean till sunset, except that earthenware bowls must be smashed. It is assumed that all metal pots are thoroughly washed in any case (Mk 7.4).

16–18. All semen discharged in normal sexual relations involves ritual uncleanness to both parties. They must bathe in spring water and be unclean till sunset. No sacrifices are involved, but only for irregular discharges.

Discharges from a Woman 19–30

19–24. These verses deal with normal menstruation. The woman is not a *zāḇāh* (verses 25–30) unless there is a discharge at least three days outside the normal seven (cf. Mt. 9.20, Mk 5.25, Lk. 8.43). Her 'impurity' (the root means 'shrink from') lasts for seven days. Any man who has intercourse with her during this period will be ritually unclean for another seven days, though some Rabbis argued it means the rest of her seven-day period.

Concluding Summary **31–33**

31. separate: the Hebrew here has an unusual use of the verb *nāzar*, which means 'sacred separation', e.g. the Nazirite and his vows. See a similar use of the verb in 22.2, where it means that a priest in a state of ritual uncleanness must keep away from the holy gifts. It is best in both cases to read 'observe strict rules in respect of ritual uncleanness'. The versions found this use of the word difficult, and tended to read *hizhartem* (warn) instead of *hizzartem*.

(f) THE DAY OF ATONEMENT 16.1–34

This chapter is certainly composite. Verses 11–28 form a parallel account to verses 6–10, but more detailed; both sections begin with exactly the same words. The first section says that the he-goat must go into the wilderness 'for Azazel', but the second section says nothing about Azazel. Verses 29–34 seem to be wholly independent. This is not surprising, since the rites of the 10th day of the 7th month are definitely post-exilic, and the two accounts of what happens to the he-goat bear every trace of very ancient origin, the first more ancient than the second. Further, here 'the holy place' apparently means the inner shrine, elsewhere P's 'holy of holies'. Here also 'the tent of meeting' is parallel to the outer court of the Temple (verses 16, 20, 33) and not to the court within the Upper Gate. Many solutions have been offered in the analysis of this chapter; see the larger commentaries and the introductions. The Azazel ceremony is an ancient annual ceremony for the purgation of the sins of the community. We have also an early rite concerning cleansing rites necessary before entering the shrine for the first time: it is unlikely that the sacrifices of 3b were made on every occasion. In any case, this must be later than the E-tradition, according to which Joshua went freely in and out of the tent, or 'did not depart from the tent' (Exod. 33.11). Aaron must have come into the tradition not earlier than the post-exilic period, since it was only then that the Aaronites had any status whatever at Jerusalem. It is unwise to attempt to sort out in any greater detail the various traditions, since all of them have been written over and adapted to successive developments.

1–2. The first verses connect the statement of verse 2 with the Nadab-Abihu story of chapter 10, though actually it has nothing to do with that incident. Verse 2 is a general statement concerning the special sanctity of the Holy Place within the veil, i.e. the Holy of Holies, where later tradition said the Ark was housed. Not even the High Priest was free to enter the inner shrine at any time. The penalty was death, as for any priestly infringement of such rules of holiness as applied to them (Lev. 10.5, etc.).

2. not to come at all times: following EVV. Presumably the writer intended to say 'not at just any time' or 'not at all except on the one special occasion'.
the mercy seat: this phrase came into our English Bibles from Luther's *Gnadenstuhl* through Tyndale's translation, which appeared in the next year or so after the publication of the first parts of Luther's German Bible. The earlier English rendering is Wyclif's *propitiatorie*, virtually a transliteration of V, itself a translation of LXX *hilastērion*. The Hebrew is *kappōreṯ*, and the problem of this word is: are we to derive it directly from the original meaning of the root and say 'cover, lid', or are we to derive it from the ritual development of the root and translate it as having to do with the covering of sin, and thence with ideas of propitiation? Undoubtedly it was a cover which fitted on the top of P's Ark, and also God was thought to be particularly present immediately above this covering. It was a slab of solid gold, forty-four inches by twenty-six, and on the top of it, of one piece with it and all of beaten gold, were the two cherubim, kneeling and facing inwards with bowed heads and wings reaching over so as to touch in the middle. These are not the two cherubim of 1 Kg. 6.23–28, giant figures some fifteen feet high, facing outwards with a wing-stretch of fifteen feet. They are a post-exilic stylization of the bearers of God in Ezekiel's visions (Ezek. 10.1–3, etc.). It was upon these cherubim that God, the Shepherd of Israel, sat enthroned (Ps. 80.1 (Heb 2)). Here, in Lev. 16.2, God promises to appear in the cloud above the mercy seat. This is the Shekinah, the luminous cloud of Mk 9.7 and Ac. 1.9, but in Lev. 16.13 it is associated with the cloud of incense.

Aaron and the Holy Place 3–5

3. thus: the Hebrew is *b^{e}zô'ṯ*, the numerical value of which, according to Gematria (the science of exegesis according to numbers) is 410, and this is held in the Midrash to be an allusion to the 410 years during which the First Temple stood.
The **young bull** is for the de-sinning rite on behalf of Aaron and all his house. They must be ritually clean before any of the special atonement rites are begun. The ram for the whole-offering is similar to the gift without which none may come before the king. In the final statement of the chapter Aaron and his successors as High Priests must use every possible ritual cleansing rite to ensure the final cleanness of themselves, the people, the sanctuary, and even the mercy seat from every possible taint of ritual uncleanness.

4. The High Priest does not invest himself with his full official garments (Exod. 28.39f.), which traditionally were eight in number, but with linen garments a near copy of those of the ordinary priest: coat, girdle, turban (not 'cap'), and breeches. We have a linen variation of the High Priest's turban, and a linen girdle, though according to the Talmud (*b. RH*, 26a) the belt of the ordinary priest was a mixture of linen and wool. All the gold work is to be kept out of his clothes, the tradition being (since the Jerusalem Targum never forgets and barely forgives) that there shall be no reminder of the golden calf over which Aaron sinned. Rashi has the answer: 'the prosecuting counsel cannot become the defending counsel', so that when the High Priest appears thus before God he must be stripped of all his finery and be a humble suppliant.

his body: as elsewhere, a euphemism, as V (*verenda*, often so used by Pliny) saw; but the Talmud (*b. Yoma*, 31b) maintains that the reference throughout the verse is to the whole body. The High Priest had to immerse himself once, and wash his hands and feet twice every time he changed his garments. This involved five immersions and ten washings. Perhaps a perfect ritual cleansing does indeed require all this.

The Two Goats **6–10**

Here one only of the goats is called a sin-offering, though in verse 5 both constitute one. Tradition says that the two goats were placed in front of the High Priest, one on his right and the other on his left. He put both hands into an urn and drew out one tag in each hand. He placed the tag 'for the Lord' on one goat and the tag 'for Azazel' on the other goat. The first goat is a sin-offering for the people, and the second goat carries all their sins away and loses both itself and the sin in the wilderness. This appears to involve two distinct sin-rites, but both combine to ensure a complete ritual de-sinning rite.

8. for Azazel: the ancient versions are, for the most part, completely puzzled by this. LXX has 'for sending away' (*'ēz*, she-goat, and root *'-z-l*, go away), and so V *caper emissarius*. Rashi thinks of the root *'-z-z* (be strong) and *'ēl* (mighty) and says that Azazel was a precipitous flinty rock in a craggy land: so *b. Yoma*, 39a (cf. Arabic *'azāz* (Lane)). Ibn Ezra says the rock was not far distant from Mount Sinai and the Jerusalem Targum says it was a rough, hard place in the rocky desert which is known as Beth-hadudun. This is said to be the modern *Khirbet Khareidan*, about three and a half miles from Jerusalem, overlooking the Kidron valley. Another suggestion is that it is associated with the Arabic *'azala* and means 'remove', i.e. the complete removal of sin. Or again, there is an association with the worship of satyrs, the goat-demons of the waste and rocky places. According to the Book of Enoch 8.1, 9.6, Azazel taught men how to make weapons of war and all ornaments and cosmetics. He taught men 'all unrighteousness on earth'. He is not named with the fallen angels, but is mentioned in that context. Ultimately he comes to be identified with the Devil, though the Rabbis were always very careful to explain that the goat was never intended in any sense whatever as a gift to Azazel. The term 'scapegoat' first appears in Tindale, and has become the technical term in the study of comparative religion for such de-sinning rites, though in popular thought it means one who takes the blame, and to some extent at least innocently suffers for others. The Talmud was on the right track. There is an Arabic word *'a'zal* (isolated sandhill), and G. R. Driver suggests 'precipice', *JSS* 1, 1956, 97f. The meaning of the Hebrew word could be simply 'the goat has gone away' (cf. *AI*, pp. 508f.).

The Scapegoat Rite in Detail **11–28**

Fuller details are to be found in the Mishnah tract *Yoma* and in the Talmud *b. Yoma*. The goat was taken away by a man detailed for this task, and finally pushed backwards over the cliff, 'and it went rolling down, and before it had reached half-way down the hill it was broken in pieces' (*Yoma*, vi, 6).

12. two handfuls: better 'a double handful'; the word is in the dual, and in any case the corresponding Arabic root means 'take with both hands'.

beaten small: it is only here that the adjective *daḳḳāh* (pulverized) is used of the spiced Temple incense. The tradition is that for this particular rite the incense used received additional pounding the day before so that it was reduced to the finest possible dust (Sifra and *b. Yoma*, 45a).

13. the cloud of incense: LXX has *atmis* (steam, vapour). V combines both Hebrew and LXX and has 'the cloud and the vapour thereof (DV)'. The intention is to create an artificial cloud which will hide the majesty of the Presence of God, lest the High Priest see God and die.

the testimony: this word *'ēḏûṯ* in the singular is used by P and once by the Chronicler. There is a plural form found in Psalms and in the Chronicler (and two or three times elsewhere) to mean 'testimonies', parallel (especially in Ps. 119) to 'statutes', and as such it is a strong word: firm evidence. It is in the first place a name given (Exod. 31.18) to the Ten Words written with the finger of God on the two tables of stone. Then we find the phrase 'the ark of the testimony' (Exod. 25.22), and similar phrases, the tent, and the tabernacle of the testimony (Num. 9.15; Exod. 38.21). Here the word denotes the Ark itself, as in Exod. 27.21 and Lev. 24.3. The word is from the root *'ûḏ* (bear testimony, originally 'repeat, emphatically affirm').

16. transgressions: the word *peša'* means 'rebellion' and the plural, as here, 'rebellious actions'. It is the characteristic word used by the prophets to describe Israel's sin. The importance of this lies in the fact that they thought of sin as a rebellion against a personal God rather than a transgression of laws laid down by him, or as an infringement of some ritual detail. The word, of course, is not always used in this precise sense, but sometimes it is clear that it is used of serious apostasy in contrast to *ḥaṭṭā'ṯ* (sin). See especially Job 34.37, 'for he adds *peša'* (rebellion) to his *ḥaṭṭā'ṯ* (sin)'.

the tent of meeting: here as elsewhere (see also note on 1.1) both LXX and V have 'tent of testimony', taking the word *mô'ēḏ* to be from the root *'ûḏ* (witness) rather than from the root *yā'aḏ* (meet, appoint). In the E-tradition the Tent of Meeting was outside the camp and at a considerable distance (Exod. 33.7), but in the P-tradition it is within the Sanctuary, which itself is in the precise middle of the camp. Since the tent therefore **abides with them in the midst of their uncleannesses,** all these minute precautions have to be taken to ensure that it is absolutely ritually clean.

17. the holy place: this must be what is elsewhere called 'the holy of holies' (lit. the Most Holy Place), the inner shrine which in the Second Temple was within the veil. See note on verse 1.

18. he shall go out to the altar which is before the LORD: this must be the altar of burnt-offering which was in front of the Holy of Holies, which is what must be meant here by 'the holy place'. This is the altar mentioned in verse 12 on which the fire was burning and Aaron took a censer of burning ashes off and then brought it 'within the veil'. The Talmud (*b. Yoma*, 58b) disagrees with this, and says that in verse 18 we are dealing with the altar of incense (the golden altar) which was within the veil. The difficulty arises from Exod. 30.10, where it is stated that Aaron is to make atonement upon the horns of the altar of incense once a year, and the previous verse lays particular emphasis that it is the altar of incense and not the altar of burnt-offering. It is best to admit frankly that we have here a variation in the traditions, and not to try to assimilate both passages as the Talmud does. In Leviticus 16 we have a tradition which apparently belongs to the days when there was no altar of incense, whilst Exod. 30.10 belongs to a time when there was such an altar. Possibly the insistence of Exod. 30.9 that it was indeed the altar of incense is itself evidence of a change in custom. Probably also, the complication caused by 'the holy place' in this chapter being elsewhere, and usually called 'the most holy place' (Holy of Holies) is part of the same problem, since presumably ultimately one altar would be in the Holy Place and the other in the Most Holy Place. Another curious difference in custom is that in the case of the normal sin-offering (Lev. 4.7) the de-sinning blood was put on the horns of the altar of incense, and doubtless this is behind the Talmud tradition concerning Lev. 16.18, yet de-sinning blood was also put on the horns of the altar of burnt-offering (Lev. 9.9). We cannot marshal all the statements concerning altars and sacrifices and holy places into one coherent scheme. If it is admitted that we have much ancient material in the P-traditions, then it must also be expected that we shall find variations in the traditions, if only because of the increasing complexity of ritual ceremonies which seems to develop steadily through the centuries in all religions.

21. both his hands: normally one hand only is placed on the head of the sin-offering (4.4), but this is to make doubly sure of the transference of the sin. In Num. 27.23 'hands' is found, but S and Sam have 'hand'. Here the definite 'two' is found, so that there can be no doubt.

who is in readiness: following RV. LXX has 'ready' and V 'prepared' which is what the AV 'fit' meant in the sixteenth century. Jewish tradition says he was a man who knew the tracks through the wilderness and able and ready to do what had to be done. He was picked the day before, and was usually a non-Israelite.

22. solitary land: following V and RV. AV 'not inhabited' is from T. The Hebrew is stronger than this; *gᵉzērāh* means 'cut off': no way back. The goat carries away all the sins of Israel to a place from which neither it nor they can return. In the modern ritual of the Day of Atonement (*Yom Kippûr*) the list of sins is long and complete.

23. Once more we find confusion. The Rabbis thought this verse should come after verse 25; Rashi thought after verse 28. But if we read 'had put on' and assume that 'the holy place' is the Holy of Holies and that here 'the tent of meeting' is equivalent to 'within the Upper Gate' (where the altar of burnt-offering was), then the passage makes sense. Whether this is what the text meant originally is another matter, but this appears to be what the P-editors meant. When the priest entered the Holy of Holies, he put on the special linen clothes. When still within, he put these clothes off, bathed himself, put on his usual clothes, and then came outside into the area where the altar of burnt-offering was. It is impossible wholly to straighten out the difficulties, except on an assumption that we have a stratum of the P-tradition in which different equations were made between P's desert sanctuary and the Second Temple. In any case, the intention of the ritual is plain: to make a complete separation between Israel and the sin so that there is no possible chance of actual contagion. Every possible precaution was taken to see to it that on the 10th of Tishri, the Old New Year's Day (see *JNYF*, p. 134), the Temple, the High Priest, and all the people were absolutely and undoubtedly ritually clean.

26. he who lets the goat go: following EVV. Both LXX and V have the stronger 'send away'. The Hebrew can have either meaning. The Targums have 'led away'.

27. Both sin-offerings are destroyed outside the camp, all except, as usual, the blood and the fat which were disposed of at the altar. The destruction of the priest's sin-offering is normal practice; he cannot get rid of his own sin by eating it. It is normal practice also for the sin-offering of the people to be destroyed outside the camp (Lev. 4.21). The difference is that it is clearly stated here that some other person had to carry the carcase out and deal with it, and that he had to bathe himself wholly before he came back inside the camp. These extra instructions show the stringent care shown to secure the absolute separation of the uncleanness from Israel.

The Day of Atonement **29–34**

Originally this section was independent of what goes before, but since by tradition the High Priest was permitted to enter the inner shrine once a year and on the Day of Atonement, the two passages come together.

29. seventh month on the tenth day: see notes on 23.23–33, where all the sacred occasions of the seventh month are discussed.

afflict yourselves: this is better than EVV 'afflict your souls', following the ancient versions. RSV has rightly seen that here the Hebrew *nep̄eš* means 'self'. With suffixes this word is a fulsome way of saying 'me, him', etc., as though Hebrew is committing the frequent error of modern spoken English by confusing the reflexives and the ordinary personal pronouns. The phrase means 'fasting' (Ps. 35.13). The Jerusalem Targum gives details of the restrictions: abstain from food, drinks, use of the bath, 'rubbing', sandals, 'the practice of the bed', and all this in addition to every kind of work whatever. This was the most stringent fast of all. It is 'the Fast' of Ac. 27.9. All must keep the fast, both native and stranger (resident alien), who may or may not be circumcised.

31. sabbath of solemn rest: see note on 23.3.

32. the holy linen garments: these are the special linen clothes, used only on this particular day (see verse 4).

FOURTH SECTION 17.1–26.46 THE HOLINESS CODE

(a) ALL SLAUGHTER IS SACRIFICE 17.1–9

The paragraph deals with the slaughter for food of domestic beasts, cattle and sheep and goats, which also are the only animals offered in the Temple. There is more than one strand here (cf. 'outside the camp' (verse 3) and 'in the open field' (verse 5)). Ancient laws are adapted to a new purpose. It is necessary to realize two things: one, the common Hebrew word for 'sacrifice' (*zeḇaḥ*) originally means 'slaughter', ordinary killing of animals; two, the so-called 'sacrifice of peace-offerings' (*zeḇaḥ šᵉlāmîm*) was eaten by the worshipper, apart from the blood and the fat, both of which went to the altar, and the breast and the right thigh, which were the perquisites of the priesthood as a whole and the officiating priest respectively. Further, the blood and the fat went to the altar whatever the sacrifice. Cf. *SOTS*, pp. 31f., 37–9.

In earliest times all slaughter was also a sacrifice. A great stone could be the 'place of slaughter' (*mizbēaḥ*, later 'altar') (1 Sam. 14.31–35). Before king Josiah destroyed the local shrines, it was comparatively simple to obey the early rule and bring the animal to the local shrine. This custom was encouraged in the interests of true religion, since the blood which was poured out on the ground could be regarded as a *šelem* (plural *šᵉlāmîm*), which in the Ugarit tablets was poured into the 'liver of the earth' as a fertilizing agent (*Baal* V, iii, 31, etc.). It was to prevent this sacrificing to the satyrs (verse 5) that the instructions were originally framed. There had to be a later adaptation to the post-exilic situation with the one central shrine, and this is embodied in verses 5f. The clear distinction made necessary by the centralization of the worship at Jerusalem is made in Dt. 12.15–26, between slaughter for food and slaughter for the sacred meal. But here we have an earlier stratum of law, confused by the P-editor's understanding of *zeḇaḥ* as the sacred meal known as *zeḇaḥ šᵉlāmîm* (RSV, sacrifice of peace offerings).

4. does not bring it: following AV. The rendering of RV (hath not brought) makes the situation more clear.

gift: this is a return to LXX *dōron*, presumably to avoid the 'oblation' of EVV, due to V, a word largely meaningless. The Hebrew is *ḳorbān* in its general sense of everything that is 'brought near' and presented in the Temple. LXX has a long interpolation which goes into details concerning whole-offerings and shared-offerings, but the introduction of whole-burnt-offerings into this context is an error. We are here concerned with offerings, none of the flesh of which went to the altar.

bloodguilt shall be imputed: the use of the word bloodguilt here is sound, but it is better to avoid the word 'imputed' because the word has all sorts of theological overtones associated with various theories of the Atonement. The Hebrew is 'shall be reckoned to'. The man is liable to the full consequence of bloodguilt, which is death.

5. their sacrifices which they slay: this means 'the animals which they slaughter for food'.

6. sprinkle: once again, the verb is *zāraḳ*, which means 'toss, throw'; cf. 1.5, where RSV actually has 'throw'.

7. Here is the purpose of the original regulations. They are against worshipping the gods of the countryside, here called the 'goats'; AV 'devils', RV rightly 'he-goats', with 'satyrs' (so RSV) in the margin. This confuses the Semitic idea with the goat-man creatures of lust of classical mythology. See the Ugarit tablets, mentioned in note at the beginning of this section. These are the goat-demons of the countryside.

play the harlot: this metaphor for the worship of the Canaanite gods is as old as the J-tradition (Exod. 34.15). These cults did involve temple prostitution, and the *ḳāḏēš* and the *ḳ^e^ḏēšāh*, male and female sacred prostitutes, were a feature of shrines throughout the whole Semitic area, nor were the Yahweh shrines always altogether free from them. Both sexes of prostitutes are prohibited in Dt. 23.18 ('dog' means male prostitute).

8–9. These verses are a separate law dealing with the whole question of animal sacrifices.

(b) PROHIBITION AGAINST EATING BLOOD 17.10–16

The prohibition against eating blood, including flesh from which the blood has not been drained, is absolute and ancient. This is the modern Jewish insistence on food being *kosher*. The **life** (verse 11, Hebrew *nep̱eš*) of any 'creature' (Hebrew *bāšār* **flesh**, but correctly 'creature' in verse 14) **is in the blood.** The later ritualistic reason is in verse 11b, it is a means of making atonement (root *k-p-r*).

11. for your souls: this should be either 'for your lives' (Hebrew *nep̱eš*, as before) or 'for your selves'. This has nothing whatever to do with any idea of an immortal soul or even of a man having a soul as distinct from his body or his spirit.

13. The blood of creatures killed in hunting (V 'and fowling') must be poured on the ground and covered; cf. Dt. 12.16, 24, with the addition here of being covered. Uncovered blood calls for revenge, and there can be bloodguilt for the shed blood of animals as well as for the shed blood of man. It is the blood that is important, more important than the fact of a human life being taken. Such is the over-all importance of a *taboo*. The metaphor of covering shed blood with dust is used in Job 16.18, where Job does not wish his death to take place or his shed blood covered, until he has had the satisfaction of seeing justice done.

14–16. What dies naturally or is mangled by wild beasts still has its blood in it, and that is why it is *taboo*, ritually unclean.

(c) SOCIAL LAWS **18.1–20.27**

These three chapters deal with a whole miscellany of social laws: matters of sexual relations within the prohibited degrees of blood relationship, then with Molech worship, and after that with a whole range of regulations, some of which have already been dealt with. Here is clear evidence of at least a second source.

I am the LORD *your God* **1–5**

The basis of all the laws is that Yahweh is the God of Israel, and they are his people. They must not therefore do as the Egyptians do (among whom they once lived), nor as the Canaanites do (in whose land they have come to live). The phrase 'I am the Lord', with its fuller forms as in 18.30, 19.36, and 21.15, is the whole basis of the Holiness Code. There are two reasons: one is that Yahweh is the God of Israel; the other is that Yahweh is holy, which means the only true God, separate, different and distinct, and Israel must be holy too, separated from the other nations in conduct as well as by race. All these rules are lifted out of the welter of pagan thought and made to stem from the work of Yahweh the Saviour of Israel. The basis of Hebrew conduct even in the ritualistic setting of Leviticus is definitely religious as against ethical; that is, these things are to be done not because they are morally right, but because they are the will of their Saviour God. This is the basis of Christian conduct; barely ethical and strongly humanitarian arguments concerning morals confuse the issue.

2. the LORD your God: the Rabbis said that the occurrence of the two Names of God means that he (*Yahweh*) is the covenant God and he (*Elohim*) is the judge. See Exod. 21.6, where the traditional translation of *'^{e}lōhîm* is 'judges'. RV and RSV rightly have 'God'.

5. shall live: this means 'keep alive' and not die because of the infringement of a *taboo*.

Unchastity with Blood Relations is prohibited **6–18**

It is always assumed that this section deals with marriage within the prohibited degrees, but the Hebrew does not say 'marriage' and some of the instances can scarcely involve marriage. The general rule is given in verse 6, where **near of kin** means 'blood relation'. The Hebrew is *š^{e}'ēr b^{e}śārô*, 'the innermost-flesh of his flesh'. The word *š^{e}'ēr* is not from *š-'-r* I (remain, be left over; Arabic *sa'ara*; AVm is quite wrong), but from *š-'-r* II (Accadian *šêru*, flesh and Arabic *ṯa'r*, blood revenge). The word strictly means the flesh near the bone as against *bāśār* (flesh near the skin). Hence the phrase above is our 'blood relation'. The further overriding consideration is that a man and his wife 'become one flesh' (Gen. 2.24).

6. to uncover nakedness: i.e. the *pudenda*, either of man or woman. The phrase can be used of the shameful exposure of a man (Gen. 9.22), but mostly of women (slaves being sold naked), but chiefly of sexual intercourse.

7. The verse is not easy to translate. It is best to say 'the nakedness of your father and mother', which is what the Hebrew actually says (note the limitations of the 'construct' construction), which is 'one nakedness', so to speak, since they are one flesh. The whole section presents difficulties of translation because all our terms are based on a monogamous system. Also, it is not necessarily marriage that is being discussed, but unchastity.

8. your father's wife: This is not our term stepmother, who is the father's second wife after the decease of the man's mother. It is another wife of the father, other than the mother of the man, e.g. Reuben's relation to Bilhah, supposing she had been his father's full wife (Gen. 35.22, 49.4. See Ezek. 22.10a). It may well be that Reuben's real offence was that he was the eldest son, and therefore the presumed heir (cf. 2 Sam. 3.7, 16.22; 1 Kg. 2.22). According to Rashi the regulation here prohibits marriage after the father's death (cf. Koran 4.26).

9. This is the case of a father's daughter, who may be a full sister or a half-sister (mother's daughter but to another man). 'Born at home' means by the same father of a woman of his household. 'Abroad' may mean of a woman not of his household. The usual interpretation is that this latter means by a different father in a previous marriage.

11. This is a different case. Here the girl is the father's daughter, but of a woman of the household who is not the man's mother.

12. The father's sister is the closest female blood relation on the father's side, just as the mother's sister (verse 13) is the closest female blood relation on the mother's side.

14. aunt: strictly the *dôḏāh* is the wife of a man's *dôḏ*, who is the father's brother (Latin *patruus*, though the Syriac equivalent of *dôḏ* is used also for the mother's brother, Latin *avunculus*). There seems to have been no prohibition involving the mother's brother's wife, and Hebrew does not appear to have any word for this relationship.

16. brother's wife: some commentators regard this as the prohibition of what is called the levirate (Latin *levir*, husband's brother) marriage. The prohibition here has to do with sexual intercourse with the brother's wife whilst the brother is still alive. There is nothing here against ancient custom (Gen. 38), which is even required by Dt. 25.5–10, where marriage is definitely involved, as also in Mt. 22.23ff.

17. your near kinswomen: RSV is correct here in following LXX; or better still, 'they are (may be) your blood relations'. The point is that if a man has intercourse with a woman, any child she bears may be of his begetting. Thus the point is not that they are her blood relations but that they may be his. Hebrew has 'a female blood relation'; not 'her', there being no *mappîḵ* in the final *hē'*.

18. This has nothing to do with marrying a deceased wife's sister. What is prohibited is having anything to do with a wife's sister whilst the wife is alive, a custom which was allowed in Jacob's time. Rashi says it means a man may not marry a divorced wife's sister.

a rival wife: whatever may be said about polygamous societies being happy, in Hebrew life jealousy and rivalry between wives was sufficiently common for the other wife to be called *ṣārāh*, rival (1 Sam. 1.6; Sir. 37.11). This verse definitely refers to marriage. LXX links this verse with Sir. 26.6. V has *in pellicatum*, make a concubine or mistress of her. DV has 'for a harlot, to rival her'.

Other Irregularities **19–23**

20. neighbour: and so LXX and V, but Heb has *'āmîṯ*, found outside H only in Lev. 6.2 (Heb 5.21), where apparently it means 'business associate'. The prohibition here is because of uncleanness. In the previous verse contact with menstrual blood is involved. Here, as V points out, contact with the other man's semen is involved, on the assumption that it has been only recently deposited.

21. devote them by fire to Molech: the usual assumption is that this involved sacrificing the children by throwing them into a raging fire. There has been considerable discussion in recent years concerning these so-called sacrifices 'to Molech'. The evidence for such sacrifices is almost entirely from Carthaginian sources. The point at issue is not whether there were child sacrifices in old Israel—nobody denies this—but whether this particular type existed, sacrificing them by throwing them into a raging fire. This distinction is made clear by O. Eissfeldt (*Molk als Opferbegriff in Punischen und Hebräischen und das Ende des Gottes Molech*, 1935) where he writes of *molk* as a particular kind of sacrifice in Punic circles. See also J. G. Février, 'Essai de reconstruction du sacrifice Molek', *JA* 248, 1960, 167–87, and de Vaux, *AI*, pp. 444–46, and *SOTS*, pp. 73–90. Because of the usual identification with the Punic rite, RSV here follows EVV in inserting the mention of fire, and has gone further still by translating *l*[e]*ha'*[a]*ḇîr* (cause to pass through) by 'to devote'. Sam and LXX read the root *'-b-d* (worship); Aq, Sym, Theod all have *parabibazō* (put aside, set aside). Rashi quotes the Talmud (*b. San.*, 64a) and says the parent handed the children over to the priests who lit two large fires and passed the children between the fires. It is significant that this reference to the children and the Molech cult occurs in the middle of a series of prohibitions of illegal sexual intercourse. In 2 Kg. 23.10 RSV has 'burn his son or his daughter as an offering to Molech', but the Hebrew text has nothing about burning. Similarly in Jer. 32.35 there is no mention of fire. See also Isa. 57.9, where some read 'Molech' instead of 'the King', and so RSV. The context is concerned largely with lascivious, idolatrous rites, and verse 9 itself speaks of journeying to Molech with oil and multiplying perfumes. The probability is that the children were given to the authorities at the shrine to be trained as temple prostitutes, male and female (cf. Lev. 20.4, 5). Burning in fire is mentioned in Dt. 12.31, but there is no mention there of Molech, and Dt. 18.10 has 'pass through in the fire'. See *VT* 16, 1966, 123–7.

Molech: the vowels are the vowels of *bôšeṯ*, shameful thing, idol. These vowels are used to denote an idolatrous association: *'aštōreṯ* for Astarte, *tôpeṯ* for *tepeṯ* (Topheth), *'iš-bôšeṯ* for Ishbaal, and *Mepîḇôšeṯ* for Mephibaal. See 7.18 for a similar use of the vowels *šiḳḳûṣ*. The god's name was Melek (king), a common name for a deity in Semitic religion. W. J. Harrelson in *DB*, p. 669, following Eissfeldt, is strongly of the opinion that we should always read *lᵉmōleḵ*, meaning 'for a child sacrifice' (see previous note).

22. abomination: usually this word *tô'ēḇāh* has to do with idolatrous actions, actions connected with the cult of other gods. This links up with the previous verse if we see there a reference to children dedicated to temple prostitution. Thus homosexuality here is condemned on account of its association with idolatry. Sexual intercourse with a beast is *teḇel* (**perversion,** verse 23). This word actually means 'confusion'. It could mean confusion in the sense of a violation of nature, but it is more likely that Rashi is right when he refers to the resultant mixture of semen, human and animal: which brings this case into the same category as that in verse 20. LXX has *museron* (something foul). DV has combined this and V *scelus* into 'heinous crime'. These all miss the point.

Concluding Exhortations **24–30**

These verses point out the moral of the fate of those earlier dwellers in Canaan who committed all these offences. Post-exilic Israelites must take warning, lest they meet the same fate.

25. I punished its iniquity: Hebrew 'I visited (root *p-ḳ-d*) its iniquity upon it'. This verb *p-ḳ-d* (visit) is the key word to much of Hebrew thought about God and the world. God does not work from inside the world, and he is in no sense immanent in it. He visits it, to the extent of coming in between (to use our terms) every cause and every effect. In particular, he visits it in two ways, with good favour and salvation or in punishment. Much popular religious thought has abandoned the idea of God's regular visitations to the realm of natural law, but keeps the idea for special visitations of divine providence or divine retribution (why has God done this to me?).

19.1–37. This chapter consists of a whole miscellany of commandments parallel to those in Exod. 20, 22.18–31, 23.1–19; Dt. 5.6–21. The order differs, and there is a section concerning the eating of sacrificial meals (5–8). Sometimes the second person is used and sometimes the third. It all shows a compilation from many sources.

2–4. An early set of commandments, involving three items: revere parents, keep the Sabbath, shun idolatry. The order is opposite to that of Exod. 20. The second person is used.

3. revere: Hebrew has *yārē'*, the usual verb for 'fear' (EVV), used in all connections, including often fearing God. Usually the word used of a man's attitude to his parents is *k-b-d* (honour) as in Exod. 20.12; Dt. 5.16, a word used comparatively rarely (about eleven times) with 'God' as the object. See further in verse 14.

his mother and his father: this is not the usual order (cf. Exod. 20.12; Dt. 5.16). LXX (cod. A) omits the reference to the mother and T has the usual order.

Speculations as to the reason for the difference are precarious. The easiest explanation is a different part of tradition.

4. idols: as EVV, following LXX and V. The Hebrew *'elîlîm* (RVm 'things of nought') provides an assonance with the regular Hebrew words for God, *'elōhîm* and the plural *'ēlîm* (*'ēl* being the regular Semitic name of the high god). The word may originally have been a genuine word for 'gods' (cf. Sabaean), but there is a Syriac word *'alîl* (weak, feeble) and the Hebrews undoubtedly associated it with the word *'al* (worthlessness, nothingness). A good rendering is 'worthless godlings'. **molten gods:** the word undoubtedly means 'made of cast metal' as against images of hewn wood or stone. So also Exod. 34.17, but Exod. 20.4; Lev. 26.1; Dt. 5.8, 4.16, 23, 25, all have *pesel* (hewn idol), whereas Dt. 27.15 gives both. The word used here is used only of 'molten images', especially the 'molten calf' of Exod. 32.4, Israel's greatest sin, but *pesel* can be used of idols generally, of molten as well as of hewn idols. It has been suggested that there were two ancient traditions, one which prohibited hewn idols but not molten idols, and the other which prohibited molten but not hewn. There is a possibility that hewn idols may have been prohibited in some circles, the theory being that the god was inside the idol and he might be harmed by chipping it. Cf. the prohibition against shaping building stones on the sacred site (1 Kg. 6.7).

Eating Sacrificial Meals **5–8**

The flesh at a sacrificial meal may be eaten the same day or the next day, but definitely not after the second day. The rule applies to all such sacrifices, but in Lev. 7.11–18 the period varies according to the type of *zeḇaḥ šelāmîm* (shared meal, 'sacrifice of peace-offerings'); if a thank-offering (*tôḏāh*), the flesh must be eaten on the first day, but otherwise it may be eaten on the second day. We thus have a different law, probably earlier, in Lev. 19. In a hot country 'dead meat' must be eaten quickly, but it is more likely that the priestly prohibitions are not so much to avoid dysentry as to avoid anything connected with fermentation and decay, which is ritually unclean and therefore not holy (cf. the *taboo* against yeast (leaven)).

5. offer: following EVV. This rendering aids in the confusion concerning this offering, of which none of the flesh went to the altar. It is better to keep strictly to the Hebrew and translate 'slaughter'.

that you may be accepted: following RV. AV has 'at your will', i.e. not on particular specified occasions, which may well be right. The usual assumption is that if the rule is broken the sacrifice will not be acceptable to God, but God did not share in this sacrifice, since none of the flesh went to the altar. The meaning might possibly be 'to gain favour (peace, good health) for yourselves' (cf. 22.19 and 29, 23.11). LXX (codd. A and B) have *dekatēn* (tenth), but this looks like a scribal error in the Greek for *dektēn* (acceptable).

7. abomination: see note on 7.18, where the same prohibition is found. Here LXX has *athuton*, not acceptable as a sacrifice; V has *sacra inauspicata*.

accepted: it is better to translate 'acceptable'.

Gleaning in Field and Vineyard **9–10**

Cf. Lev. 23.22; Dt. 24.19–21. It is maintained that the original reason for the prohibition against making a clean sweep is that the odd stalks and grapes are for the fertility spirits. Here the reason is humanitarian. They are to be left for the poor and the resident alien, those who have no property and no protector. Elsewhere the widow and the fatherless are added.

9. reap . . . to its very border: lit. 'finish to reap the edge of your field'. We must think of the reapers beginning at one end of the strip and moving steadily in a line across the field. V and DV seem to have read *pᵉnê* (surface of) and have 'you must not cut down to the very ground'. The 'corners' of EVV comes from T. Rashi thinks of the last corner that is left.

the gleanings: the *leḳeṭ* is what can be picked up, as a bird picks up seeds. It is prohibited to go over the field again and pick up every stalk not in a sheaf. The Mishnah (*Peah*, vi, 5) says that three stalks together make a bundle and are not 'gleaning'.

10. strip bare: the EVV 'glean' is too weak. Hebrew '*-l-l* means 'deal severely', hence the reading of RSV, but the Arabic '*alla* means 'do a thing a second time', and probably this is what we have here. The reference is to odd grapes left when all the clusters have been picked.

fallen grapes: the noun *pereṭ* is found only here. The corresponding Aramaic word means 'small change'; cf. the Israeli currency of 1949–60 when 1,000 *peruṭas* equalled one Israeli pound. The word here refers to single grapes which have fallen to the ground and also to grapes which are neither *kāṯēp̱* (growing on a stalk out of the central stem and in a cluster) nor *neṭep* (hanging directly from the central stem). All true grape clusters are to be gathered; odd grapes are to be left.

General Anti-social Behaviour **11–16**

These are offences of varying degrees of seriousness, but all uncharitable and improper in any society, especially among a holy people.

11. lie: cf. Accadian *taškirtu*; better than EVV 'deal falsely'. LXX has 'be a sycophant', literally one who shows figs, which normally are hidden by the leaves, and so 'informer' in ancient Greece.

to one another: the Hebrew is '*āmîṯ* (associate, close neighbour, business associate) (Lev. 6.2 (Heb 5.21)).

12. swearing falsely: this refers to swearing an oath in the Sacred Name with intent to deceive, which is 'to play the hypocrite with Heaven' (Sir Walter Scott, *Quentin Durward*, ch. viii).

13. oppress: the verb '*āšaḳ* is usually used of extortionate, tyrannical behaviour, but the Syriac equivalent means 'accuse, slander', whence the 'calumniate' of V and DV.

wages of a hired servant: the day labourer must be paid at sundown (Mt. 20.8). Rabbinic tradition turned consideration for the employee into consideration for the employer, and this by making full use of the phrase 'until the morning': he fulfils the law if he pays the man before dawn. Similarly, Dt. 24.14f. is held to refer to the night worker, so that the employer has the whole of the next day in which to find the money: he must pay the man by sundown the next day (see Mt. 15.6; Mk 7.13).

14. The deaf man cannot hear the curse and the blind man cannot see the obstacle. Thus both men are helpless and are therefore the special concern of God (Ps. 10.14, 72.12). The phrase stumbling-block has become part of the English language because of this use of it: it means taking unfair advantage of a man's disability.

fear your God: not only revere, stand in awe of, but actually fear the punishment inflicted by the God of Israel who is the helper of the helpless. The original idea behind the phrase is the terror inspired by the 'numinous' (Otto, *The Idea of the Holy*), the *deima panikon* of the Greeks, the 'horror of Pan', whence our 'panic'. This is more than ordinary fear, but full horror, involuntary and uncontrollable. The idea becomes sublimated in the awe of worship and deep reverence, and tends gradually to pass out of modern religious thought. The essential 'faith' of Protestantism depends on the prior experience of the complete helplessness of the human being before God, so that man can do nothing except trust completely in God's redeeming grace. See this common element in the experience of Paul, Luther, and their successors.

15–16. These two verses deal with justice in the courts and general slander. The justice is absolutely impartial, the blindfolded figure with the scales and the sword.

15. righteousness: the Hebrew *ṣeḏeḳ* is usually interpreted here to mean 'strict justice', which, at any rate in later times, is *dîn*. According to the Tosefta, *San.*, i, 3: 'Wherever there is justice (*dîn*) there is no 'righteousness' (*ṣeḏeḳ*, *ṣᵉḏāḳāh*), and wherever there is 'righteousness' there is no *dîn*. Based on such ideas the Talmud (*b. San.*, 30a) interprets this verse to mean that one must always judge with mercy rather than with justice, but this must be extended equally to both rich and poor.

16. stand forth against the life: lit. against the blood. The general interpretation is witness falsely against a man on a capital charge. This involves taking into account the first part of the verse also, with its reference to going about slandering others (Rashi says it means spying on others) and then appearing in court afterwards. The ancient Jewish interpretation (the Sifra and *b. San.*, 73a) is being able to rescue a man, but standing by and doing nothing, and the examples given are drowning in a river and being attacked by a robber or a wild beast.

17–18 deal with personal hatreds and vendettas. No man must nourish hatred against a brother Israelite. V and DV say he must reprove him openly. The Sifra says: frankly but not in public, because that would bring shame on him and it would be a sin to do that. If the aim is to heal the breach, the Sifra is right and V and DV are wrong.

18. love your neighbour as yourself: according to Rabbi Aqiba, 'this is a fundamental principle of the Torah', and so also the Sifra and the Talmud *j. Ned.*, ix, 3. Jesus said that this is a commandment second only to the opening words of the Shema‘ (Dt. 6.4), whose verses (Dt. 6.4–9, 11.13–21; Num. 15.37–41) every Jew is enjoined to repeat morning and evening. The first verse became a declaration of adherence to the Kingdom of God during the Bar-Kokba revolt in the time of Hadrian. The meaning here is neighbour Jew. Jesus included the Samaritan (Lk. 10.29–37). See also Rom. 13.9; Gal. 5.14; and 'the royal law' of Jas 2.8. Christian commentators have tended to ascribe the first universal application of this saying to Jesus, but see such passages as Isa. 56.1–8 and various sayings attributed to Hillel.

Separatism for Cattle, Seed, and Clothes **19**

The principle of Habdalah (separation) must be applied to every detail of life.
statutes: the word *ḥuḳḳôṯ* (only here in these regulations) refers to that which is decreed. Rashi says it refers to enactments of the king for which no reason is given.
stuff: the Hebrew *ša‘aṭnēz* is used only here and in the parallel Dt. 22.11, where it is defined as 'wool and linen together'; hence AV here. Köhler (*Lexicon*) thinks it means 'stuff of large meshes', but it is better to accept it as a Coptic loanword meaning 'false woven' (cf. LXX *kibdēlos* (spurious)). The reference is to cloth woven wrongly, that is, from yarn of two different materials. Many modern cloths would thus be barred.

20–22. Intercourse with a slave girl, who is allocated to another man, but she has not yet been bought by him nor given her freedom.

20. a woman who is a slave: the term is *šipḥāh*, a concubine, but certainly a woman wholly at the disposal of her master. In Arabic the verb means 'pour out blood, water, semen'. The word is used of a female slave belonging to her mistress, e.g. Hagar (Gen. 16.1) and Zilpah and Bilhah (Gen. 29.24, 29), but in all three cases the husband, with the permission of the wife, had access to them. The tradition is strong that no Jewess can be a *šipḥāh* (she is an *'āmāh*), who must be at least half-Canaanite.
betrothed: following EVV. This is misleading. The 'marriageable' of DV (V *nubilis*) is inadequate. The word means 'assigned to, acquired for' (see LXX 'a house-slave guarded for a man'). There has been an agreement whereby the girl is to go to a certain man as his concubine, but nothing further has been done. The agreement has been neither implemented nor cancelled. If the woman is a betrothed free woman, the penalty is death for both (Dt. 22.23).
not yet ransomed: the 'redeemed' of EVV is no clearer. The girl has not been bought. The root *p-d-h* is here used in its strict sense: a payment is made and the payer receives what was not his originally. Thus this is the right word for the 'redemption' of Israel from Egypt; Israel did not belong to God until Mount Sinai. On the other hand, the other redemption root (*g-'-l*) is the right word for the redemption from Babylon, since God 'sold' Israel into captivity (Isa. 50.1f.). See article 'The Hebrew Root G-'-L (I)', *Annual of Leeds Univ. Oriental Soc.*, 3, 1963, 60–67.

given her freedom: he had not cancelled the agreement under which she was to be his bed-slave.

an inquiry shall be held: the renderings vary from AV 'she shall be scourged' to RSV and to RVm 'there shall be an inquisition'. The Hebrew is *biḳḳōreṯ*, which certainly means 'inquiry, investigation'; hence LXX *episkopē* in its original sense of 'inquire, oversee', especially if he visits in order to do so. Thus the *episkopos* is the man who is always travelling (cf. the gaiters, etc., of earlier travelling clothes) to superintend those who are under his care. The rendering 'scourged' goes back to the Targums, which both say that the woman is liable to scourging. V and DV both say that both the man and woman are to be scourged (*vapulabunt ambo*), and so AVm. Rashi secures the rendering 'scourge' by a *tour de force*, by reading *biḳ^e rî'āh* (by reading aloud), since the Rabbis laid it down that whoever is subjected to lashes must also listen to the reading aloud by the judges of Dt. 28.58f. Ibn Ezra achieved the same result by reading *bāḳār* (cattle), the connexion being that the lashes were applied with a lash of calfskin.

21. guilt offering: the man's punishment was to bring an *'āšām*, the usual ram as an offering. But no payment was made because, although theoretically loss was sustained, that loss was negligible.

A Close-period for Newly Planted Trees **23–25**

23. count its fruit as forbidden: lit. 'you shall treat as uncircumcised its uncircumcision in respect of its fruit'. LXX has 'you shall thoroughly cleanse their uncleanness'. V has 'you shall take away their foreskin (DV: first-fruits)', and T says 'you shall put away its fruit . . . to be destroyed'. Rashi explains by saying 'you shall close its closing', close it up and bar it off so that no benefit may be derived from it. They are all saying that the fruit is *taboo* for three years, just as religiously the uncircumcised male is *taboo*. Possibly the original reason was that the fruit belonged to the spirit of the land (the baal), just as all increase of every kind is always regarded as belonging to God. In any case it is a sound agricultural principle; it gives the tree time to make wood and ultimately bear better crops (which is what verse 25 says).

24. all their fruit shall be holy: better, all their fruit shall be a *ḳōḏeš*, a holy gift. The whole crop is regarded as first-fruits in the first year when the tree is permitted to bear, and thus all of it goes to the priests.

an offering of praise: RSV has added 'an offering of', and this confuses the matter. The Hebrew is *hillûlîm* (cf. Jg. 9.27 of the merry-making of the vintage feast at Shechem. But Sam read *ḥillûlîm* (with a *ḥēṯ* instead of a *hē*')). This is from the root *ḥ-l-l*, which is used regularly of 'profaning a vineyard', i.e. making it 'common' in the sense of beginning to use its fruit for human consumption (see Lev. 10.10).

The Cult of the Dead **26–28**

The religious leaders evidently had the utmost difficulty in abolishing the cult of the dead in Israel. This is not surprising, considering the many pagan ideas and customs which still persist today in so-called civilized countries. People are very loth to do away with customs connected with the 'passage times' of life (cf. note on 'seven' (Lev. 4.6)).

26. any flesh with the blood in it: this is a strange rule to be found in this context which is dealing with witchcraft and necromancy. Lit. the Hebrew is 'ye shall not eat upon the blood', but LXX has 'on the mountains' (reading the consonants *hrm* instead of *hdm*, and involving in the square script only the slightest of changes) (cf. Ezek. 18.6, 15, illegitimate sacred meals on the mountains; also Dt. 12.2; Isa. 57.7, 65.7). The Talmud (*b. San.*, 63a, b) says the meaning is: no funeral feasts for a man who has been executed.

practice augury: the versions refer to the taking of omens. The ancient Jewish explanations are: making prognostications from the cries of weasels or the twittering of birds (the Sifra and *b. San.*, 65b), from bread falling from the mouth or a stag crossing one's path (*b. San.*, 66a). The Roman *augur* was an official who declared the future from his observation of birds (cf. LXX).

witchcraft: AV follows Jewish tradition with 'observe times', understanding it to mean those who believe in auspicious days, ideas which still persist in superstitions concerning Friday and Sunday. V and DV think in terms of dreams. The connection is probably with the Arabic '*unnat* (nasal twang) and has to do with necromancy (Jg. 9.37; Dt. 18.10f.). The reference is to the nasal twang of those who speak for ghosts and to their supposed twittering and chirping. See Isa. 8.19, which apparently defends this type of necromancy.

27. round off the hair on your temples: the Jewish tradition is that a man must not make his temples like the back of his ears and forehead; i.e. if he shaves his side-whiskers there will be a complete circle round his head. Extreme sects in Israel today wear long ringlets hanging down in front of their ears. See Jer. 9.26, where this difference in the cutting of the hair is one of the distinctions between circumcised and uncircumcised.

mar the edges of your beard: in V and DV this has become a command not to shave the beard. Jewish tradition says it involves the five corners of the beard: two near the temples, two at the angles of the jaw, and one in the middle of the chin.

28. cuttings in your flesh: the Hebrew is *śereṭ* (cf. Arabic *šaraṭa*, of slitting the ear of a camel). The reference is to gashing the skin in mourning, not so much to express sorrow in masochistic fashion, as to provide life-blood for the spirit of the dead. The *tašrîṭ* is the name for the gashes on the cheek-bone which distinguish the inhabitants of Mecca.

30. reverence my sanctuary: the traditional signs of irreverence were: entering with staff in hand, shoes on the feet, money in the belt, dust on the feet (the Sifra and *b. Ber.*, 54a; *b. Yeb.*, 6b).

More against Witchcraft **31**

mediums, which is what EVV mean by 'them that have familiar spirits', that is, spirits supposed to attend at call. The Hebrew is *'ôḇ*, a ghost that speaks out of the ground (Isa. 29.4). V has *magi*, which DV has turned into 'wizards'. LXX has 'ventriloquists' (*engastrimuthoi*, those that speak from their stomachs). Rashi says that the 'lord of the *'ôḇ*' places a corpse under his arm and thus speaks from his armpit.

wizards: following EVV. V and DV have 'soothsayers' (*ariolus*, said to be connected with Sanskrit *hira*, entrails). The Hebrew is *yidde'ônî* ('familiar spirit', Latin *famulus*, attendant), most likely meaning 'the knowing ones', whose who have secret knowledge of hidden things (cf. Ewald's *vielwisserisch*). Rashi says that the rite involved putting the bone of an animal (Maimonides says it was a bird) in one's mouth, and the bone speaks; so *San.*, vii, 7.

Care for the Aged and the Alien **32–34**

33. stranger: as always, this is the resident alien. This care for the alien is sometimes said to be a characteristic of Deuteronomy, but it is found in Exod. 22.21, 23.9 in the so-called Book of the Covenant, which is said to be as old as any Israelite legislation.

do him wrong: following RV. This is too weak and the AV (vex) is out of date. V and DV have 'upbraid', but 'oppress' is best, as LXX. It is immaterial whether 'neighbour' in Lev. 19.18 means 'neighbour Israelite' or 'neighbour everybody', since here a man is bidden to love the resident alien as himself. Rashi interprets: 'do not reproach thy fellowman for a fault which is also thine own', referring (verse 34) to the reason given there, that the Israelites were once 'strangers in Egypt'.

Crooked Deals in Business **35–36**

These verses are against false measurements of length, weight, and quantity. Scales were used not only for weighing what was sold, but also for weighing the money paid, the coins, such as they were, being by no means standardized or secure from clipping. The *ephah* mentioned here is a dry measure equal to forty litres, seventy pints. The *hin* is a liquid measure, about six litres, ten and a half pints. All measures used in trade shall be honest and correct. T (Pal) develops the theme and refers to the shovel which was used for heaping up and the *miḥḳā'*, the leveller which was used to ensure that the receptacle was exactly full, no more and no less.

20.1–27: this chapter in part covers the same ground as the previous two chapters. We have compilations of laws and customs from different sources, all brought together without any real attempt at editing or correlation.

The Cult of Molech **1–5**

See note on 18.21. This section is not so much an extension as a variant, belonging to a separate collection here embodied in H. There is nothing here concerning burning children as sacrifices. The phrase is 'giving any of his children'. Possibly even these five verses are not from a single source; cf. 'put to death' (verse 2) and 'cut him off' (verse 3). The giving of the children to Molech is said to 'defile the sanctuary', which makes very good sense if the reference is to the dedication of the boys and girls to temple prostitution, especially if this is done in the name of Yahweh ('profaning my holy name').

2. the people of the land: this must mean the whole people as a body, all the people, as in 2 Kg. 11.14, etc. See note on 4.27.

5. against his family: following EVV. V and DV have 'against all that consented with him', following T (all that support him). The Hebrew *mišpāḥāh* is occasionally used of a whole tribe (Jg. 13.2, 17.7, etc.), but strictly means a much smaller unit, such as a clan, a family, or even 'a father's house'. Possibly, it originally meant a definitely subsidiary group; see note on 19.29 and the derivation of the word. According to the Sifra and the Talmud (*b. Sheb.*, 32a), the reason for the mention here of the man's family is that they will always try to protect him, and in any case it is reasonable to assume that he could not dedicate any child of his in this fashion without the knowledge of the whole family. This may be why T equates the family with the man's abettors. It may be that corporate personality is involved, but there is no need to apply such a theory to this case.

Laws against Necromancy **6–8**

See notes on 19.31.

Law against Cursing Parents **9**

It must be remembered that a curse is not simply an impious wish. It was believed to be effective and itself capable of being realized in fact and action. See also Exod. 21.17, where also the penalty is death. The phrase his blood is upon him means that when the man is put to death, the laws of blood revenge do not apply. This phrase is found only in this chapter and in Ezek. 18.13. Another phrase is 'no blood shall be reckoned to him' (RSV freely: he shall not be guilty of blood) (Num. 35.27). Yet another phrase is 'his blood I will require at your hand' (Ezek. 3.18). Solomon went to great pains to secure that the deaths of Joab and Shimei were their own seeking and not his, and David was very concerned that he should not be involved in a blood feud because of the murders of Abner and Amasa. Further, the whole system of refuge cities was designed to prevent the chain-reaction of murder for murder (Num. 35). It is still 'a life for a life' in parts of Arabia in this present generation, even if the death be accidental.

Illegal Sexual Intercourse **10–21**

Cf. 18.6–20, 22f. One difference is that here the writer is dealing definitely with adultery and incest as well as with irregular intercourse in general. Further, here there are penalties prescribed, whereas in 18.6ff. the penalties are not stated.

10. RSV rightly omits 'if a man commits adultery with the wife of', which is an accidental repetition in Hebrew.

11. father's wife: see 18.8. This does not refer to the man's own mother, but to another wife of his father.

12. incest: this is indeed incest in that it is sexual intercourse between parties whose marriage is prohibited by law, but Hebrew has *teḇel*, which is used in 18.23 of intercourse between a woman and an animal, and is there translated 'abomination'. The meaning is 'confusion', possibly of established laws, but more likely confusion of semen.

13. abomination: following EVV. The Hebrew term *tô'ēḇāh* is a wide one, and means 'repugnant', an offence in the sense of being an offence against both God and man. It is used of various objectionable actions, especially when idolatrous practices are involved. In this case, and in the cases of other words of a similar nature, all versions, both ancient and modern, are seeking to find equivalents, but no one is quite sure what the Hebrew terms mean.

14. wickedness: the Hebrew *zimmāh* is used of unchastity generally, incest, adultery, and as a figure of speech for idolatry.

17. a shameful thing: the Hebrew is *ḥeseḏ*, a word which (if it is indeed the same word) in all cases except two, here and Prov. 14.34, means 'steadfast love' (see note on Num. 14.18). The root originally seems to have involved the idea of 'eager zeal, desire', and came to have a good meaning in Hebrew and a bad meaning in Arabic (*ḥasada*, envy) and in Aramaic (*ḥissûḏā'*, shame, reproach). Here is a case of the bad meaning surviving in Hebrew, but in either case is the idea of strength and power involved. Rashi quotes the ingenious use of the double meaning of the word made by the Rabbis (the Sifra and *b. San.*, 59b). It was due to God's *ḥeseḏ* (loving-kindness, mercy) that Cain was allowed to marry his sister, thus committing this *ḥeseḏ* (shame), but thus ensuring the survival of the human race. Besides, as he says, it all happened before the Law was given.

shall bear his iniquity: that is, bear the responsibility, and perhaps also pay the penalty (see 5.1). The words for 'sin' can all mean the consequence also.

18. fountain: following EVV. The reference is to the continuing discharge.

19. The aunt, whether father's sister or mother's sister, is the closest female relation on either side. Both are 'next of kin' (Hebrew *še'ēr*); see 18.6.

20. uncle's wife: The *dôḏāh* here is the wife of the *dôḏ*, which, as a technical term for a relationship, certainly means 'father's brother' (*patruus*) in Hebrew (cf. 18.14). But apparently in Exod. 6.20 it can also mean 'father's sister' (cf. Exod. 2.1 and Num. 26.59).

childless: the root means 'stripped', but this particular word *'ărîrî* has been understood to mean 'stripped of children' and so 'childless', ever since LXX so translated it in Gen. 15.2 of Abram. This may well have been the case with Abram at that time, since the birth of Ishmael is recorded in the next chapter. Nevertheless, the context there has to do with the fact that Abram had no heir. The translation 'childless' is not satisfactory in Jer. 22.30, where LXX has *akēruktos* (excommunicated). Jeconiah had children (1 Chr. 3.17f.), and a tablet has been found giving details of the daily rations allowed him and his sons in Babylon (*DOTT*, pp. 84–6).

Nor is 'childless' suitable here, in spite of LXX and V. It probably means 'stripped of posterity', 'proscribed', i.e. having no true son (son of a full wife) to keep his name in remembrance (2 Sam. 18.18), and thus no place in the genealogies, nor in the continuing Israel. Thus 'struck off the list' is a good interpretation. The Arabic '*arîr* is 'a stranger to the tribe'.

21. The verse deals with adultery, the brother being still alive. There is thus no contradiction of the levirate law of Dt. 25.5.

Exhortation and Promise **22–24**

Cf. 18.24–30.

22. statutes: Hebrew *ḥuḳḳîm*, those which are 'carved in', decreed, sometimes contrasted with ordinances (*mišpaṭîm*), that which is customary. The first refers to decrees laid down by God once and for all (the Rabbis said, without any reason being given), the second to customs which God has ordained for man to follow (cf. Jer. 8.7). The two terms thus comprise the whole of the laws and are 'all the commandment' of Dt. 8.1.

24. inherit: as usual this means 'take possession of' by dispossessing the earlier inhabitants.

flowing with milk and honey: this is the traditional way of describing the fertility of Canaan as the Land of Promise (Exod. 3.8, JE, and regularly in JE and D) The milk is *ḥālāḇ*, fresh milk and not curds. The honey is the Arabic *dibs*, which is wild-bee honey, or, as in Gen. 43.11 and Ezek. 27.17, date honey.

25–26. Holiness means separation, separated to God, separated from the nations.

27. Another prohibition of necromancy; see 19.31.

(d) SACRED PERSONS AND SACRED THINGS **21.1–22.33**

Precautions to be Taken by the Priests against Defilement **1–9**

These rules are strict, but not so strict as those for the High Priest (verses 10–15). There is nothing ethical involved here. The rules are concerned with ritual uncleanness and the copying of idolatrous rites.

1. the priests, the sons of Aaron: this phrase is rare: only here in the Pentateuch and thrice in Chronicles (2 Chr. 26.18, 35.14 (twice)). The usual P-phrase is 'the sons of Aaron the priests'. This chapter and succeeding chapters bear many signs of editing and successive revisions, and perhaps this phrase is one of them. It may well be that the original was 'the priests' and that the rest was inserted at a time when the Jerusalem priesthood was called Aaronite (see pp. 13f.).

defile. This refers to ritual uncleanness caused by touching a dead body (cf. Num. 19).

for the dead. The Hebrew is *nepeš*, the word which is often in EVV wrongly translated 'soul' (see 19.28). Here it means 'a dead body'.

among his people: following EVV and some versions. The Hebrew has the plural, which strictly means 'his kinsmen', referring to the father's rather than to the mother's side. This plural is found also in verses 4, 14, 15, in all of which LXX and Sam have the singular 'people'. V and DV have 'citizens', partly influenced by Jewish tradition, which says that the verse applies to situations where other Jews and relations are available, but where there is no other Jew and where the deceased's relations are unknown, then the priest may act as undertaker and handle the corpse as necessary.

3. his virgin sister: the sister who is married belongs to her husband's family. The priest's wife is not mentioned either here or in the similar list in Ezek. 44.25–27. The Sifra and the Talmud (*b. Yeb.*, 22b) therefore say that 'his nearest of kin' (properly 'any blood relation') denotes the wife.

4. as a husband among his people: thus finding the expected reference to the wife: EVV follow V in translating *baʿal* as 'chief, principal man', but this is a counsel of desperation. LXX reads *ballaʿ* (suddenly). The text is corrupt. The most satisfactory solution is to read *liḇ*^{e}*ʿûlaṯ baʿal* (for one married to a husband). We now have the statement that the priest may not defile himself for a married sister. V and DV follow T and interpret: not even for the prince of his people.

5. shall not make tonsures: this involves any intentional bald patch, but has nothing to do with Roman priests. The Hebrew is *ḳorḥāh*, a form used only in connection with mourning for the dead, which LXX rightly adds here. See also 19.27f. Ordinary baldness in Hebrew is *ḳāraḥaṯ*.

6. bread: better 'food'. See 3.11, 16, where the fire-offerings are called 'food for God', i.e. all that is burned on the altar.

7. defiled: EVV have 'profane' and RVm 'polluted', and possibly this is the meaning: a girl who has been seduced or violated. But the Hebrew *ḥ*^{a}*lālāh* is exactly the Latin *profanus* (not sacred), available for human use and not divine use only. When the first-fruits have been presented at the shrine, the crop is no longer *ḳōḏeš* (holy), belonging exclusively to God, but is *ḥôl* (common, profane), proper for use by man. Thus the *ḥ*^{a}*lālāh* is a woman who has been 'used by man'. She is a woman who is no longer a virgin. The context suggests that violation is involved, but there is no proper justification for the 'vile prostitute' of V and DV. Jewish tradition is that the word means a woman born of a marriage forbidden to a priest, a daughter of a High Priest and a widow, or of an ordinary priest and a divorced woman.

9. profanes her father: she renders him ritually unclean since she is so close of kin to him. The source of uncleanness must be utterly destroyed, that is by fire. Some say this penalty means being burned alive (cf. the threat to Tamar, Gen. 38.24), but see Jos. 7.15, 25, where death is by stoning and the body is then burned. The essential thing is to bring about the death without shedding blood, thus avoiding the blood feud.

Additional Restrictions on the High Priest **10–15**

The High Priest is defined by three things. He is **chief among his brethren**, still *primus inter pares*, though already in H we have the development of the process by which he became separate in holiness, even from the priests. He must also have the anointing oil poured over his head (8.2), and he must 'fill his hand' (have been installed), i.e. he must take into his hands the first sacrifice he offers (8.33). Then he may wear the specially holy garments of the High Priest (Exod. 30.23f.). See also note on Lev. 10.6.

13. LXX adds 'from his kindred', doubtless under the influence of verse 14, where of his own people means 'of his own kinsfolk' and not 'of any Israelite'.

14. widow: according to Ezek. 44.22 no priest may marry a widow unless she is the widow of a priest. The High Priest is prohibited from marrying any widow whatever. She must be a virgin of his own kindred. If he breaks this rule then the child of the marriage will be 'profaned'. The daughter would be a *ḥªlālāh*, a defiled woman under verse 7; a woman is one born of a 'mixed' marriage, priestly and non-priestly.

Physical Disqualifications for a Priest **16–24**

The priest may have no physical blemish of any kind. The list of disabilities is similar to those which prevent a man in ancient Sippar from being a soothsayer: 'the son of a diviner who is not of pure descent, or is not perfect in stature and in the members of his body, who has a cataract in the eyes, broken teeth, a mutilated finger, who suffers from any disease of the stones or of the skin'—quoted from *KAT*³, p. 534, by A. R. S. Kennedy (*Cent. Bible*, p. 143).

18. mutilated face or a limb too long: EVV have 'flat nose' for the first phrase, following LXX *koloborrin* (stump-nosed). Jewish tradition (the Sifra and *Bekh.*, vii, 3) says this means that the man's nose is so flat between the eyes that he can paint both eyes with one stroke of the brush. For the second phrase EVV have 'anything superfluous'. In the early midrashes and in the Talmud *sāra'* is 'to be abnormally long', especially (*b. Bekh.*, 45a) one of a pair of members being longer than the other. Similarly the Arabic *šara'a* and *'ašra'* mean 'long-nosed'. RSV is probably correct, especially since the Arabic *ḫarama* (cf. first phrase) means 'slit, pierce nostrils, lip, or ear'. V and DV have 'a little, or a great, or a crooked nose'.

20. hunchback: this is the generally accepted meaning of *gibbēn*, which means something that is curved. The form of the word (short-*i*, doubled middle letter, and long-*e*) denotes a physical deformity. But the T's think of eyebrows so long that they curl over the eyes, and so Rashi. The association with the eyebrows is confirmed by the Syriac and Aramaic evidence, and the next item has to do with eyesight. Possibly the reference is to over-arched eyebrows. The association with the back is due to *Bekh.*, vii, 2 which mentioned the word *gaḇ* (back).

dwarf: following EVV, a rendering with astonishingly little support among ancient authorities. The Hebrew is *daḳ* (thin, small, fine) and hence AVm 'too thin'. The traditional explanation has to do with the eyes: LXX (a white spot in the eye), V (blear-eyed), T (withered spot), S (one whose eyebrows have withered). Rashi

thinks of the Old French *toile* (web) and so of a membrane over the eye, and probably this is best, though it does not necessarily mean a cataract.
with a defect in his sight: to be more specific, Rashi refers to a white spot or line across into the central black iris of the eye, thus mingling (Hebrew root *b-l-l*) the white and the black. It is such a defect in the eye as prevents the white being all white and the black all black.
an itching disease or scabs: both words are found together only here and in 22.22. The first undoubtedly refers to the scab, and the second is some eruptive affection of the skin. Rashi says that one is wet and the other dry, but there is doubt as to which is which. He identifies the latter with the Egyptian lichen, following the Sifra and the Jerusalem Targum, an eruption of red solid pistules over a limited area. He says also that the first word *yallepeṯ* is from a root which means 'embrace' (cf. Arabic *walafa*), and that it therefore clings to the body till death: all of which involves some incurable eruption of the skin.

22. For the distinction between 'most holy things (gifts)' and 'holy things (gifts)', see p. 34. The disqualified man of priestly descent thus becomes like the provincial priests of 2 Kg. 23.9, who were permitted to share the unleavened bread with the Jerusalem priests, but not to approach the altar.

Restrictions as to Holy-gifts **22.1–16**

All priests that are ritually clean may eat the holy-gifts, provided that they are not involved with non-priests. A priest's slaves may eat of them, whether home-born or bought. But no visitors and no hired servants may eat of them.

2. This verse is misleading in RSV, and so also are EVV. It is not a matter of the Aaronic priests having to keep away from these holy gifts. Jewish tradition is that they must keep away from holy things when they are ritually unclean. But the Hebrew *nāzar* does not always mean 'keep aloof'; it means 'dedicate, consecrate', and here the meaning is that the priests must observe the consecration rules concerning holy gifts. Thus LXX has *prosechō* (give heed to, hold fast to).

4–5. Here is a comprehensive list of the ways in which a man can become ritually unclean (see 13, 15.1–12). Verse 8, based on 17.15, looks like an addition to the original list.

9. my charge: the Hebrew *mišmereṯ* is the proper word in P and in Ezek. 40–48 for the official and ceremonial duties of priests and Levites.
bear sin: so EVV, and a literal translation. V and DV have 'fall into sin', but 'bear the guilt, pay the penalty' is nearer to the modern mode of thought. The Hebrews thought of sin as being some kind of stuff, a stain, a miasma, something material which clung to a man until it was cleansed off him, and in some cases this could only be by death. We have no precise way of expressing this.
die thereby: that is, die because of the sin, as a result of it. Rashi says it means by direct visitation of God and not through the courts (see *b. San.*, 83a). V and DV have 'in the sanctuary' (the Hebrew is *bô*, lit. 'in it, by it'), thinking presumably of the fate of Nadab and Abihu (10.2).

10. outsider: EVV have 'stranger', which is probably what LXX and V think. The word here means 'layman', one who is not a priest.
a sojourner of the priest's: the *tôšāḇ* was a temporary guest as against the *gēr* (often translated 'stranger') who was a permanent resident alien. The LXX *paroikos* (neighbour) is too indefinite to be helpful.

12. offering: this is the *tᵉrûmāh*, the 'heave-offering' of EVV. It is the share of the offerings of the people which were the perquisite of the whole body of priests (see p. 58).

13. The essence of this verse is that a priest's daughter who is separated from her lay husband either by his death or by her divorce, and has no child who is of mixed (i.e. priestly and lay) parentage, reverts to her original status and is a member of the priest's family. She is therefore sufficiently a holy person to be able to eat the holy gifts.

14–16. The priests must take care that the holy-gifts offered by the Israelites are not profaned, that is, subjected to common use, eaten by non-priests. They are, for instance, to stop the non-priests from incurring guilt and the repayment that is involved through eating the holy-gifts which are the property of the priests. RSV has iniquity and guilt, but probably 'guilt and repayment' is better. It is because non-priests thus cause loss to the priesthood that repayment, compensation (Hebrew *'āšām*) is necessary (cf. 5.15).

Details concerning Offerings **17–25**

This section is concerned with whole-offerings (animals wholly burned on the altar) and the so-called 'peace-offering' (none of the flesh of which went to the altar). No mention is made of sin-offerings (*ḥaṭṭā'ṯ*) or of compensation-offerings (*'āšām*). This is in accordance with the general pattern of H, which has no knowledge of these latter two types.

18. This is the only place where whole-offerings are divided into vows and freewills. All whole-offerings brought by the people are freewill offerings, according to Ezek. 46.12. It is the animal for the sacred meal (the so-called peace-offering) which may be either a vow or a freewill. It may also be a *tôḏāh* 'thank-offering' (see verse 29).

23. a part too long or too short: see 21.18, where *šārûa'* means 'stretched', especially one of a pair of parts of the body. The other word here (*ḳālûṭ*) means 'stunted' (cf. Arabic).

Further Details concerning Offerings **25–30**

27. seven days: see Exod. 22.30. These are the seven days of birth (see note on 4.6).

28. Cf. Dt. 22.6f., where the same regulation is applied to birds and their young. The regulation is generally held to have a humanitarian basis, an explanation which is as old as the Palestinian Talmud; but the origin is doubtless to be found in more primitive notions.

31–33. This is the concluding exhortation of H, where the essential holiness of God is regularly linked with the rescue of Israel from Egypt.

(e) THE SACRED CALENDAR **23.1–44**

This chapter is composite, as is clear from the double introduction, verse 2 and verse 4. Scholars who carry literary analysis into minute details find they have to speak of more than one P-editor, apart from the allocation of verses between H and P. It is generally agreed that 1–8, 21, 23–38, 44 belong to P, though of different strata, and that 22, 39–43 are H, with the rest mixed, basically H but with P-elements of varying degrees of recognizability. Generally speaking, the agricultural emphasis is characteristic of H, and the ecclesiastical element of P. Indeed, it is these differences that are mostly used as criteria.

The Sabbath **1–3**

This section is entirely ecclesiastical and is full of P's technical phrases. The origin of the sabbath is disputed. Some maintain that it was a seventh-day festival and a day of rest from the beginning. Indeed, P's teaching is that the sabbath began with Creation and is fundamental to the whole structure of heaven and earth. J. Meinhold (*Sabbat und Wocke im Alten Testament*, 1905) maintained that the *ḥōḏeš* (new month day) and the *šabbāṯ* were both originally monthly festivals, the one coinciding with the new moon and the other with the full moon, and that the sabbath became a seven-day festival later. But it has also been argued (*JNYF*, pp. 103–24) that whilst the two festivals were originally monthly festivals, *šabbāṯ* meant originally 'the end of the month', since the root *š-b-t* does not primarily mean 'rest' but rather 'come to the end of a period, come to a stop'. It is also argued that in pre-exilic times the month began with the full moon, and that it was only during the exile that the new month day became the day of the new moon, following the Babylonian calendar of Nippur, which the Jews adopted in post-exilic days. Thus *ḥōḏeš* means new month day, which was at the full moon before the exile, and the *šabbāṯ* coincided with the days when the nights were dark, and thus always had something of the nature of a *taboo*, since these were held to be times when demons were active. In the old Assyrian calendar the seventh days and the new moon days were days of the strictest *taboos* (see Langdon, *Babylonian Menologies and the Semitic Calendars*, pp. 78ff.), seven being the sacred number in all areas influenced by Mesopotamian régimes. The Israelites came under Mesopotamian influences in pre-exilic times and thus came to regard both new month days and seventh days as *taboo* days, but after the great calendar reforms of Asshurbanipal only the seventh days were *taboo* days, when men must not stir out of the house and physicians must not lay their hands on the sick. Thus the sabbath became the only *taboo* day and the new month day received only attentuated recognition. There is a considerable amount of literature on the subject available in commentaries and biblical dictionaries, and much variation of opinion (cf. *AI*, pp.

475–83). For sabbath regulations in Israel, see Exod. 20.9f. and Dt. 5.12f.; Exod. 23.12, 34.21.

2. appointed feasts: following AV (feasts) and RV (set feasts), but RVm is better with 'appointed seasons'. The term *mô'ēḏ* is P's technical term for religious times and occasions, and is a wider term than *ḥaḡ* (feast), which was essentially a pilgrimage, and in post-exilic times to the Central Sanctuary at Jerusalem (cf. the *ḥajj* of Islam, the pilgrimage to Mecca. According to P (Gen. 1.14) the purpose of the sun and moon is not only to make a distinction between day and night but to fix the ecclesiastical seasons (*mô'ᵃḏîm*) and the calendar with its days and years. These things were of paramount concern to P, and there have always been those, both in Judaism and in Christianity, who 'esteem one day as better than another' in the sense of Rom. 14.5. Disputes concerning the proper date have caused great divisions in both religions: disputes concerning the proper day for the observance of the Feast of Weeks among the Jews, between Babylonian and Palestinian Jews, Karaites, Ananites, and among Christians, between the Celtic and the Roman churches in Britain, between east and west concerning Easter and Christmas, and so forth.

holy convocations: this is P's phrase for religious gatherings on all appointed occasions. They are 'that which is proclaimed' (*miḵrā'*), times when the people are summoned, just as the Muslim is summoned by the muezzin. The word was in use in pre-exilic times for 'the calling of assemblies' (Isa. 1.13, 4.5).

3. a sabbath of solemn rest: the phrase *šabbāṯ šabbāṯôn* is used of the weekly sabbath (Exod. 31.15, 35.2 and here; also Exod. 16.23), of the Day of Atonement (Lev. 16.31, 23.32), of the sabbatical year (Lev. 25.4 and 5). The word *šabbāṯôn* itself is used of the Festival of Trumpets (23.24) and of the first and eighth days of the Feast of Tabernacles. The meaning of *šabbāṯôn* is not agreed. It has been compared with the Babylonian *šabattu*, explained by Assyrian scribes as being 'in the middle of the month'. It has nothing to do with the seven-day system, just as the seven-day system has nothing to do with the lunar month. The Babylonians called it 'the day of the resting of the heart' (*um nu-uḫ libbi*). Primarily the word means 'be complete' (Accadian *gamâru*) or 'come to an end' (Accadian *ḳâtu*); then 'the end of the first half of the month' (cf. Egyptian *samadt*). There seems to be adequate reason for equating the Hebrew and the Babylonian words, and some such meaning as the easing of heart and conscience is adequate for all occasions.

4–5. passover: after a new introduction, we come to the fixing of the date of **the LORD'S passover** (Exod. 12.1–13 and 43–50, and Dt. 16.1–7). This rite was observed on the night of the spring full moon, the full moon of Abib, six months away from the harvest full moon, which in Old Israel was the beginning of the year. When the Nippur calendar was adopted by the Jews after the Exile, the date of the Passover became the night of Nisan 14, this now being the first month. It is commonly said that the pre-exilic Abib became the post-exilic Nisan, but see *JNYF*, pp. 94–103, where it is argued that the new month day of Abib became the 14th of Nisan, since the new month day of Abib was the full moon and the new month day of Nisan is the new moon. The Passover was an ancient spring festival and was originally an apotropaic rite, designed for the turning away of evil spirits. It was always essentially a home rite, and never a temple rite, though in the last days of the Second Temple the actual slaughtering of the lamb took place in the Temple. The rite was transformed to celebrate the rescue from Egypt and in the last years of the Temple it became the festival of the expected deliverance, the time when Messiah would appear. See the commentaries and the biblical dictionaries; also most recently J. B. Segal, *The Hebrew Passover*, 1963, and *SOTS*, pp. 1–26. The word *pesaḥ* may mean 'limp, pass over' (cf. 1 Kg. 18.26 of the limping dance of the Baal prophets). Some maintain that the Passover was a new-year festival and so think in terms of 'passing over' from one year to another. Rashi favours the meaning 'leap over, spring over', but quotes Menahem ben Seruk, who associated the word with the root *p-s-ḥ* (spare, cf. Accadian *pasaḫu*), quoting Isa. 31.5 as meaning 'sparing and delivering'.

5. in the evening: as the note in RSV indicates, the Hebrew is 'between the two evenings', and so ten times elsewhere, including Exod. 16.12 where RSV has 'twilight'. This was the time of the evening offering, the second part of the *tāmîḏ*, the regular daily offering. Jewish tradition fixes it between noon and darkness, from the time when the shadows incline towards the east and the day declines, or between the darkening of the day and the darkening of the night. Thus 3 p.m. (Mk 15.33–37) is the middle of this period, and according to the Mishnah (*Pes.*, v, 1) the daily whole-offering was slaughtered at 'a half after the eighth hour' and offered up at 'a half after the ninth hour', though at Passover these times were put forward by two hours in order that the Passover lamb could be slaughtered at the proper hour. Possibly the original time was between sunset and dark, a much shorter time in Palestine than in more northerly latitudes. See *AI*, p. 182.

The Feast of Unleavened Bread **6–8**

See Exod. 12.14–20; Num. 28.17–26. The Feast of *Maṣṣôṯ* was a *ḥaḡ*, a pilgrimage, when every Israelite had to appear at the shrine, as is proper, since it is a harvest celebration. The *maṣṣôṯ* were unleavened cakes, though there is nothing laid down in the Law concerning shape or size. Seven days was always the length of *Maṣṣôṯ*, though according to Dt. 16.8 it was six days with the seventh day reckoned as an '*ᵃṣereṯ* (not 'solemn assembly', but 'closing ceremony'). This seventh day is a 'holy convocation', and regarded, like the first day, as being a special day at all periods. The first day of *Maṣṣôṯ* marked the opening of the grain harvest, the barley being the first to ripen.

8. no laborious work: cf. verse 3, where the phrase is 'no work'. The difference is the addition of '*ᵃḇôḏāh*, obligatory service. This word can mean both 'servile work', as here, but also 'divine worship', since that is obligatory on man. The ancient Jewish tradition (*Tôraṯ Kôhᵃnîm* on 23.36) is that 'laborious work' includes even work which may reasonably be regarded as a necessity, e.g. 'necessary' household daily duties.

The Waving of the Omer **9–14**

This ceremony is observed with diligent care throughout Jewry. See *JEn.*, ix, article 'Omer', where there are illustrations of the 'calendar' on the walls of synagogues, kept to facilitate the counting. The first sheaf is to be presented to the priest and 'on the morrow of the sabbath' (and for fifty days in all) is to be waved to and fro before the sacred shrine. This is the Counting of the Omer. This continues until the Feast of Weeks (again *seven* weeks, as is proper), which marks the end of the harvest period. This is why the Feast of Weeks is called an '*ᵃṣereṯ* (closing ceremony) in the Targum and by Josephus (*Ant. Iud.* III, x, 6).

11. wave: this may indeed involve waving horizontally to and fro, but as elsewhere neither LXX nor V understand it so (see on 7.30).

on the morrow of the sabbath: strictly Heb has 'from the morrow of the sabbath', beginning on that day and continuing. Orthodox Jewish tradition maintains that the counting begins on the second day of *Maṣṣôṯ*, so that Pentecost is always the 6th of Sivan. This is also the opinion of LXX, the Mishnah, and the Talmud, Philo (*de septen.* ii, 10) and Josephus (*Ant. Iud.* III, x, 5). Orthodox Jews say that a 'sabbath' here means the first day, which is such a surprising statement that it must be right, since it is obviously wrong if 'sabbath' must always mean the seventh day of the week. Indeed, Samaritans and Sadducees say that 'sabbath' must mean the sabbath which falls within the seven days of *Maṣṣôṯ*. This was the belief of Anan and the Karaites (from *c.* A.D. 840). This is the basis of the Christian fixing of Pentecost on a Sunday, adopted by the Council of Nicaea (A.D. 325). V and DV (the next day after the Sabbath) follow the Council of Nicaea and the heretical Jews.

13. two tenths of an ephah is fourteen pints. **A fourth of a hin** is two and a half pints (see on 19.36). This *minḥāh* (grain-offering) is an *'iššeh* (fire-offering) and part of a whole-burnt-offering (*'ôlāh*), all of it being burned on the altar.

14. neither bread nor grain parched or fresh: the intention is to prohibit the eating of any of the new barley harvest until the first-fruits have been presented The bread is grain, ground and baked into loaves. The rest is grain, either fresh or cooked: *ḳālî* means 'roasted' (cf. Arabic and Ethiopic) and was a common food (Ru. 2.14; 1 Sam. 17.17). *Karmel* is fresh, fully ripened grain. Rashi says that *ḳālî* is flour from *karmel* (tender ears), dried in the oven and scorched.

The Feast of Weeks **15–22**

As it is called in Exod. 34.22 J; Dt. 16.10, 16; Num. 28.26 P. It was a pilgrimage and closed the harvest period.

16. a cereal offering of new grain: lit. 'a new *minḥāh*'. The Talmud (*b. Men.*, 84b), that this was from the new wheat, and so was distinct from the new *minḥāh* of 16th Nisan, which was of barley (23.13f.).

17. baked with leaven: these two loaves were for the priests. They were 'waved'. No piece of them went to the altar, since nothing leavened could be placed on it.

19. sacrifice of peace offerings: this is unusual, since the normal shared-offerings were eaten by the worshippers and the priests received only the thigh and the breast. Perhaps it was because of the anomaly that LXX repeats 'with the bread of first-fruits', found in the next verse. They were the perquisite of the priest who presented them, as LXX makes quite clear. Probably the apparent anomaly arose because these were animals which did not go to the altar, and *zeḇaḥ šᵉlāmîm* was the best description out of the technical terms available.

22. see 19.9, 10.

The Feast of Trumpets **23–25**

In post-exilic times this festival was celebrated on 1st of Tishri (which in Accadian means 'beginning'), the seventh month. This was a day of *zikkārôn* (remembrance) of *tᵉrû'āh* (trumpet blowing), and a holy convocation, all men being summoned to a sacred celebration. It is the ecclesiastical New Year, since in pre-exilic times the new year began with the autumnal festival. The pre-exilic Feast of *'Āsîp* (ingathering) was celebrated for seven days beginning with the all-night festival at the harvest full moon. Some of the ceremonies remained with the full moon of Tishri; others gravitated to the 10th Tishri and yet others to the 1st Tishri. See *JNYF*, pp. 131–49 and 150–94. The trumpets were blown for remembrance before God (*b. Sh̲abb.*, 131b), but Rabbi Saadiyah (tenth century A.D.) gave ten reasons for blowing the ram's horn on New Year's Day (*Rō'š hašŠānāh*). See Jewish prayer-books and a translation in *JNYF*, pp. 160–62.

The Day of Atonement **26–32**

Yôm Kippûr, the great Jewish fast. The 10th Tishri is 'old New Year's Day', ten days being the difference between twelve lunar months and a solar year according to Jewish calculations. All the penitential elements of the pre-exilic feast gravitated to the first ten days of Tishri, reaching their climax on the tenth day. See Mishnah *Yoma* and compare the Babylonian eleven-day period called *zagmuku* (Sumerian for the Accadian *rēš šatti*, head, beginning of year). This was New Year's Day for the Year of Jubilee and in *c.* A.D. 900 Daniel ben Moses al-Kumasi broke away from the Karaites, insisting that New Year's Day was 10th Tishri, according to Ezek. 40.1. This verse belongs to the transition period.

27. atonement: Hebrew has the plural, i.e. of special expiation, the plural being one of the ways in which Hebrew expresses the superlative: 'full atonement'. The scapegoat ritual is given in fuller detail in 16.1–34.

afflict yourselves: this is much better than 'afflict your souls' (as EVV and D). The meaning is 'fast' (16.29).

32. from evening to evening: in the Old Testament the day begins at sunset (Gen. 1.5).

The Feast of Booths (Tabernacles), P **33–36**

Until the last years of the Second Temple, this was the most popular and important of all the feasts. In the Fourth Gospel 'the feast' (without further specification) is Tabernacles. The all-night festival with its lights and dancing remained with the full moon when the pre-exilic feast broke up, and so also did the rite of water-pouring with its special procession before dawn from the Pool of Siloam. It was originally a seven-day feast, but later an eighth-day closing (*'ᵃṣereṯ*) festival was added.

34. booths: temporary shelters made from intertwined leafy boughs (Neh. 8.15). The 'tabernacles' of EVV is from V. LXX has 'tents'. The origin of this custom is lost in antiquity, but the later explanation makes them commemorative of the journey through the wilderness.

37–38. P's conclusion to the festal calendar.

The Feast of Booths, H **39–43**

But probably with P insertions. No name is given in this paragraph, but the feast is to take place when everything of every kind has been gathered in. It is to last seven days with an extra (P) day added (cf. Dt. 16.13). The first and eighth days are *šabbāṯôn*, days of special *taboo*. This is probably why not even 'necessary' labour might be done.

40. the fruit of goodly trees: most associate *hāḏār* with the idea of beauty, adornment, splendour; hence LXX, V, and EVV. But Jewish tradition reads *haddār* from the root *dûr*, and meaning that which remains on the tree from year to year (*b. Sukk.*, 35a). This means a non-deciduous tree, an evergreen, and is taken to mean any kind of citrus fruit, this word now including lemon, lime, orange, and kindred fruits. The Jews called this citrus fruit the *'eṯrôg*, and the worshipper carried it in his left hand. When Alexander Jannaeus contemptuously poured the libations on the ground, the people pelted him with the citrus fruits they were carrying (*b. Sukk.*, 48b; Josephus, *Ant Iud.* XIII, xiii, 5).

branches of palm trees: Jewish tradition is strong that this means one branch for each worshipper. He took the palm frond, placed a myrtle branch on one side and a willow branch on the other, and bound them together with strands of similar pieces. Some used gold thread, but others said the gold thread was inside and the similar pieces inside (*Sukk.*, iii, 8). This bundle was the *lûlāḇ* and was carried in the right hand. It was waved at prescribed intervals during the recitation of Psalm 118. The palm frond had to be at least three hand-breadths long.

boughs of leafy trees: these are the myrtle boughs, because *'āḇôṯ* mean 'plaited, interwoven' and not 'leafy' (*b. Sukk.*, 32b) and the myrtle is said to have boughs plaited like ropes because it has three leaves growing from one point and covering it.

willows of the brook: this is commonly identified as a poplar, *populus euphratica*, but see *DB*, p. 1037, where it is said that the phrase applies equally well to two types of willow plentiful in Palestine by the brooks, *Salix fragilis* and *Salix alba.*

(f) THE LAMPS OF THE TABERNACLE **24.1–4**

This section is generally agreed to be from P, and so the whole chapter except verses 15–22 (H). It is doubtful whether it is possible to separate the sources accurately, and it is more than likely that the P-editor was editing much earlier material. This is the great seven-branched candelabra of the Second Temple (cf. the bas-relief on the Arch of Titus). In Solomon's Temple there were ten candelabra, five on the north side and five on the south side of the inner shrine (1 Kg. 7.49).

2. beaten olives: these were pounded in a mortar and then strained to make sure the oil is pure (*zaḵ*).

continually: following EVV and V. The word is *tāmîḏ*, which here means 'regularly'. The light was to burn until dawn (so LXX; cf. 1 Sam. 3.3). The word is used of the regular daily allowance made to king Jehoiachin (2 Kg. 25.30). This lamp was to be kindled regularly. The Rabbis worked out (*b. Men.*, 89a) how much oil was necessary to keep the lamps burning till morning during the longest nights (in Tebet). This was half a pint per lamp, and this became the fixed amount.

4. the lampstand of pure gold: so the Jewish traditions, but the ancient versions make 'pure' refer to the lampstand: whence 'the lampstand that is ritually clean', which is the natural meaning of the Hebrew.

(g) THE SHEWBREAD **24.5–9**

So EVV in Exod. 25.30, where RSV has 'the bread of the Presence'. This consisted of twelve perforated flat cakes, each containing fourteen pints of fine flour, which had been sifted eleven times (*b. Men.*, 76b). Each cake must therefore have been of considerable size, since one pint of flour weighs just under twelve ounces. Josephus (*Ant. Iud.* III, vi, 6) says the cakes were made of unleavened flour. There were twelve loaves set out as *akal panu* (food of the presence) in Babylonian temples, and a table as at Delphi (Josephus, *Ant. Iud.* III, vi, 6). The custom was ancient in Israel (Nob, 1 Sam. 21.6). The origin of the rite may well have been astral and associated with the twelve signs of the Zodiac, but in Israel the twelve loaves came to stand for the twelve tribes.

6. table of pure gold: as before, there is no reference to gold in the Hebrew: it was the table that was ritually clean.

7. The Hebrew says that the frankincense was put on the pile(s), and LXX adds salt. For the use of frankincense as a memorial, see 2.2. Josephus (*Ant. Iud.* III, x, 7) says the frankincense was in two cups, which probably was the case, since the priests afterwards ate the loaves.

8. continually: better 'regularly'. The High Priest himself changed the loaves every sabbath. The old loaves were 'most holy', i.e. at one time regarded as food for the god and later eaten by the priests alone. The Talmud (*b. Sukk.*, 56a) says half were eaten by the outgoing priests, the 'course' which had completed its week of service, and half by the incoming course. In Josiah's time the Temple guards were changed on the sabbath (2 Kg. 11.5).

(h) LAWS AGAINST BLASPHEMY AND ASSAULT **24.10–23**

The pattern of this section is found elsewhere: first a statement of the law (verses 15–22), in this case regarded as from H, with a P-editor adding an actual example, so that here is case law (cf. Num. 15.32–36).

11. blasphemed the Name: during a fight with a full-blooded Israelite, the half-caste uttered a curse containing the Name of God. This passage was used to support the custom of substituting 'Name, Place, Heaven' for the divine Name itself.

the tribe of Dan: the mother was a Danite. Dan was the apostate tribe, because they set up a graven image (Jg. 18.30). This tribe has no place in the world to come, and hence is not found in Rev. 7.5–8.

12. declared: the word is *pāraš*, 'make distinct, declare distinctly'. In later Hebrew and in Syriac the root can mean 'separate', like the LXX equivalent here (*diakrinō*). This is the word from which the word 'Pharisee' is derived; hence its disputed derivative meaning.

14. lay their hands on his head: this rite can plainly mean more than one thing: transmission of holiness or sin; declaration of ownership. Here it signifies that the man's blood is on his own head, and there is no blood guilt on those who stone him to death. The man shall bear his own sin (verse 15).

17–21. Various examples of *lex talionis*. This is sound Amorite law, in force over the whole area in and before the time of Hammurabi (see *HDB*, extra vol., pp. 584–612, article 'Code of Hammurabi'. See also Exod. 21.12–35).

(i) THE SACRED CALENDAR (continued) **25.1–55**

The chapter is a mixture of H and P, and the general opinion is that verses 2–7 (seventh year) are from H and verses 8–16 (jubilee) mostly P. Then verses 17–34 and 35–40a are almost wholly H, and the rest mostly P. It is certain that the sabbatical year was observed; see also Exod. 23.11, which does not say that all fields must lie fallow in the same year—plainly the intention here. In Ezra's time (Neh. 10.31) the people covenanted to forgo the crops of the seventh year and also to cancel all debts. Josephus testifies to the observance of the sabbatical year in the time of Alexander the Great (*Ant. Iud.* XI, viii, 6) and also in the time of the Hasmonaeans and the Herods (*Ant. Iud.* XIII, viii, 1 and XIV, xvi, 2; also 1 Mac. 6, 49, and 53. Tacitus says (*Hist.*, v, 4) 'it was sheer laziness on the part of the Jews'. This rigorous ecclesiastical law must have caused the poor considerable hardship, and not a little inconvenience for the rich. It is most unlikely that the jubilee fallow was ever observed, involving two fallow years in succession, but Neh. 10.31 refers to the cancellation of debts. See, however, 2 Kg. 19.29. The chapter ends with details concerning the redemption of property and kindred matters arising from the liberations of the jubilee year.

The Sabbatical Year **1–7**

The system of the sacred (*taboo*) seven is applied with increasing thoroughness through the centuries.

4. a sabbath of solemn rest: see note on 23.3. Not even 'necessary' work is to be done in field or vineyard. There was to be no gathering of a harvest, but there was *sapîaḥ*, that which grows in the next year from seed fallen to the ground the previous harvest. There was probably more of this than is the case with the modern farmer.

5. undressed: i.e. unpruned. The Hebrew *nāzîr* (one who is consecrated) here means 'untrimmed' because the Nazirite vow involved unshorn hair.

The Jubilee Year **8–17**

forty-nine years: the extension of the *taboos* associated with seven to seven times seven is paralleled by the specially strict *taboos* for the 49th day of Assyrian months (19th of following month), restrictions abolished by Asshur-bani-pal.

9. send abroad the loud trumpet: i.e. send the ram's-horn trumpet round the country to sound a loud blast. This took place on the 10th Tishri, the 'old New Year's Day' (see note on 23.26). Originally this day was a day of great rejoicing, and it was one of the two days in the year when the maidens of Jerusalem went out to dance in the vineyards, apparently a betrothal dance. The other day was the 15th Ab. See *Taan.*, iv, 8; also 'The Song of Songs: the dances of the virgins', *AJSL*, 50, 1934, 129–42. The penitential sorrow of the Day of Atonement is a later development.

10. liberty: the word is *d^erôr* (free run, liberty), used in Arabic of streams flowing freely, horses freely galloping. See Isa. 61.2, the freedom of the captives when 'the year of the Lord's favour' is proclaimed. Rabbi Judah derived the word from *dûr* (dwell), and said it means the man may dwell at an inn (i.e. where he pleases). Hence the word came to involve freedom of residence.

jubilee: the word is *yôḇēl* (ram, ram's horn), such as were used at Jericho (Jos. 6.4). The English word is due to V's transliteration of the Hebrew, helped by the first-century Latin *jubilum* (loud shout, shepherd's cry).

11. what grows of itself: but this is what grows of itself in the second year, and is not *sāpîaḥ* but *sāḥîš* (or *šāḥîš*) (2 Kg. 19.29; Isa. 37.30). P has transferred the H-regulations of the seventh year to his jubilee year. This supports the contention that we have ecclesiastical theory rather than actual custom.

14. neighbour: the word *'āmîṯ* is found eleven times in H and once elsewhere. Neither party is to cheat or drive a hard bargain. Probably the meaning is 'business associate' (cf. on 5.21).

15. No land is to be sold outright, but only the crops to the next jubilee. P's principle is sound Israelite tradition. Naboth could not sell his vineyard to Ahab (1 Kg. 21.3) because it was the inheritance of his fathers and belonged not only to them but to his heirs after him. The price paid is the value of the crops till the next jubilee, and the land reverts to the original owner, if not previously redeemed, at the jubilee without further payment.

The Difficulties of the Seventh (fallow) Year **18–24**

18. securely: EVV have 'in safety', but V and DV are best, *absque ullo pavore* (without any fear), without worry concerning the prospect of not having enough to eat (see following verses and Jer. 17.8).

21. blessing: the word here has overtones of special blessing. Cf. Arabic *barakat*, the equivalent of *mana*, that supernatural power of primitive belief.

for three years: the writer is being realistic. The Israelite is not to depend only upon what he can cull from the land without proper harvesting (verse 12). He must store the produce of the sixth year to provide a carry-over till he can harvest another crop. This means sufficient to maintain him and his family for three years, but the reasoning is not clear. Some commentators have suggested that the writer is really dealing with the two fallow years, when the jubilee year followed the seventh sabbatical year. Possibly the confusion is due to a pre-exilic rule with its autumnal new year being copied without proper amendment for a post-exilic period with its spring new year.

23. the land is mine: the pre-exilic theory was that the land belonged to the family and was inalienable. But behind this is the theory that all are wholly dependent upon God the owner of the land, and live on it more (*gēr*, resident alien) or less (*tôšāḇ*, passing guest) permanently.

Detailed Regulations concerning the Redemption of Property **25–34**

25. your brother: the LXX adds 'with you', being well aware of the difficulties caused by the Dispersion.

part of his property: Jewish tradition takes this to mean that no man ought to sell all his property, no matter how hardly his poverty bears upon him.

next of kin: the Hebrew is *gō'ēl* (redeemer, vindicator, executor, next of kin). See the articles in the dictionaries. The root *g-'-l* means to get back (usually by payment) what was originally one's own. The root *p-d-h* means to redeem what was not originally one's own. Both words are often used in a general sense, but there are times when the exact meaning is important. The *gō'ēl* sees to it that his helpless kinsman gets his proper rights. He must see to it that the property is secured to a man's descendants, in spite of poverty or death (see verses 48f.; Jer. 32.8–12; Ru. 4.1ff.).

27. overpayment: this is little better than the 'overplus' of EVV and D. It should be 'balance'. The man who is redeeming the property must deduct from the original price the value of the crops which have been taken off the land. He pays the balance, that is, the value of the crops for the remaining years of the jubilee. The Rabbis ruled that no redemption can take place under two years.

29–34. The growing urbanization of the country made it difficult to observe the ancient right of redemption, so that modifications were more and more necessary for walled towns. The *'îr* (city) was a concentration of houses enclosed by a wall, and often far short of a modern town in size. The *ḥāṣēr* (village) was a settlement, sometimes of tents, but definitely without a surrounding wall. Houses within a wall may be redeemed within one year, but after that must remain with the purchaser. Houses in villages are reckoned as open country and are subject to the regular rule. But houses belonging to Levites within walls follow the ordinary jubilee rules, and the Rabbis said that the two-year rule did not apply. The grazing grounds outside the Levitical cities could not be sold at all. For details of these grazing lands, see Num. 25.2ff.

The Care for the Poor **35–38**

These are the H instructions concerning the problem of the poor. No profit is to be made out of him, either through loans or by the sale of food.

36. interest . . . increase: these are two types of interest. The first (*nešeḵ*) means interest paid regularly, and in the end the original loan is repaid in one payment. The second (*tarbîṯ*) involves no interim payment of interest, but an increased sum being repaid in the end. Exod. 22.25 (Heb 24); Dt. 23.19f. deal only with the first type. Probably this later legislation is to block a loophole which the money-lenders had discovered.

37. profit: the Hebrew is *marbîṯ* and the meaning is the same as that of *tarbîṯ* in the previous verses (cf. Egyptian Aramaic and *NSI*, p. 404).

The Laws concerning Slavery **39–46**

A Hebrew could sell himself as a slave to another Hebrew, but apart from not receiving wages he is to be treated as a hired servant or as an alien living in the house. According to the Sifra, he may be ordered to do field-work or to follow some craft, but he must not be made to carry his master's clothes publicly to the baths or to put his boots on for him. These tasks involve humiliation. Originally the rules prohibited the harsh, brutal treatment associated with slavery: the *pereḵ* of verse 43 and Exod. 1.13. All were to be released on the 10th Tishri, having been feasted for the previous 10 days, which were a sort of intercalary period (cf. 'the twelve days of Christmas').

42. servants: the Hebrew says 'slaves' and this is important. When God redeemed Israel from the Egyptians, whose slaves they were, they became his slaves, his own particular property (*s*ᵉ*ḡullāh*, 'peculiar treasure'), Exod. 19.5 E and in Dt. D. Daube (*The Exodus Pattern in the Bible*) makes the motif of the change of slavery to Egypt to slavery to God to be of fundamental importance in Hebrew religion. Cf. Paul's use of the Greek *doulos* and the distinction in LXX, which is sometimes important, between *doulos* and *pais*.

43. rule over: the word *rāḏāh* is much more violent, as LXX (*katateinō*, hold down tight) and V (*affligo*, DV afflict) have realized. The word means 'drive hard, bully' (cf. Syriac, Aramaic, and Accadian).

44. Non-Israelite slaves have no right to freedom at the jubilee, and can be left by will to heirs.

The Hebrew who is Slave to a Foreigner **47–55**

The ordinary jubilee rules apply, and the redemption price is to pay for the remaining period to the jubilee reckoned at the wages of a day-labourer (hired servant). The theory is that all Israelites are God's property (his slaves) and that at most he is hiring them out for a limited period. In verse 53 **servant** is right, but in verse 55 it should be 'slaves'.

(j) CONCLUDING EXHORTATION **26.1–46** (H, with perhaps P elements in verses 1, 2, 46)

1–2. H's fundamental requirements: no idolatry; observe the sabbaths, revere the sanctuary.

1. idols . . . graven image or pillar: following EVV and the accents of Hebrew. LXX with V and DV have: do not make things made by hand or carvings, neither erect a pillar. There are three things involved: *'ᵉlîlîm* (nothings, false gods), *pesel* (hewn from wood or stone), *maṣṣēḇāh* (erect stone pillar).
pillar: the *maṣṣēḇāh* was a sacred stone at one time wholly legitimate in Hebrew worship. The patriarchs regularly set up a pillar as a memorial of a theophany and to establish a sacred shrine (Gen. 28.18 E; 35.14 J, etc.). Moses erected twelve (Exod. 24.4 E), according to the twelve tribes of Israel. Hosea regarded their absence as a deprivation (Hos. 3.4), but in the Deuteronomic Code they were condemned (Dt. 16.22, etc.; 1 Kg. 14.23, etc.) because of their Canaanite associations. The single pillar was originally not so much an image of a god as his dwelling-place. When a stone pillar and a wooden pole (*'ᵃšērāh*) were erected beside an altar, they are said to represent the fertility deities of Canaan, Baal, and Astarte-Asherah. At Gezer, many stone pillars have been found and some were altars (*QSPEF*, 1903, pp. 23–26).
figured stone: following AVm and RV; usually taken to be an image to which men bow down, but see RVm (thereon) which is a strictly accurate rendering of the Hebrew. The word *maśkîṯ* is found also in Num. 33.52. It is something at which or from which one looks. LXX has this with *skopos*, whilst V and DV make it 'a remarkable stone'. According to Rashi, it may be an image at which one looks or a mosaic on which (so Hebrew *'āleyhā*, not **to them,** though sometimes there is confusion between *'el*=to and *'al*=upon) men prostrate themselves (hence RVm). The Jer. Targum allows such a pavement inside a sanctuary, but says men must not worship upon it.

4. rains: the *gᵉšāmîm* are the seasonal rains of Palestine, the early (October–November) and the latter (March–April) rains. In the J-story of the Flood (Gen. 7.12) the Flood is caused by the rains. In the P-account the waters above and below the firmament break through, and the bow is put in the sky to hold up the firmament for ever. The Arabic *gasuma* means 'be bulky'. The meaning is that the rains will be regular, but some Jewish traditions make a great deal of '*your* rains' and say it means that the rains will come when pious Israelites wish: on Friday nights (the sabbath darkness) when nobody goes out!

5. cf. Am. 9.13, so great a harvest that there will be not enough time to deal with it.

10. old store long kept: the Sifra and the Talmud (*b. B. Bath.*, 91b) say that *yāšān* means last year's crop and *nôšān* the year before that. Hence LXX: 'the old and the old of the old'.

11. my soul: idiomatic form: 'I myself', common in poetry and in ornate prose.

13. the bars of your yoke: these consist of heavy cross-pieces which rest behind the hump of the ox and have the appearance of holding the ox down. This is the picture the writer has in mind: when the yoke is removed, Israel can stand upright. V and DV change the figure of speech and have 'the chains of your neck'.

The Penalties for Disobedience **14–39**

There are five stages, increasing with a persistent refusal to be warned and repent; 16–17, sickness and defeat in battle; 18–20, drought and famine; 21–22, overrun by wild beasts; 23–26, war and siege; 27–32, the last stage of all when men eat their own children towards the end of the siege, and this is followed by complete destruction and exile.

15. your soul: i.e. 'you yourself' (cf. verses 11, 30).

16. appoint over you: this is *pāḳaḏ*, God's special visitation to save or, as here, to punish (cf. 18.25).

sudden terror: as in Accadian, but in Aramaic *behālāh* means 'helplessness, dejection, dismay', whence LXX *aporia* and V and DV (poverty).

consumption: as in Arabic and Jewish Aramaic. It is found only here and in the similar catalogue of disasters (Dt. 28.22). LXX has 'scurvy', and Rashi says it involves pustules. The next word *ḳaddaḥaṯ* is found only here and in Dt. 28.22. LXX has 'jaundice', but **fever** is probably right.

25. a sword: this is archaic. The modern equivalent is 'war', just as **staff of bread** (verse 26) is 'food supply'.

30. your high places: these are the hill-shrines of Canaan, declared illegal and destroyed by king Josiah (2 Kg. 23.5–20), but at one time legitimate (cf. Elijah on Mount Carmel (1 Kg. 18.20, 32)). Such shrines and temples can be seen on hilltops in India to this day (cf. especially the shrine on the rock in Tirichupali). They are copies of, substitutes for, the holy mountain of the Gods away in the north, the Mount Zaphon of the Ugarit tablets, the Olympos of the Greeks, and Mount Zion itself is described in such terms (Ps. 48.1–2). See the dictionaries.

incense altars: cf. Ezek. 6.4ff.; 2 Chr. 34.4, and perhaps correct, but there was a Phoenican god *Ba'al-ḥammān* and they seem to be some kind of stone that is set up, either a pillar or an altar. Rashi says they were set up on the roof of a temple and so placed in the sun, but this may well be no more than a guess (EVV 'sun-images').

idols: the word *gillûlîm* means 'logs', but it has the vowels of the word *šiḳḳûṣ*, short-*i*, doubled middle consonant, and long-*u*; and this involves idolatrous associations.

31. sanctuaries: fifty-three Hebrew MSS, Sam and S have the singular, which makes the verse refer to the Temple at Jerusalem.

your pleasing odours: this is the soothing smoke of the whole sacrifices (1.9 and often in P).

36. faintness: the word *môreḵ* means 'weakness, timidity'. LXX has 'slavery', V has 'fear', T 'brokenness'. Evidently the ancient versions did not recognize the word.

Repentance means Restoration **40–46**

These verses are capable of another interpretation, dependent on translating the *'ap̱* ('so that': beginning of verse 41) as 'yet still' and retaining the future of the verb. Though the people confess their sins, I will yet still walk contrary to them and bring them into exile. When they are truly humbled and have made amends in full for their sins, I will remember the covenant and rescue them once more as I did from Egypt.

41. make amends: cf. Isa. 40.2, where the same words are found in Heb.

42. remember: when God 'remembers', he takes action to help and save.

FIFTH SECTION 27.1–34 THE COMMUTATION OF VOWS AND TITHES

(a) VOWS **27.1–29**

This chapter has been added at the end of the H-material. It is from the latest stratum of P, since it assumes the existence of the jubilee year.

A Person Vowed to God **1–8**

In early times this involved the sacrifice of the person vowed (cf. Jephthah's daughter, Jg. 11.29–40). Ultimately the sacrifice even of the first-born was prohibited, so that all such vows had to be commuted. Virtually therefore this vow became a payment of cash, the amount theoretically estimated by the priests, but in practice fixed according to age and sex. For a male between twenty and sixty years old the payment was fifty silver shekels of 224 grains (see note on 5.15). The silver holy shekel weighed a little more than the British silver half-crown. The whole amount was a little less than £6, pre-1914 standards. For a woman of the same age the price was half this; for a youth between five and twenty years old, £2 10s; and half that for a girl of the same age. For a boy from a month old to five years old the amount was 12s 6d; and 7s 6d for a girl of the same age. For a man over sixty years old the amount was £1 7s 6d; and £1 5s for a woman of the same age. The purchasing power of money was very much higher than it was even in 1914. There was an overall direction: if the man is too poor to pay, the priest must assess him according to his ability to pay.

An Animal Vowed to God **9–13**

A distinction is made between beasts ritually clean, which can be presented as a holy-gift, and those which are ritually unclean and cannot be so presented. The ritually clean animal becomes holy, and can never return to *ḥôl* (common, 'lay') life. No exchange or commutation is permitted. If the beast is ritually unclean, the priest must estimate its value, good or bad. If the man wishes to redeem it (buy it back: *gā'al*; cf. 25.25), then he must pay that price plus 20 per cent. If he does not wish to redeem it, the priest sells it at his valuation (verse 27).

10. substitute ... exchange: the two words are near synonyms, and both LXX and V used one word to cover both. But there is a difference. The first means 'substitute an exact equivalent' (Phoenician); the second means 'exchange', but not by what is an exact equivalent (e.g. not for cash).

14–15. A house can be bought back in the same way as an unclean animal: assessment plus 20 per cent.

A Piece of Land Vowed to God **16–25**

A distinction is made between land inherited and land bought. Inherited land may be bought back at the stipulated price plus 20 per cent. If the land is not bought back it belongs to the priests. The land must not be sold whilst involved in the vow (verse 28). There are two interpretations of this restriction. One is: if the man who made the vow sells the land, he forfeits all right to it and the land does not revert at the jubilee. Rashi says it means: if the treasurer of the Temple sells the land; this would be as sharp practice by the priests, as such a sale would be illegal for the man. Land that has been bought may be redeemed by the man, but at the jubilee it reverts to the original owner, the man who inherited it.

16. a sowing of a homer of barley: this is as much land as can be sown with eleven bushels of barley: about $3\frac{3}{4}$ acres (see *HDB*, iv, p. 910). The value of such a plot was about £6 5s, pre-1914 equivalent. The value of the plot depends on the number of harvests due before the next jubilee. It works out at a shekel a year for each of the forty-nine years and one shekel for them all (Rashi).

21. devoted: the word *ḥērem* means set apart absolutely and irrevocably. Whatever was *ḥērem* to another god was ruthlessly and completely destroyed; thus *ḥērem* can mean 'the sacred ban'. This was the practice in early warfare, both as fought by the Israelites (Jos. 6.17) and as fought by surrounding nations, e.g. the Moabites (MI 17). But the word is also used, as here, of that which is devoted to God and cannot under any circumstances be redeemed. The Arabic *ḥaruma* means 'be prohibited, forbidden, become sacred'; *el-Ḥarām* is a sacred place, which only the faithful Muslim may enter, and there are three of them, Mecca, Medina, and the mosque at Jerusalem; a *ḥurmat* is a woman, and the plural is *ḥarîm*, which also means the women's quarters.

25. twenty gerahs: the earliest mention of this coin (weight) is Ezek. 45.12, and it is the Babylonian *giru*, a small coin of Nebuchedrezzar's time. Originally the word meant a seed, either that of the carob or of the lupin. It was the equivalent of the Hebrew *mᵉ'āh* and the Greek obol, one sixth of the Attic drachm. Twenty obols equal one shekel (cf. Josephus, *Ant. Iud.* III, viii, 2). The plural *mā'ôṯ* (of m^{e}'*āh*) means 'small change'.

26–27. firstlings: the firstlings of clean animals cannot be vowed to God, because they are his already (Exod. 13.2, 34.19). The firstlings of unclean animals also belong to God, but they must be redeemed or sold; they cannot become the property of or be eaten by the priests.

Devoted Things **28–29**

See verse 21, above. See also ***HDB*, i, article** 'Ban', A. R. S. Kennedy.

The Law of Tithe **30–33**

Cf. Dt. 14.22–29, 26.12–15; Num. 18.21–32 P. No permission is given elsewhere to commute any tithe, though D allows the tithe to be sold locally and the money spent at the central shrine to provide the sacred meal. Nowhere else is any cattle tithe mentioned. By the time of 2 Chr. 31.6 both cattle and sheep tithe had been established and the tithe belonged to the Levites, who had to give a tithe of the tithe to the priests. The origin of the tithe is lost in antiquity, and is general to mankind, apparently as a variation of first-fruits (all belongs to the god) or as thankfulness for mercies received. The patriarchs paid tithes (Gen. 14.20 and 28.22), and the Bethel sanctuary was closely allied in Israelite tradition with the institution of the tithe. The king could levy a tithe (1 Sam. 8.17), though this may be an early form of the sacred tithe.

32. the herdsman's staff: this was used for counting the sheep (Jer. 33.13 and *b. Bekh.*, 58b). It had to be the tenth animal and no substitution was allowed, good for bad or bad for good.

THE FOURTH BOOK OF MOSES
COMMONLY CALLED
NUMBERS

THE FOURTH BOOK OF MOSES
COMMONLY CALLED

NUMBERS

FIRST SECTION **1.1–10.10** WHAT HAPPENED AT SINAI

This section is entirely from the P-tradition, though from more than one layer. The first two chapters deal with the numbers of the people and the layout of the camp. The next two explain who are the true priests, and then fix the status and duties of the Levites. Then follow various rules and regulations.

(a) THE FIRST CENSUS **1.1–54**

According to P, the people were numbered twice: at Sinai in the second year, and thirty-eight years later on the plains of Moab at the end of the journey through the wilderness. For a comparison of the figures, see the notes on 1.17–46. The ancient belief was that it was wrong to number the people (2 Sam. 24; 1 Chr. 21). It was presumptuous of David, since the people belonged to God and not to him. The ancient theory was that God alone is king of Israel and the monarch is his regent, the *nāḡîḏ* (leader) as in 1 Sam. 9.16, 13.14, 1 Kg. 14.7; 2 Kg. 20.5, or the *nāśî'* (prince) as in Ezek. 44–48. Rashi says that God 'counts them every now and then', because they are dear to him (Exod. 12.37, 30.16; Num. 1.2).

1. wilderness of Sinai: see on Lev. 7.38. Also, for Tent of Meeting, see Lev. 1.1.

2. congregation: see on Lev. 4.13.

by families: there were twelve tribes (*šēḇeṭ*, P *maṭṭeh*, each with a primary meaning of 'rod, staff'). In each tribe there was a number of clans or families (*mišpāḥāh*). Within each clan there were 'father's houses' (*bēṯ 'āḇ*). It is rare for *šēḇeṭ* to be used other than of a full tribe, and *maṭṭeh* never, but the other terms are used more loosely (*RS*[2], p. 276, and *BDB*).

head by head: lit. 'by their skulls'. The older English versions retain the word 'poll', not used today except of an election and of cattle.

3. go forth to war: the root *y-ṣ-'* (go out) can be used, as here, of going out to battle, going to war (Jg. 2.15, Isa. 41.12, etc.). Cf. Arabic *baraza* (go out), *bāraza* (go to battle), *mubāraza* (challenge to single combat). Better, 'go out on a campaign'. since *ṣāḇā'* (cf. Arabic *ṣaba'a*, go out against someone) is the militia, the call-up, when every able-bodied man was summoned to serve for a limited period. This was the army in the field, of which Joab was commander, distinguished from the king's bodyguard, of which Benaiah was David's captain. The word can mean 'campaign' and even 'period of hard toil' (Job 7.1). The plural *ṣ^eḇā'ôṯ* is found in the title 'God of Hosts'. Here the reference may be to astral bodies whose worship in Israel–Judah was revived in Manasseh's time (2 Kg. 21.5), or to the armies of Israel fighting in a holy war (Arabic *jihâd*). See fuller discussion in *DB*, pp. 590f., 401.

4–16. Moses chooses one leader (*nāśî'*, chief, prince) from each tribe. They assist him in the census, and lead the tribes (2.3–31, 7, 10.14–28). The order of Leah's and Rachel's children is the order of their birth (Gen. 29.31–30.23), but that of the four sons of Bilhah and Zilpah is different from the Genesis order. Gad comes between Simeon and Judah, because Simeon and Gad are both allocated to the south of the Tent of Meeting (2.10–16). The names of the leaders are not found outside Numbers, except for the two Judahite names, **Nahshon** and **Amminadab** (Exod. 6.23; Ru. 4.18–21). For the meanings of the names, see G. B. Gray, *HPN and Numbers* (*ICC*), pp. 7f., and the dictionaries. Most of the names are theophorous and apparently any one name could have the name of the God either first or second. **Elizur** means 'God is a rock'. 'Rock' is found thirty-three times to describe God and sometimes (e.g. Dt. 32.4) is apparently used as a proper name. The form Zuriel is found in Num. 3.35. **Shedeur** (Shaddai is light) is the only case where Shaddai is found as the first component. The name Shaddai is of disputed meaning, and the traditional 'Almighty' is due to V *omnipotens*. **Shelumiel** (God is prosperity) and **Zurishaddai** (Shaddai is a rock) have no parallels. **Nahshon** (serpent) is one of those animal names (full list in *HPN*, pp. 88–96) which are alleged to be evidence of totemism in Israel in early times (see W. Robertson Smith, *Kinship and Marriage in Early Arabia*, p. 219, etc.; Oesterley and Robinson, *Hebrew Religion*, 2nd ed., p. 52f.). Such names could arise in other ways, e.g. English surnames such as Bull, Sparrow, Crow, Whale. **Amminadab** is 'the (divine) kinsman is generous'. **Nethanel** (God has given) is one of the commonest of names. **Zuar** means 'little one'. **Eliab** (God is father) is another common name. **Helon** is of uncertain meaning. **Elishama** (God has heard) is common and has a parallel form Ishmael. (Samuel means 'name of God'.) **Ammihud** (the kinsman is glorious), **Gamaliel** (God is a reward—common name of Rabbis from first century), **Pedahzur** (the Rock has redeemed), and **Abidan** (the divine father has judged; cf. Daniel) has no parallels. **Gideoni** is a variant of Gideon (? hewing down). The other names are **Ahiezer** (the divine brother is a help), **Ammishaddai** (Shaddai is kinsman), **Pagiel** (God has encountered), **Ochran** (? trouble), and **Eliasaph** (God has added). **Deuel** is probably an error for Reuel (God is companion), J's name for Moses's father-in-law. **Ahira** is probably an error for Ahida (so S here: my brother knows); cf. the name Jehoiada (Yahweh knows). The meaning of **Enan** is uncertain.

16. clans: EVV have 'thousands', as LXX, RVm 'families', and V 'army'. It is argued that *'elep* (thousand) came to mean 'a company of a thousand men'. In Jg. 6.15 the meaning is a *sept* (?), a section of a tribe larger than a 'father's house'. There is no clear evidence to fix the relative size of the *mišpāḥāh* (clan) and the *'elep* (sept).

The Details of the Census **17–46**

The same formula is repeated for each tribe, virtually without variation. The first three verses are introductory. The numbers are (ch. 1 first and ch. 26 second): Judah 74,600 and 76,500; Dan 62,700 and 64,400; Simeon 59,300 and 22,200; Zebulun 57,400 and 60,500; Issachar 54,400 and 64,300; Naphtali 53,400 and 45,400; Reuben 46,500 and 43,730; Gad 45,650 and 40,500; Asher 41,500 and 53,400; Ephraim 40,500 and 32,500; Benjamin 35,400 and 45,600; Manasseh 32,200 and 52,700. The remarkable features of these lists are the comparatively small size of Ephraim; the very large decrease in Simeon and the very great increase in Manasseh. If these figures are at all trustworthy, then Simeon must have met with some disaster, which is usually associated with Gen. 49.6–7 and 34.25–31. But the figures may belong to any century, and any deduction made from the figures must be unreliable.

17. named: lit. 'pricked off', often in Chronicler and in Isa. 62.2. Compare the way in which the Queen of England chooses the Lord-Lieutenants.

18. registered themselves: i.e. declared their pedigree, said whose sons they were.

32. The comparative grand totals are 603,550 and 601,730. The total number of both Israel and Judah in David's census was 1,300,000 (2 Sam. 24.9) or 1,570,000 (1 Chr. 21.5). In 2 Sam. Israel outnumbered Judah by 8 to 5; in 1 Chronicles it was a little more than 11 to 8. The two lists in Numbers work out as 6 to 1 and 5 to 1.

The Duties of the Levites **47–54**

For the census-number, see 3.21–28. For changes in the nature and status of the Levites, see pp. 13f.

50. tend: EVV have 'minister', following V. The verb *š-r-t* is used of higher than domestic service, of chief servants and royal officials. Joshua was 'minister' to Moses (Exod. 24.13), Elisha to Elijah (1 Kg. 19.21), and the angels are God's ministers (Ps. 103.21). The verb is used at all times of ministrations in worship, and in P mostly of the Levites, though occasionally of priests.

51. any one else: the Hebrew is *zār* 'outsider', but here, as usually in P, one who is not a priest, a layman unqualified to perform priestly duties.

52. standard: the Hebrew is *degel* (standard, banner; cf. Accadian *diglu*, from *dagalu*, look at; cf. Ca. 5.10). LXX thought of 'company', V of the *cuneus*, the wedge-shaped battle formation with which Spartacus achieved such success in the great slave revolt. Thus the four sets of standards were one set on each of the four sides of the camp, with the Levites between the tabernacle and the secular tribes.

(b) THE DISPOSITION OF THE TRIBES IN CAMP **2.1–34**

The whole chapter is an idealistic reconstruction to fit in with later religious ideas, whilst the disposition of the tribes reflects the genealogies. The Tent of Meeting is no longer outside the camp (Exod. 33.7f. E) but in the centre, reflecting the position of the Temple in Jerusalem and declaring that God is in the midst of his people. There is an inner ring of sacred groups. To the east, in front of the entrance (cf. the Temple), the sons of Aaron were stationed. They were the most sacred of all in the post-exilic system. The Levites were disposed on the other three sides. The most important of these was the south, occupied by the Kohathites. Kohath was the second son of Levi, and it was through him and his eldest son Amram that the Aaronite priests claimed descent from Levi (Exod. 6.18 and 20). They had the care of the most sacred of the Temple furniture (4.1–16) and the most important place, after the Aaronites, round the Tent of Meeting. The sons of Gershon, Levi's eldest son, were to the west, and the sons of Merari, Levi's youngest son, to the north. In the outer ring of the secular tribes, precedence of birth is followed to a similar and not complete extent. Judah occupies the principal place, was leader of the eastern group and led the march. He was the fourth son of Leah, and in his company were Issachar and Zebulun, Leah's fifth and sixth sons. The second position was to the south, where Reuben was leader. He was Jacob's first-born and Leah's first son. With Reuben was Simeon, Leah's second son, but since Levi (Leah's third son) was now a sacred tribe, his place in the second group was taken by Gad, the elder of the two sons of Leah's handmaid. The third position was west, and here the leader was Ephraim, the greatest of the three Rachel tribes (though in P's second census (ch. 26) it was the smallest), Manasseh and Benjamin completing this group. The fourth position was to the north, and the leader was Dan, the elder of the two sons of Rachel's handmaid, Bilhah, and the oldest of the sons of the concubines. With him there were associated his full brother, Naphtali, and Zilpah's second son, Asher. The camp of Israel was a complete square with the Tent of Meeting in the centre. The whole scheme is a development of the scheme for the new Jerusalem in Ezek. 48. This is thus evidence of the important place which these last nine chapters of Ezekiel play in the development of post-exilic ecclesiastical theory. See Ezek. 44.10–16, where it is stated for the first time that the Levites are to be penalized and no longer allowed to act as sacrificing priests, the Zadokites alone being allowed to have this status (see pp. 13f.).

2. ensigns: the Hebrew is *'ôṯôṯ* (signs, tokens), and the natural interpretation of the text is that the standard (*deḡel*) of each group was that of the leader of the tribe, whilst the ensigns were the banners of the separate tribes, here called **fathers' houses.** There is a tradition that each tribe had a piece of cloth attached to its ensign the same colour as its particular stone in the High Priest's breastplate (Exod. 28.21). **facing:** the Hebrew is *minneḡeḏ*, which can mean 'opposite', as LXX and RV have understood it. But the more likely meaning is 'at a distance' (Dt. 32.52; 2 Kg. 2.15, etc.). This is the ancient Jewish interpretation: the secular tribes were two thousand cubits away, roughly a thousand yards, the traditional sabbath day's journey. The interpretation is based on Jos. 3.4. The secular tribes would thus be as far away as possible from the sacred enclosure, but near enough to come to the Tent on the sabbath.

3–31. The tribes are allocated to their positions in the camp and on the march. The names of the leaders and the numbers of the tribes are repeated from chapter 1.

32 Depends on 1.44f. and **33** repeats 1.47.

(c) THE DESCENDANTS OF AARON **3.1–4**

This section serves to introduce the rest of the chapter by separating the sons of Aaron from the rest of the Levites. The details are based on Exod. 6.23 and Lev. 10. According to verse 3, all four sons were anointed priests and had been instituted into the priest's office, but the two elder sons offered unholy fire, and were destroyed. These two left no heirs, so that Eleazar and Ithamar alone were the fathers of the post-exilic priesthood. See pp. 13f.

1. and Moses: this is found in all the versions and undoubtedly is the correct text. In point of fact Moses has nothing to do with the genealogy, and the name is probably the accidental repetition of a scribe who was accustomed to the occurrence of the two names. The Talmud (*b. San.*, 19b) makes the most of it: it is because Moses taught them the Law, and Scripture regards the teacher of the Law as a father to his pupil.

3. This verse seeks to make P's description of the post-exilic priesthood a strictly accurate one. They were all of them 'sons of Aaron' and all the sons of Aaron have always been consecrated to the priesthood. But Nadab and Abihu left no heirs. It is difficult now to explain why the fire was *zārāh* (lay, **unholy**), since in Lev. 10.1 it was because they were not priests.

ordained: see note on Lev. 8.22.

4. in the lifetime of: the Hebrew is *'al-pᵉnē*, which can mean 'in addition to' (Job 16.14), but more often 'in the presence of' and probably twice 'in the lifetime of', here and Gen. 11.28. The two younger sons continued to act as priests whilst their father was still alive.

(d) THE LEVITES ARE TO SERVE THE AARONITES **3.5–13**

Cf. Ezek. 44.10–16, where the Levites are degraded priests. Here they are given by God from among the people.

7–10. The Levites are to perform all duties except those directly connected with the service of the altar.

11–13. Here is a second explanation of the status of the Levites. They are a compensation to God for the first-born of Israel. This explanation is continued in verses 40–51, so the Levite genealogy (verses 14–20) and the census and list of duties (verses 21–39) are a later insertion.

13. I am the LORD: this phrase is generally recognized as a characteristic of H. If this section is P, then H and P are not as separate as some suppose. See also verse 41.

(e) THE CENSUS OF THE LEVITES **3:14–51**

It was essential to have an estimate of the numbers of the Levites before the calculations involved in verses 44–51.

14–20. This list is based on Exod. 6.16–19. The tradition of Gershon, Kohath, and Merari as the ancestors of the Levites is found also in Num. 26.57, but in 26.58 a different tradition is preserved: Libni, Hebron, Mahli, Mushi, and Korah. The first four of these appear in 3.18–20 as sub-families of Gershon, Kohath, and Merari; in 16.1 Korah is a son of Kohath.

21–26. the Gershonites: their number is 7,500; their place in camp was west, and on the march they followed the Kohathites. They were in charge of all that covered and screened Tabernacle and Tent and Court (Num. 4.24–28; Exod. 26.1–37; 27.9–19).

27–32. the Kohathites: their number is 8,300 (so LXX). The scribe accidentally omitted the middle consonant of *š-l-š* (three) and wrote *š-š* (six). Their place in camp was south, and on the march they followed the priests. They carried all the holiest of the Tabernacle furniture, too holy to be transported in wagons (Num. 4.4–15, 7.9).

33–37. the Merarites: their number is 6,200. Their place in camp was north and they were last on the march. They had charge of the wooden framework and all pegs and cords and sockets (4.29–33).

40–51. The surplus firstborn: the number of Levites proved to be 273 less than the number of the firstborn. Since the Levites are God's compensation for his surrender of the firstborn, payment has to be made for the surplus firstborn at five shekels a head. This money went to the priests. The idea of the cattle of the Levites being a compensation for the surrender of the first-born of cattle is curious and looks like ecclesiastical theorizing, because the Israelite could redeem these if he wished.

51. redemption money: the Hebrew is *pᵉḏuyyîm*, which is strictly correct; it means payment to obtain what was not one's own originally.

(f) THE DUTIES AND NUMBERS OF ADULT LEVITES **4.1–49**

This is a census only of males eligible for the sacred duties.

2–20. The duties of the Kohathites.

3. from thirty years old: the lower limit for service varies. Num. 8.24 has twenty-five and so LXX (cod. B) here; but 1 Chr. 23.24, 27 have twenty and so LXX (cod. A) here. The Chronicler gives no upper limit. Evidently the age-limit was gradually lowered. LXX is seeking to harmonize the various statements.

the service: the word *ṣāḇā'* is used in 1.3 of the militia, and in Isa. 40.2, Job 7.1 of hard toil and trouble.

4. the most holy things: following EVV but not inserting a preposition, since the two words *ḳōḏeš ḳᵒḏāšîm* are out of construction. There are three possibilities follow Exod. 30.10, 29.37 and make the phrase refer to the sacred furniture and the altar, which is what EVV do; assume the reference is to the sacred duties of the Kohathites; regard the phrase as a gloss 'holy of holies' on the Tent of Meeting and an identification of the Tent of the Wilderness with the innermost shrine of the Second Temple. This last is the most satisfactory solution.

5. the veil of the screen: according to P, there were three screens: one at the gate of the court (Exod. 27.16), one at the entrance to the tent (Exod. 26.36; Num. 3.25), one within the tent (Exod. 35.12). P thinks of this innermost curtain of all as having been used to cover the Ark during the actual journeys.

6. goatskin: LXX and V understood this to refer to the hyacinth colour of the skins, but Jewish tradition has always been that it is some kind of fish or animal. Hence AV 'badger', RV 'sealskin'. In Arabic *taḫas* is the dolphin. Some suggest 'porpoise', and others 'dugong', which is the Malay word for 'a large, aquatic herbivorous mammal inhabiting the Indian seas' (*OED*). In Ezek. 16.10 RSV has 'leather', after a suggestion that we are dealing with an Egyptian loanword. This skin was the outer cover for all sacred objects, and it was only the Ark itself which had the additional blue cloth over all.

blue: there are two shades of purple involved. One is *tᵉḵēleṯ* (as here), a bluish purple; the other is *'argāmān*, a reddish purple (verse 13). Both colours were obtained from the *murex trunculus*, a shellfish found on the Phoenician coast and the foundation of the prosperity of the Tyrian trade in purple cloth, famous throughout the ancient world (cf. Lydia, Ac. 16.14, and *DB*, art. 'Colours', p. 170).

put in its poles: but compare Exod. 25.15, according to which the poles were to be left in permanently.

7. the table of the bread of the Presence: following EVV which insert the reference to 'the bread'. This is the only place where the phrase 'the table of the Presence' is found. EVV and RSV are assimilating to the rest.

the continual bread: but *tāmîḏ* means 'regular' rather than 'continual' (Exod. 25.30 and note on Lev. 24.5–9).

the plates: the Arabic *ḳa'ara* suggests that these were deep dishes. LXX has *trublion* (cup, bowl). In Syriac the word is used of the calyx of a flower or an acorn cup, and V has 'censer'. The nearest English equivalent is 'bowl'.

dishes for incense: the word *kap̱* means 'hand', so that some small hollowed dish is being described. V and DV have 'little mortars' and EVV have 'spoons'. The reference to incense is due to LXX, and is probably right.

bowls: these were cups for drawing wine out of a bowl (LXX).

flagons: these were jugs, urns, jars (Ethiopic), and were used in pouring the libations, though the Arabic *ḳaśwat* (basket of palm leaves) suggests that the utensil is being described by its shape rather than by its texture (see Exod. 25.29).

9. lampstand: see Lev. 24.4. The reference is to the seven-branched candelabra.

trays: the Hebrew word denotes some kind of utensil for catching falling material. Rashi says they were small ladles with flat bottoms and no ridge in front, used to receive the ash raked from the lamps, which were containers in which the wick rested, protruding from a spout at the side. The *maḥtāh* was also used as a firepan for the ashes from the altar (Exod. 27.3) and as a receptacle for incense (Lev. 10.1; Num. 16.6). Presumably there were pans of different sizes.

10. carrying frame: the word is *môṭ* which means a yoke, such as the pole (Num. 13.23) on which the spies carried the bunch of grapes from the valley of Eshcol. So AV and RVm.

11. the golden altar: this is 'the altar of fragrant incense' (Lev. 4.7) which is said to have stood in the Second Temple within the Veil, but it certainly did not exist before the exile.

14. firepans: this is the word used in verse 9 and there translated **trays**. All these ashes from the altar were deposited at the east side of the ramp which led up to the altar, except for a small portion, which was called a *t^erûmāh*, because it was lifted off. This was returned to the altar-fire to preserve continuity (Lev. 6.10 (Heb 3)).
forks: the shape of the *mizlāḡāh* is unknown except that the *mazlāḡ* of 1 Sam. 2.13 was a three-pronged fleshhook. Hence V has 'trident' and LXX has *kreagra* 'fleshhook'. Tradition says they were copper hooks used to turn the limbs of the animal over in the fire to ensure they were wholly consumed.
basins: these were used for tossing the blood against the corners of the altar. At the end of this verse V and Sam have an addition and thus complete the list of utensils (cf. Exod. 30.28): 'and they shall take a purple cloth and cover the laver and its base, and they shall put them within the covering of goatskin (dugong?), and shall put them on the carrying frame'.

16. Eleazar: ancestor of the Zadokites (1 Chr. 6.4–8, etc.) was in charge of the Kohathites, who had the care of the most sacred Temple furniture, but he was personally responsible for the oil (for the lamps), the regular *minḥāh* (grain-offering), and the anointing oil. The regular grain-offering (*minḥaṯ tāmîḏ*) is included here because in P's time it was divided into two portions, one offered in the morning and the other in the evening (Lev. 6.19–23 (Heb 12–16)), so that theoretically it would be necessary to carry one half for the full day's march.

The Duties of the Gershonites **21–28**

These Levites, who were in charge of the less holy Temple furniture, were under the charge of Ithamar, the younger surviving son of Aaron and the father of the Aaronites. Thus the Zadokite Levites had precedence over the Aaronite Levites. Details of the curtains and screens and how they all fitted together are to be found in Exod. 26.1–14.

25. goatskin: as in verses 6, 8 (early editions of RSV have 'sheepskin'); it was probably the skin of the porpoise or the dugong.

The Duties of the Merarites **29–33**

These Levites were responsible for all the frameworks and accessories (see Exod. 26.15–30).

The Census of the Three Families **34–49**

The number of males eligible for Temple service was Kohathites 2,750 Gershonites

2,630, and Merarites 3,200. The total, given with P's characteristic preciseness, is 8,580.

49. This verse is confused and actually untranslateable. RSV has made some necessary emendations as all the translations have had to do.

(g) MISCELLANEOUS REGULATIONS **5.1–6.27**

Containing especially the ordeal of jealousy (5.11–31), the Nazirite laws (6.1–21 and the Aaronic blessing (6.22–27).

1–4. Unclean persons: all are to be excluded from the camp. All types of ritual uncleanness come under this ban. In Lev. 13–15 men and women suffering from 'issues' (haemorrhages from the sex organs), or because of contact with the dead, are not stated to be excluded from the camp. The regulation there applies only to lepers, i.e. people with running sores. All these regulations depend upon the idea that God dwells in the midst of the camp (verse 3) and therefore the whole camp must be ritually clean.

5–8. Breach of trust: see Lev. 6.1–7 (Heb 5.20–26). Both there and here, damage has been done or loss sustained; compensation is due plus 20 per cent. And an offering must be brought. In Leviticus 6 this offering is called an *'āšām* (so-called guilt-offering), but here that term is used only of the compensation. The offering is here called 'the ram of atonement'. There is an additional regulation to provide for the case where the man is dead and has no heir. The compensation in this case is to be paid to the priests, who thus receive both the ram and the money.

9–10. These two verses define the *tᵉrûmāh* (the so-called 'heave-offering'; here RSV has 'offering'); see p. 58. Further, for **holy things** read 'holy gifts', offerings of the people which went to the priests.

The Ordeal of Jealousy **11–31**

This law concerns the case where a man's wife is found to be pregnant and he suspects he is not the father. She is given a potion, and in case of guilt this produces a miscarriage. This is the only case in the Old Testament of that trial by ordeal which was common in ancient time and persisted in Britain until well on in the Middle Ages, when it was applied to witches and for offences generally: grasping red-hot irons, trials by combat, etc. See Gray, *Numbers* (*ICC*), pp. 43–49.

12. goes astray: the verb *śāṭāh* is used regularly of marital unfaithfulness on the part of a wife (cf. Ethiopic 'to be seduced'). Sexual misconduct on the part of a man was reckoned 'to be different', as it still is by many.

14. spirit of jealousy: this use of *rûah* in the psychological sense of an over-mastering rush of feeling is true to the essence of the word. When used of the wind, it denotes a strong, powerful wind, the wind of the desert. The *rûaḥ* of God rushes (*ṣālaḥ*) suddenly and powerfully on a man (Jg. 14.6, etc.; Ac. 2.2). See articles on 'Spirit' in the dictionaries, and also 'The Spirit of God in Jewish Thought' (*The Doctrine of the Spirit*, Headingley Lectures, 1937, pp. 11–37). A man can be dominated by his 'spirit' (Pr. 16.32). Jealousy is a powerful emotion, and men and women do actually find themselves controlled by it and driven to do the most extraordinary things, from petty misconduct to wilful murder. This changing of a man is a characteristic feature of the work of the Holy Spirit in the New Testament and in Christian experience.

15. a tenth of an ephah is a little under seven pints.

meal: this is coarse flour (*ḳemaḥ*). Everywhere else in P *sōleṯ* (fine, sifted flour) is required in a grain-offering. The Rabbis (the Sifra and *b. Soṭah*, 14a) point out that this is food for beasts, and it has to be this here because she has done a beastly thing. But such coarse meal was offered on ordinary occasions in ancient times. The absence of oil and frankincense distinguishes this offering from the ordinary grain-offering and allies it with the sin-offering (Lev. 5.11).

jealousy: the Hebrew has the plural and the Rabbis made the most of this saying that there was double 'jealousy', God and the husband, but this comment depends on the strict meanings of the Hebrew word, which can mean both jealousy of and zeal for or against anything or anybody.

remembrance: usually the meaning is 'remembrance before God' (Lev. 23.24) or a reminder of what has happened in the past (Jos. 4.7), but here the meaning is 'bring to knowledge'. This is another indication of the fact that many ancient rites of diverse origin have been forced into one pattern. There is more than one type of *zikkārôn* (remembrance).

16. before the Lord: this is said to be the Gate of Nicanor in the Second Temple (*Soṭah*, i, 5), but there is considerable difference of opinion as to which gate this was, whether the Upper Gate, which led up from the Court of the Women, or the Beautiful Gate, which led up from the Court of the Gentiles. Probably this ceremony took place in the Upper Gate.

17. holy water: following EVV and V and it is Heb. But Sam has 'sanctified', LXX has 'pure, running' water, and T and the Mishnah (*Soṭah*, ii, 2) say it was water taken from the bronze laver. The basis of this is the tradition that the bronze laver (Exod. 38.8) was made from the mirrors of devout and chaste women who 'ministered at the door of the Tent of Meeting'. Other explanations are: it came from a holy spring; it was mixed with dust from the sacred floor.

18. unbind the hair: the analogy is the leper (Lev. 13.45), whose loose hair was a sign of uncleanness. Rashi says it was by way of disgrace and that it involved pulling away the plaits which were bunched on the top of the head.

water of bitterness: following EVV which are based on T and V, and assume the root *mārar* (Arabic *murra*). But Sam has 'testing' and so LXX (*elegmos*, proof). Another possibility is the root *mārar* (Arabic *marra*, pass by, and *marmara*, cause to flow), so that the meaning may be 'cause an abortion'. The safest rendering is 'waters of proof', especially since the whole ceremony is a trial by ordeal.

21. The first part of this verse is a rubric and RSV rightly places it in brackets.

your thigh fall away: Jewish tradition makes this phrase and the next to be euphemisms. Her sin started with 'the thigh' and finished with the womb, so the punishment must include both. Possibly 'fall away' (*nôpeleṯ*) should be connected with *nēpel* (abortion). This gives two expressions for miscarriage, the one occurring at an early stage and the other much later. See Gray, *Numbers* (*ICC*), p. 48.

23. in a book: it was on a piece of parchment (*Soṭah*, ii, 4). The curses are washed off the parchment into the water, and the woman drinks the mixture. If she has been unfaithful there is a miscarriage; otherwise she comes to no harm.

26. its memorial portion: this is the *'azkārāh*, the token portion which is burnt on the altar, the priest taking the rest (Lev. 2.2).

28. shall conceive children: the reference is probably to the child she is carrying. But the Jews had difficulty with the verse, and interpreted to mean: if formerly she had pain in delivery, she shall have no more pain; if she has borne ugly children, they shall henceforth be beautiful.

The Nazirite **6.1–21**

The rules first define what is involved in the Nazirite's vow; next, what he must do if the *taboo* is accidentally broken (verses 9–12), and finally, the ceremonies to be observed on the completion of his vow. The Nazirite vow is one type of the special vow (Lev. 22.21, 27.2).

2. Nazirite: the *nāzîr* is a man who has made a vow (Arabic *naḏara*) with specially stringent conditions. There is nothing in the Hebrew itself to justify the translation of either noun or verb by 'separate', though separation and abstinence are necessarily involved. LXX translates the noun by *hagneia* (purity, chastity) and the verb by *aphagnizō*, which in Plato means the strict observance of religious duties. The Nazirite must abstain from everything connected with the vine, even to the pips and skin of the grape. He must remain unshaven and unshorn, and must not touch any human corpse, not even of his nearest of kin. He must keep himself sacred (RSV **separate himself**) scrupulously for the whole period of the vow. Particular reference is made to the hair, which is *taboo* among many early peoples, and the hair of all sacred persons must remain untouched. Either the head must be completely shorn (Egyptian priests, Buddhists, Romans) or it must never be shorn at all. Samson was a Nazirite from birth and his strength was in his hair (Jg. 16.17, 22). Kings wore their hair long, and it was contained with a fillet. This is how kings came to wear crowns, and *nēzer* means both 'consecration' and 'fillet, crown'.

5. grow long: the same root is used in 5.18 of the woman's hair. See also Jg. 5.2 of the sacred hair of the devoted leaders of the tribes.

9. defiles his consecrated head: the vow is rendered void if a man suddenly falls dead beside the Nazirite and accidentally touches him. The hair is no longer sacred. Indeed, it is held to be utterly unclean, and when shaved off it had to be buried, like one of the birds brought for the cleansed leper or the ox that gores a man to death (*Tem.*, vii, 4), being unclean to the lowest degree. This shaving is to take place at the beginning and again at the end of a seven-day period, the 'passage' time (Lev. 4.6, note). The Nazirite must bring the appropriate offerings and start again. He must bring two pigeons, one for a burnt-offering, because he appears before God, and the other for a sin-offering, because his fault was inadvertent. He must also bring an *'āšām* (compensation-offering) because of the time lost (cf. the rite of the cleansed leper, Lev. 14.12 and 21).

13–20. The completion of the vow: the Nazirite was brought forward, just as the priest to be installed was brought forward (Lev. 8.6). He had to bring all the regular offerings; compare the offerings brought on the eighth day of the priest's installation ceremonies (Lev. 9.7–22). But this time the hair was not buried; it was burned on the altar with the fat of the shared-offering (*zeḇaḥ*). Like the fat, it was holy-*taboo*. This dedication of hair to the god is attested almost all over the world, Australia, Syria, ancient Greece (Achilles), West Africa.

19–20. The officiating priest takes the normal *t^e^rûmāh* (thigh), and the priests receive the normal *t^e^nûpāh* (breast), but there is an additional *t^e^nûpāh*, the shoulder, one cake, and one wafer. The statement that this *t^e^nûpāh* was for the priest is a loose statement saying that all these went to the priesthood, since the individual priest certainly did not receive the breast.

21. The man could make extra vows, just as he could prescribe the length of time for keeping the vow. Queen Helena of Adiabene made a seven-year vow, and when she came to Israel at the end of the seven years the School of Hillel made her start again, because other lands are unclean as the uncleanness of death. At the end of this second seven years she contracted uncleanness and had to start once more, making twenty-one years in all (*Naz*., iii, 6).

The Priestly Blessing of the Aaronites **22–27**

In his description of the splendour of Simon the High Priest, Ben Sira (Sir. 50.20f.) places this blessing at the end of the service. In the Temple it was pronounced as a single blessing, but in the synagogues as three, with the congregation responding 'Amen' at the end of each blessing. The Sacred Name was pronounced in the Temple, but not in the synagogues (*Tamid*, vii, 2; *Soṭah*, vii, 6). In the Temple the priests raised their hands above their heads, but the High Priest only as high as the plate on his turban (Exod. 28.36), though Rabbi Judah said he raised them higher. In the synagogues the priests raised their hands only as high as their shoulders.

24. keep: preserve, guard, care for.

25. make his face to shine: the Hebrew means 'shine forth' rather than 'shine' (cf. LXX *epiphainō*); not a steady, continuous shining but an ever-renewed access of light; not a state so much as an action. The phrase indicates outgoing activity in goodwill.

26. lift up his countenance: the Sifra says this means suppressing his anger, since 'to hide the face' (Dt. 31.18) means 'be angry'. Hence 'turn away his anger from thee' and V 'turn his countenance to thee'.

peace: all translate literally, but *šālôm* has a much wider meaning and involves prosperity, good health, wholeness and completeness in every way. Like the Arabic *salām*, it is the proper mode of greeting.

27. put my name upon: the actual speaking of the Sacred Name was supposed to have in itself effective power: cf. the magic incantations and formulae which were little more than a recital of names in the hope that one would be effective (cf. Lk. 9.49). The word 'name' was used in antiquity as a substitute for the actual Divine Name itself, and to know a person's name was to have power over him (Gen. 32.29). The actual placing of the Divine Name on Israel not only declares that they belong to God, but also ensures prosperity.

This verse is not part of the blessing, and in LXX it follows verse 23.

(h) THE OFFERINGS OF THE LEADERS OF THE TRIBES 7.1–89

The leaders of the tribes set the example in generosity for all future generations, and freely bring all that is necessary for the service and transport of the tabernacle and all its appurtenances. They bring in all six wagons and twelve oxen for the transport, and then on successive days gold and silver vessels and all the regular offerings and everything needed for the dedication of the sanctuary and the first offerings. The leaders are those of Numbers 2, and the order is the same. The gifts are identical for each tribe. After slight variations in the first two paragraphs the formulae are exact, the only changes being the names of leader and tribe.

1. Moses finished setting up the tabernacle on the first day of the second month in the second year after the Exodus (Exod. 40.17), the day of the census (Num. 1.1). This chapter is later than, and independent of, the earlier chapters, since Moses had already consecrated the vessels of the altar (verse 1), which yet had to be brought (verses 11–83).

3. The wagons and a pair of oxen for each wagon were allocated, two to the Gershonites and four to the Merarites. None were given to the Kohathites because they had to carry the holiest of the sacred objects, including the Ark, on their shoulders.

covered wagons: the word *ṣāḇ* means 'wagon' (Accadian *ṣumbu*, cart), but the tradition that they were covered carts is as old as the Sifra and T and most ancient versions. But Sym has *hupergias* (wagons for military service), perhaps reading *ṣāḇā*. S and the Jerusalem Targum have 'prepared, made ready', and the Palestinian Targum has both interpretations. The same word is translated 'litters' in Isa. 66.20.

9. the holy things: the Hebrew is in the singular and strictly means 'the sanctuary', as EVV. Either will do, provided it is understood that 'the sanctuary' means the holiest place of all and everything in it.

10. dedication: the word *ḥ^{a}nukkāh* is not found earlier than P. The earlier usage of the verb is 'to train', possibly from training horses by controlling the lower jaw with bit and bridle; Arabic *ḥanak* means upper or lower jaw, both of horses and men.

11–88

Each day a leader of a tribe brought a silver plate and a silver basin, both full of sifted flour mixed with oil, a gold dish full of incense, a bull and a ram and a yearling ram for whole-offerings, a male goat for a sin-offering, and two oxen, five rams, five male goats, and five yearling lambs for shared-offerings. The sin-offering is not mentioned at the dedication of the First Temple (1 Kg. 8.64) or at the rededication of the Second Temple (1 Mac. 4.53, 56), but is included here by P to make the generous gifts of the leaders of the tribes complete for the whole service of the post-exilic Temple.

13. plate: EVV 'charger' (see 4.7). They were deep dishes rather than shallow plates. The weight was *c.* 60 oz. Troy.

basin: it was a bowl for tossing, and conical in shape; the weight was *c.* 33 oz. Troy.

14. dish: this was a small dish like the hollow of a hand; hence EVV 'spoons' and V's 'little mortar'. The weight was a little less than 5 oz. Troy.

incense: Jewish tradition uses the method of interpretation known as Gematria (counting up the value of the consonants) to great effect throughout the whole of this section, especially using the additional device whereby the values of the consonants are reversed, so that both the first and last consonants have the value 1, and so on. Thus *ḳᵉṭōreṯ* (incense) has the numerical value 613, and this is the number of the commandments of the Law. Indeed, in this section, every kind of homiletical device is used.

89. This verse fulfils Exod. 25.22. Here with 'the voice' (RV Voice) we have the first stage of development from Dt. 4.12, which ends with the idea of the Bath-kol, the heavenly voice of the Rabbis, mostly heard in the thunder. The 'thunder' of Exod. 19 is the Hebrew 'voice' (cf. Jn 12.29).

from between the two cherubim: these are not the two giant figures of 1 Kg. 6.23 whose huge wings guarded the inner shrine of Solomon's Temple. Cf. the guardian spirits at the gate of the Garden of Eden (Gen. 3.24). They were the smaller figures which were of one piece with the slab of solid gold, which constituted the 'mercy-seat'. The figures in Solomon's Temple were made of olive wood, plated with gold, and were fifteen feet high (1 Kg. 6.23–28, 8.6–7). The golden cherubs of the Second Temple faced each other with wings stretched inwards above them. Between (above) these cherubim the Glory of God rested and from there he spoke (Exod. 25.18–22, 37.7–9). They were the throne of God, as though the invisible God was sitting on them. Divine thrones of Syrian gods were sometimes flanked by winged sphinxes, and some scholars see an association here; so W. F. Albright, *Archaeology and the Religion of Israel*, 1946, and his earlier article in *BA* 1, 1938, 1–3. See also Dhorme and Vincent, *RB* 35, 1926, 328ff., 481ff.; de Vaux, *AI*, pp. 299f. It has been suggested that the *kappōreṯ* (mercy-seat) took the place of the Ark after the exile (1 Chr. 28.11), but even this had disappeared long before the final destruction of the Temple (Josephus, *Bell. Iud.* V, v, 6). For further details, see *DB*, p. 133, where L. H. Brockington points out that the Accadian *karibu* is 'one who prays, an intercessor', which certainly is more apt for the praying figures on the mercy-seat than for the giant spirit guards. It seems best to assume that the two types are wholly distinct: one type guardian spirits, and the other angelic intercessors. The origin may well be in the twin-spirits of the thunderstorm (cf. Ps. 18.7–15 (Heb 8–16), especially verse 10); compare the carved horses standing by the roadside at the entrances of villages of south India. They are for the guardian gods who are believed to ride round the village at night.

The chapter is incomplete, though the break is disguised in most translations. The end is: 'and he said to him', but the speech itself is missing.

(i) THE LIGHTING OF THE LAMPS **8.1–4**

See Exod. 25.31–40 for the original instructions, and Exod. 37.17–24 for the account of the making. Here the lamp is set up and lighted. It was made all in one piece, central shaft, six branches, and the knobs and cups shaped like the calyx and the petals of flowers.

2. set up: either this (as RVm) or light it (EVV). LXX and V favour the first and Jewish tradition the second. The former is to be preferred, because we are dealing with placing the lampstand in its position and fixing the direction in which the lamps shall shine.

in front of the lampstand: this word *mûl* (towards the front of) is always difficult to translate (cf. Dt. 1.1 where RSV has 'over against'). It seems to mean 'in front of', but in some sense 'opposite'. The Talmud (*b. Men.*, 98b) says that the three lamps on each side of the central shaft had their wicks turned inwards towards the central lamp, and that this was to signify that God has no need to shine out and make things clear for him to see. V and DV borrow from Exod. 40.22–25, where it is said that Moses placed the table to the north side of the Tabernacle and the lampstand opposite it on the south side. According to Exod. 25.37 the lamps were intended to send light straight ahead to where the table was on the north side. This seems the better explanation, and the other is fanciful exegesis to support a contention which doubtless is true in itself.

4. hammered work: i.e. beaten-work. Elsewhere LXX has *toreutos* (worked in relief), but here seems to have read the root *ḳ-š-ḥ*. It was made from a talent (130 lb.) of solid gold, beaten out and cut with a chisel (so Rashi).

from its base to its flowers: the Hebrew is difficult, but usually *yārēḵ* means 'side, flank (AV shaft)' and not 'base' (cf. LXX *kaulos* (stalk) and also V and DV). Rashi says the reference is to a box-shaped swelling just above the base. The meaning apparently is that the lump of gold was beaten out as if from the middle of the central stalk, one way towards the base and the other way towards to flower-shaped oil-cups. This explanation does exact justice to the Hebrew.

(j) THE PURIFICATION OF THE LEVITES **8.5–26**

The general opinion is that the nucleus of this section is verses 6–13, and that the rest consists of variants of these verses plus an expansion of 3.5–13.

6. cleanse them: the word *ṭāhēr* means 'cleanse ritually'. But the priests are 'sanctified' (*ḳiddēš*, RSV consecrated) (Exod. 28.41; Lev. 8.12). P regards the

Levites as 'taken from the people', but the priests as being apart from them from the beginning.

7. the water of expiation: lit. 'water of sin', de-sinning water. LXX and V have 'purification', whence AV 'purifying'. Rashi says it was water in which the ashes of the red heifer had been mingled (Num. 19). Also, all the hair of every part of the body had to be shaved off. See Herodotus, ii.37, where he says that Egyptian priests shaved their whole bodies every other day.

wash their clothes: here is another difference between Levites and priests. The priests had completely new clothes (Lev. 8.13).

11. offer . . . as a wave offering: RSV has tried to make the verse more intelligible by translating *wᵉhēnîp* (and he shall wave) by **and shall offer**, assuming that the original significance of the word and the ceremony have both been changed (see note on Lev. 7.4). The word does not mean 'wave'. It means 'special contribution' (*nûp* II), and especially a *tᵉnûpāh* is an offering allocated to the use and service of the whole priesthood. This is why the whole body of Levites is a *tᵉnûpāh*.

16–18. This is based on Num. 3.11–13. P has two theories concerning the origin of the Levites as secondary officials in the Temple. They were a substitute for the firstborn of Israel; they were wholly given *nᵉṯûnîm nᵉṯûnîm* (Num. 3.9) by the people. In either case, they were a *tᵉnûpāh*, for the service of the priesthood.

19. gift: Hebrew once more has *nᵉṯûnîm*, as in verse 16, and LXX has the word twice, as in verse 16.

to make atonement: the root *k-p-r* is here used in its original non-religious sense: cover. The Levites are to act as a screen between the Holy Place and the common people; compare the layout of the camp. In this way there would be no plague (*neḡep*, stroke, sudden smiting) breaking out against and among the people because of any infringement of the holy *taboo*.

21. purified themselves from sin: lit. 'de-sinned themselves'.

24. The lower age-limit for Levitical service is here twenty-five. See 4.3, where it is thirty.

to perform the work: Hebrew uses the root *ṣ-b-'* for both noun and verb (see 1.3). The reference is to active employment. In the next verse 'withdraw from the work of the service' could very well be translated 'retire from active service'.

(k) THE SUPPLEMENTARY PASSOVER 9.1–14

All its statutes and all its ordinances (verse 3) refer to Exod. 12, 34.25; Dt. 16.1–7. The chapter is a late stratum of the P-tradition. Here is case law. Some of the people were prevented by ritual uncleanness through contact with a corpse from keeping the Passover at the proper time. This was made the occasion of a general rule for this and other cases in which a man may be prevented from keeping the festival at the proper time.

2. keep the passover: Hebrew has the root *'-ś-h* (make), used regularly for the preparation of an animal for food (Gen. 18.7), but also for keeping the sabbath (Exod. 31.16), feasts (Dt. 16.10, 13), and festivals (Est. 9.31).

passover: for the meaning of the word and the significance of the festival, see Lev. 23.5.

3. in the evening: lit. 'between the two evenings' (see Lev. 23.5).

6. Moses and Aaron: this is followed immediately by 'to him', and Aaron is not mentioned elsewhere in this section. Apparently the name is a later addition.

7. kept: the root *g-r-'* means to take away a part from a whole. A small group is excluded from participation. Thus V has *fraudamur*; they thought they were unjustly deprived of their privilege as sons of Israel.

8. In all cases where there was no precedent, the case is adjourned till Moses makes special inquiry within the sanctuary, where God speaks to him (Exod. 25.22). This is an excellent illustration of the difference between *mišpāṭ* (judgment) and *tôrāh* (law, teaching, instruction). The *mišpāṭ* was primarily case law, a judgment established by precedent. If there was no precedent, the divine oracle (in Old Israel: sacred lot, etc.) had to be consulted, and this involved a *tôrāh* (instruction, law). Thus, the statement in 9.3–5 is a *mišpāṭ*, the law having been previously declared, but the law concerning the supplementary Passover is a *tôrāh*, a law now declared for the first time. Homiletical comments are given in the Palestinian Targum, which says that some judgments of Moses were deliberated, those concerned with life and death. In others, for instance those involving money, he was quick to decide. This was to teach the Sanhedrin two things: one, when to be slow in giving judgment and when to be quick; two, not to be ashamed to ask for advice.

11. unleavened bread and bitter herbs: the eating of bitter herbs at the Passover is probably an original Passover rite. The main reason is that eating the lamb and eating bitter herbs are both apotropaic rites. The eating of unleavened bread belongs to the Feast of *Maṣṣôṯ* (unleavened bread), and has to do with the first meal from the new harvest. The connection between the two begins with the establishment of the Central Sanctuary, and grows until, in New Testament times, the two celebrations are equated (Mk 14.1, 12). LXX identifies the bitter herbs with *pikris*, which is either succory (a type of chicory) or endive; V identifies them with wild lettuce.

12. Nothing is said about daubing some of the blood on the doorposts and lintel. Probably this custom was not involved in the supplementary rite.

13. The supplementary rite is not to be abused, and any man eligible to keep the rite on the proper date, and who is at home, must observe the rite or suffer the severest penalty—possibly death, possibly excommunication (Ezek. 18.32).

shall bear his sin: suffer the consequences of it, pay the penalty (see Lev. 5.1).

14. It is a feature of Israelite law that the resident alien shall be subject to the same laws as the native Israelite. He is the newcomer (cf. Old English and modern Cumberland 'offcomer'). Special care has to be taken that he must not be deprived of human rights, because, like the widow and the fatherless, he has no protector. He can share the privileges, but he has also to obey the rules.

(l) THE FIERY CLOUD **9.15–23**

This section is an extension of Exod. 40.34–38. This is the theophanic cloud which descended on the mount when God spoke with Moses (Exod. 19.9). The cloud was dark by day and luminous by night. This luminous cloud is a sign of the presence of God (Mt. 17.5, 24.30; Ac. 1.9). It is the Shekinah of later Jewish thought. The brightness declares God's majesty, the darkness shrouds his glory (1 Kg. 8.12).

15. cloud: the Hebrew is *'ānān*, which etymologically means 'appear, present oneself as an obstacle', and the Arabic *'anân* means 'clouds as intervening'. Mostly the various words for 'cloud' retain their etymological significance no more than the English word does, which properly is a *conglomeration* (cf. clod of earth), but in this case *'ānān* is exactly right. The cloud intervenes to shroud God's glory, and sometimes can be as blindingly bright by day as by night (cf. the Transfiguration).

16. by day: RSV rightly inserts this, which is in the major ancient versions and is probably an accidental omission in Heb.

22. a longer time: the Hebrew is *yāmîm*, and this in fact means a whole year (cf. Lev. 25.29), as Rashi points out.

(m) THE SILVER TRUMPETS **10.1–10**

These trumpets were made of beaten silver, and were long straight metal tubes with flaring ends and three to four feet long. See representations on the Arch of Titus and reproductions on Jewish coins. They were blown to bring the people to God's remembrance or to summon the people. For the latter of these there was a code of signals. Jewish tradition is that the *tᵉḳî'āh* (root is *t-ḳ-'*, RSV blow) was a protracted sound and the *tᵉrû'āh* (root *r-u-'*, RSV blow an alarm) was a succession of three tremolo notes. The Mishnah (*RH*, iv, 9) says a *tᵉḳî'āh* (sustained blast) was equal in length to three *tᵉrû'āhs* (quavering blast), but that three of the latter equalled three *yabbāḇā*'s (broken sound, *b. RH*, 34a).

2. breaking camp: this phrase is much better than 'the journeying of the camps' EVV, and is exactly right, since the verb *nāśa'* means 'pull up [tent pegs]'.

3. One long blast on two trumpets brought all the people together, but one long blast on one trumpet brought the leaders. For the time in the wilderness: long blasts for gathering, short quivering blasts for setting out. At the first *tᵉrû'āh* (rapid succession of three notes, RSV alarm), Judah and her two associate tribes set out, at the second Reuben, and so on.

9–10. In the Promised Land, the priests are to blow the silver trumpets in fighting against oppression, though all wars are always said by both sides to be against oppression and aggressors. They are also to be blown on all happy religious occasions, and this is most pronounced in the work of the Chronicler, 2 Chr. 20.18–23, 13.12, and also 1 Mac. 4.40, 5.33.

10. I am the LORD your God: this phrase was taken by the Jews as equivalent to the declaration of loyalty to the Kingdom of God (cf. Rabbi Aqiba and the opening sentence of the Shema' (Dt. 6.4) during the time of the Bar Kokba revolt in the time of Hadrian).

SECOND SECTION 10.11–20.13 WHAT HAPPENED IN THE WILDERNESS

This section contains all that survives concerning the journey through the desert. It is a mixture of J, J and E, mostly P editing and supplementing a combined JE tradition.

(a) THE ISRAELITES BREAK CAMP 10.11–28

Everything is done according to the instructions in Num. 2.1–31. We have the additional information that the Kohathites march behind the other Levitical families, so that the Tabernacle was already set up when they arrived.

11. The time spent in the Wilderness of Sinai was a few days under a year, from the first day of the third month to the twentieth day of the second month in the second year.

12. the wilderness of Paran: this was the home of Ishmael (Gen. 21.21 E). The exact location is uncertain, but it was definitely west of the Arabah, the great rift which continues south from the Dead Sea towards the Gulf of 'Aqaba. It was south of the Negeb (Num. 13.17) and between Midian and Egypt (1 Kg. 11.18). According to Grollenberg, *Atlas of the Bible*, map 9, p. 44, it is roughly the north-centre of the Sinai peninsula.

21. the holy things: EVV have 'the sanctuary', the natural translation of *miḳdāš*. The reference must be to the holy things of the sanctuary, and perhaps *kᵉlê* (vessels of) has been accidentally omitted. There is a similar difficulty in 18.29. Possibly we should read the plural *ḳoḏāšîm* (holy things).

(b) HOBAB RETURNS HOME 10.29–32

The name varies. In Jg. 4.11 he is Hobab. In Exod. 2.18 J he is Reuel, and here he is the son of Reuel. In Exod. 18.2 he is Jethro, but later in that chapter, verses 13–27, the name is not given, all E. Various harmonizing suggestions have been made, even to substituting 'brother-in-law' for 'father-in-law' (RV in Jg. 4.11). There are three separate traditions and three distinct names. Further, here he is a Midianite and so also in Exod. 2.16, 18 J, but in Jg. 1.16; 4.11 he is a Kenite. Also, Jg. 4.11 can be interpreted to infer that Hobab and his Kenites did not separate from Moses and his Israelites. There is a strong tradition that the Kenites settled among the Amalekites south of Judah (Jg. 1.16) and this is confirmed by Saul's warning to the Kenites before he massacred the Amalekites (1 Sam. 15.6). Modern scholars assume that whatever the name of Moses's father-in-law was, he was a Kenite: hence the 'Kenite hypothesis' as to the origin of the name Yahweh (cf. von Rad, *OTT*, i, p. 9).

29. father-in-law: strictly *ḥōṯēn* is the wife's father (not the husband's father), because he was originally the man who circumcised the bridegroom prior to the marriage in the days before circumcision, like baptism, became associated with birth rather than with maturity. Partly because of the variation of the traditions, the ancient versions have harmonized. LXX has *gambros*, which can mean any male in-law, as also V *cognatus*, any close male kinsman. T *ḥâm* originally meant husband's father, but by that time it could mean wife's father also.

do you good: that is, we shall share with you our coming good fortune.

31. you know how we are to encamp: a better parallel to the end of the verse (**serve as eyes for us**) can be secured by reading *hanḥōṯēnû* (to lead us) instead of *ḥᵃnôṯēnû* (our encamping). LXX paraphrases: 'you were with us in the wilderness and you will be our elder', *presbutēs*, but V has *ductor* (guide).

(c) THE PEOPLE SET OUT **10.33–36**

33. the mount of the LORD: elsewhere this phrase means Mount Zion. In J and P the name is Sinai, but in D and usually in E the name is Horeb. The phrase 'the mount of God' is also found in E, Exod. 3.1, etc. Possibly the editor has been influenced by the occurrence of the Sacred Name in this and the next verse, probably under the influence of D.

three days' journey: the second occurrence of this phrase says that the Ark kept a three days' journey ahead of the people. It is difficult to see any reason for this, and S substitutes 'one-day journey'. Either follow S or, better still, omit the phrase altogether as an accidental repetition.

34 looks like a clumsy attempt to harmonize the ancient tradition of supernatural movement with P's tradition of the cloud which acted as a signal.

35f. These verses have all the marks of great antiquity and date from the time when the Ark was the palladium, the object on which the success of Israel depended especially in time of war (1 Sam. 4.1–10; 2 Sam. 11.11). There is much to be said for Ps. 24 as a song celebrating the return of the Ark after victory in battle.

35. Arise: this is often used of attacking in battle, and especially of a sudden attack (Dt. 19.11; Ps. 27.3; Ob. 1, etc. See also Ps. 132.8, which is a modernization of the ancient battle-call).

36. Return: Budde suggested reading *šᵉḇāh* (dwell) for *šûḇāh* (return), but this involves a theological refinement similar to that in Ps. 132.8. The meaning is: return home after the victory to abide peacefully with Israel's countless people.

(d) THE PLACE CALLED TABERAH **11.1–3**

The journey through the wilderness was characterized by the grumbling and inconstancy of the people. This is the first of a series of incidents in this chapter and the next, all of which, except the story of Eldad and Medad, illustrate the ungratefulness of the people and the trials of Moses. The story of Taberah is generally held to belong to the E-tradition, mostly because of Moses as intercessor.

1. complained: this verb *'-n-n* is found elsewhere only in Lam. 3.39, but Accadian *unninu* means 'sigh'. Jewish tradition supposes that they were complaining of hunger (verses 4f.), and so some critics would read *rā'āḇ* (hunger) for *ra'* (misfortunes). Then, since they had plenty of meat (Exod. 12.38; Num. 32.1), the suggestion is that the verb is really *'-n-h*, and means 'were seeking a pretext' (2. Kg. 5.7).

the fire of the Lord: fire is a sign of the presence of God: the bush (Exod. 3.2), on Mount Sinai (Exod. 19.18), and often in Deuteronomy (4.11, etc.). He is 'like a devouring fire' (Exod. 24.17 E) and blazes out in destructive anger. Some seek the origin of the idea in tropical storms or electrical phenomena, but it is doubtful whether anything is to be gained by this type of modern rationalization. These stories belong to an age when a supernatural explanation of natural phenomena was accepted just as uncritically as any specious so-called scientific explanation is accepted by modern people. Fire is a natural metaphor for the terrible power of God among a people who live under the scorching sun.

3. Taberah: i.e. 'burning'. The site is unknown, though it is assumed in Grollenberg (*Atlas of the Bible*, map 9, p. 44) to be ten miles south-east of Mount Sinai.

(e) THE QUAILS AND THE MANNA **11.4–35**

Cf. Exod. 16 where, as here, the story of the flight of the quails and that of the manna are interwoven (11.4–15, 31–35, and 11.7–9). Here the J-tradition of the quails and the manna is interwoven with the E-tradition concerning the appointment of the seventy elders and particular emphasis on what happened to Eldad and Medad.

4. the rabble: the word *'asapsûp* is found only here and it describes the miscellaneous collection of people who came out of Egypt with the Israelites (cf. Exod. 12.38, where the word is *'ēreḇ*, from the root *'-r-b* I (mix)). So LXX which has *epimiktos*, whence the 'mixed multitude' of EVV. The trouble was started not so much by the Israelites, but by what V calls the *vulgus promiscuum*.

had a strong craving: the words mean 'strong desire, longing', not necessarily in a bad sense (Job 23.13; Ps. 132.13, 14).

5. fish: there is considerable evidence of fish as the staple diet of the poor in Egypt, and for others also. The fishermen in the Nile used both nets and lines (Isa. 19.8) and it is said that fish were exported to Palestine.

cucumbers, melons: LXX identifies these as two kinds of cucumbers, one eaten before it was ripe and the other when fully ripe. The cognate words in Arabic confirm EVV and RSV, a cucumber (*cucumis chate, L*) and a water-melon (*cucumis citryllus, L*), both well attested as cultivated in Egypt in both ancient and modern times.

leeks: the Hebrew *ḥāṣîr* means green-stuff generally, but in Aramaic it sometimes means leeks, and so LXX and V. The technical name is *allium porrum, L.* The fame of the Egyptian leeks spread to Rome (Pliny, *HN*, xix, 33) and Herodotus (ii, 125) writes of the radishes, onions, and leeks eaten by the workers on the pyramids. All the food mentioned in these verses was evidently the regular diet of slaves and the poor in ancient as in modern times.

6. strength: the Hebrew is *nepeš*, regularly translated 'soul' as EVV here, but 'strength' is much better here. The word can mean 'appetite', which is probably better still.

manna: this spelling is due to LXX, whereas V (*man*) transliterates the Hebrew. The P-tradition concerning the manna is in Exod. 16.13–36, where the whole affair is definitely miraculous. The P-editors here have not preserved any details of the J manna tradition.

7–9. This is an editorial insertion to explain what the manna looked like, what it tasted like, and how it was prepared for eating. It is the Arabic *mann*, a juice which exudes in heavy drops from the *ṭarfa* tree (*tamarix gallica mannifera*) in the western part of the Sinai peninsula towards the end of May and in June. It is sweet, sticky, dark yellow, and tastes like honey. If the Israelites left the wilderness of Sinai towards the end of the second month (10.11), this would bring them into the proper area at the proper time. The manna is a natural phenomenon. It falls to the ground during the night and melts with the heat of the sun. Out of this actual experience there has grown the tradition of the heavenly manna which God provided for them till they came to Canaan. The popular Hebrew explanation is in Exod. 16.15. The people said *man hû'* (what is it?), *man* being the old form of the classical Hebrew *māh*. Here the comparison with coriander seed is for size; in Exod. 16.31 it is for colour. The coriander is an umbelliferous plant with small grey-white seeds, which have a spicy flavour and are still used, like caraway seeds, to mix with bread and to give a flavour to sweets. It looked like bdellium, a gum-resin known to the Greeks (Gen. 2.12). Exod. 16.31 says the taste was like 'wafers made with honey'. Here the taste is said to be cakes rich with oil. LXX has *enkris*, a cake made with oil and honey. Hebrew says the taste was 'a *lāšād* of oil' (Ethiopic word means 'butter'; Arabic verb, 'suck, lick'). The Palestinian Targum explains by a sort of transubstantiation: when it came down on the ground it was like coriander, but when it was sanctified it was like bdellium.

8. mills: these were the household handmills, still to be seen in the Near East and in village India, consisting of the upper (rider) and lower millstone. The sound of the millstone is the common sound of home life (Jer. 25.10). LXX understood all this and used the word *mulē*, used in Homer (*Od.*, vii, 104) for the handmill turned by the women.

10–15. The story of verses 4–6 is now taken up again after the interlude mentioning the manna (cf. Exod. 16, J and P). The story is now concerned not only about the people longing for flesh, but also about Moses being overwrought and finding the sole responsibility for the people too much. Hence we have the introduction of the story of the seventy. Moses claims that God has treated him unfairly in expecting him to be able to deal himself with all the vagaries of the people. It is unreasonable to expect him to breast-feed them.

16–17. Moses is bidden choose seventy experienced elders and officers of the people.

16. officers: LXX translates *šōṭēr* as *grammateus* (scribe), following the basic meaning of the word (cf. Accadian and Arabic). Presumably the *šoṭer* was originally a scribe or secretary who developed into a subordinate official. This account is held to belong to the E-tradition, with Exod. 24.1, 9f. as a remnant of the J-tradition. **seventy:** perhaps the number 70 has a symbolic meaning here, since it is the number of all the nations on earth (Gen. 10), though LXX there makes it 72. Cf. Lk. 10.1–20 where Jesus chooses 70 (codd. B and D have 72). RSV and many moderns think that 72 is right in Lk. 10 on the ground that 'there would be a tendency to make 72 into a round number' (J. M. Creed, *The Gospel according to St Luke*, p. 144). The suggestion that Lk. 10.1–20 depends on Num. 11.16 is as old as pseudo-Clement (*Recognitions*, i, 40), but 70 is a frequent number in the Old Testament as a moderately large number and 72 can be accounted for as seven times twelve tribes. The general policy was to choose from each tribe equally (Num. 1.4, 13.2), and seven is the right number for a holy choice. It is difficult to see why the number should be changed to 72. There is an easier explanation. In Exod. 24.1 there are 72 if Nadab and Abihu are added, and in Num. 11.24, 26 Eldad and Medad are apparently additional to the 70. LXX both times has counted the extra two; Hebrew both times has not counted them.

17. The Rabbis (Sifre) pointed out that this is one of ten times in the Law where it is said that God 'comes down' to manifest himself on earth. Also, they point out that he talks with Moses and not with the seventy. Moses is still unique (Num. 12.8). **take some of the spirit:** the translation 'take from' is due to LXX and V, and is satisfactory, though the Hebrew root *'-ṣ-l* strictly means 'join with, share'. T takes the verb as a denominative from *'āṣîl* (chief, leader (Exod. 24.11)): 'and I will make them chiefs'. Here *rûaḥ* (spirit) is a supra-human power that can be assessed in quantity (cf. 2 Kg. 2.9f.). It is not conceived as being material, because the idea belongs to a time when the modern distinctions between 'personal' and 'impersonal', or between 'material' and 'spiritual', were not made. The idea of *rûaḥ* (spirit) here is akin to that of *mana* in primitive religion, also an animistic concept and so neither material nor spiritual, and neither personal nor impersonal. This 'spirit' possesses persons, not things; and so also the 'Spirit of the Lord'. See note on 5.14.

18–23. God now proceeds to deal with the people, but he promises to give them fresh meat in such quantity as to nauseate them. Their dissatisfaction with the manna is regarded as virtual rejection of God.

18. consecrate yourselves: the promised fresh flesh is a sacred meal and the people must be ritually clean in order to eat it (cf. Gen. 35.2; Exod. 19.10). Rashi refers to Jer. 12.3 where a similar hallowing is a preparation for punishment. In both cases (Jer. 12.3 and here) we have a 'sacrifice' (*zeḇaḥ*, the flesh is eaten by the worshipper as a sacred meal) provided by God himself. Cf. Isa. 34.6; Jer. 46.10; Ezek. 39.17, 19; Zeph. 1.7, 8, where God provides a sacred meal for the vultures as punishment for the victims. Here we have a sacred meal, but one for punishment and not for new life and strength.

20. becomes loathsome: the Hebrew *zārā'* is found only here and in the margin of Sir. 39.27 as a comment on 'evil': 'All these things are for good to the godly;

so to the sinners they shall be turned to evil.' Both instances deal with a gift of God that is double-edged: good to saints, evil to sinners. Possibly, we should compare Isa. 28.21, where God's deed to Israel becomes *zārāh* (strange, foreign) to them because of their wickedness. Cf. also Exod. 30.9 where incense which ought to be good can be *zārāh*, or the strange (*zārāh*) fire offered by Nadab and Abihu (Lev. 10.1; Num. 3.4, 26.61), which was completely destructive to them. LXX has *eis choleram*, which refers not so much to the cholera itself as to the sickness and diarrhoea associated with it. The idea of loathsomeness is due to V.

21. six hundred thousand: this is the number given in Exod. 12.37 as liable for military service.

22. The Palestinian Targum refers to 'the flocks of Araby and the cattle of the Nabataeans'.

23. hand shortened: for this idiom, see Isa. 50.2, 59.1. The phrase is not used except for 'the hand of the Lord', and is the opposite of it being stretched out to save (Exod. 6.6), and often. LXX has 'not sufficient' and V 'made ineffective'.

The Elders are Appointed **24–30**

Following the instructions of verses 16–17. Two of the seventy remained in camp, but they 'prophesied' just the seme.

25. came down in the cloud: this is not P's cloud, which stayed over the Tabernacle when the camp was stationary, but E's cloud of a special descent of God for a particular purpose.

they prophesied: this is the frenzy, the ungoverned behaviour erroneously equated with the mad frenzy of the dancing dervishes, who are a comparatively late development in Islam (cf. Saul, 1 Sam. 10.11, 19.20 and especially 19.23f.). See also 1 Chr. 25.1, 2, 3; 2 Kg. 3.15 for the use of music in producing this hypnotic state. See also 2 Kg. 9.11, where the soldier refers to the prophet as a *mešuggā'*. (madman). The theory is that all actions and words are controlled by a person. If therefore a man acts or speaks and is obviously not in control of himself, then some supernatural person must be in control. If he is a Yahweh-man or is in Yahweh's shrine, then it must be Yahweh who is controlling him. Similarly, the casting of the sacred dice is controlled by the God. No human person could make the marks on the liver of a newly opened animal, and such marks do not just happen. This is the theory of hepatoscopy. The sixty-eight to seventy men round the sacred tent were suddenly overcome by this divine frenzy, for the first and only time. It was their introduction into their sacred office, and comparable to the priestly installation.

26. Eldad: the name means 'God has loved' and is a genuine early formation (cf. Gray, *HPN*, pp. 61, 221). There was an Elidad, a prince of the Benjaminites, 34.21.

Medad: this name is not found elsewhere. LXX and S have the spelling Modad, which may well be the original, with the Hebrew spelling designed to produce an assonance (Gen. 4.20f.). Jewish tradition says that Eldad prophesied that Joshua was to succeed Moses, and hence Joshua's modesty in verse 28. There is also a tradition that they were both Jochebed's sons, whom she bore to the Zebulunite leader Elizaphan (34.25) after she had been divorced by Moses' father, Amram.

27. a young man: tradition identifies this young man with Gershom, son of Moses (so the Yalkut).

28. one of his chosen men: some LXX MSS have 'his chosen one', but S and T 'from his youth', which may well be correct.

29. jealous: it is sometimes difficult to decide whether the Hebrew *ḳānā'* means 'jealous' or 'zealous' (cf. 25.11, where AV has 'zealous' and RV and RSV have 'jealous'). Cf. the Greek *zēlos*, which normally is distinct from *phthonos* (envy) and sometimes is equated with it. The Arabic *ḳana'a* means 'become intensely red, black' and the Syriac *ḳannî'* 'become livid'. The verb is found with the two meanings in most Semitic languages. It means primarily 'get excited, worked up' either with zeal or with jealousy.

all the Lord's people . . . prophets: Moses does not desire in the least degree that the office of prophet shall be in any way limited. He wishes on the contrary that all men shall experience to an equally full degree the power of the spirit of God. The verse is usually allocated to the E-tradition and it is an outstanding example of the two types: the openness of the one, and the narrow exclusiveness of the priestly tradition. These two attitudes stand for two distinct types of religion (cf. Jer. 31.33f.).

31–35. The editor now returns to the quails and tells how God dealt with the people and their longing for fresh meat.

31. there went forth: the same verb (*nāsa'*) is used of the people pulling up their tent-pegs and setting out. This is the only place where this metaphor is used of God deliberately sending a wind. Other examples of sending a wind are Exod. 10.13, 19, 14.21 J and Gen. 8.1 P, and Ps. 104.4, 148.8; Jon. 1.4.

and it brought quails: the common quail (*coturnix communis*) is still called *salwā* in modern Egypt, and this identification is favoured by Josephus (*Ant. Iud.* III, i, 5), and by V *coturnix*. LXX has *ortogometra*, the land-rail (*rallus crex*), a bird which is said to accompany the common quail in its migrations. All authorities point out that this story is based on a regular annual phenomenon. These birds cross the eastern edge of the Mediterranean in considerable numbers in March and April, and back again to the south in September. They fly short distances at a time and are netted in considerable numbers (see *DB*, p. 826). They travel up the Red Sea, across the Sinai peninsula, and on towards the Jordan valley and north Palestine. It is said that eating to excess causes more than ordinary indigestion. The natural phenomonen has become part of the saga of Israel.

let them fall: the Hebrew is *wayyiṭṭoš*, which Jewish tradition translates as in Jg. 15.9; 2 Sam. 5.18, 22; Isa. 16.8, that the quails were spread out and covered a width of a two days' journey as they crossed the camp flying at a height of about three feet from the ground. So also V. This is more in accordance with the traditional method of netting these migratory birds.

32. The least quantity that any man gathered was over a hundred bushels. **spread them out:** most assume that the Israelites spread the dead quails out to dry in the sun (cf. Jer. 8.2 of bones so spread). This is strange if the trouble was caused by the birds being eaten fresh. Perhaps this is why some LXX MSS read *šāḥaṭ* (slaughter) instead of *šāṭaḥ* (spread out).

34. Kibroth-hattaavah: this has been identified tentatively with *Ruweis el-Ebeirig*, close to Taberah, a few miles north-east of Mount Sinai (Grollenberg, *Atlas of the Bible*, map 9, p. 44). The name means 'graves of craving'. All these identifications depend on a southern site for Mount Sinai. Similarly **Hazeroth** may be *'Ain Khuḍra*, a few miles farther on.

(f) MOSES IS UNIQUE **12.1–16**

This is an E-story designed to emphasize the uniqueness of Moses the prophet. Miriam is punished, but not Aaron, though he was equally guilty. Possibly Aaron was punished in the original E-tradition, but this is impossible to say. Certainly the P-tradition, and therefore the final editors of the Pentateuch, exalt Aaron to be at least the equal of Moses. It is in Jewish post-biblical tradition that the sin of Aaron is remembered, that he was the priest of the Golden Calf, and items in the ritual are often explained as a reminder and a warning of Aaron's leading part in the greatest of all the sins of apostate Israel.

1. the Cushite woman whom he had married: there is a strong tradition that she was an Ethiopian, and so LXX and V. Ancient Jewish tradition sought to identify this Cushite with Zipporah, referring to Hab. 3.7 where Cushan and Midian are mentioned. According to the homiletic system of gematria, the letters of *kûšîṯ* and those of *yᵉpaṯ mar'eh* both add up to 736, so the first word also means 'a woman of beautiful appearance' (the Sifre and T). The last phrase of the verse is omitted by V and T has there: 'because he had sent far away the fair woman he had married'. This means Zipporah (Exod. 18.2), where the usual translation is 'after he had sent her away', but the normal translation is 'divorced'. Thus another explanation is that he had divorced his former Cushite wife. There are many traditions about Moses, concerned as often in such cases, with the gaps in the record of his birth, youth, experiences in Egypt and in Ethiopia before he fled to the desert. In particular, he was commander-in-chief of a campaign against Ethiopia, when Tharbis, the king's daughter, saw him, fell in love with him, helped him to capture the city, and finally married him. It is impossible to say how much solid fact there is in these ancient tales. A popular account is to be found in E. Fleg, *Moses*.

3. meek: this word *'ānāw* usually refers to the humble, trustful attitude of the truly devout Israelite (Lk. 2.25; Ps. 37.11. See *DB*, 'meekness', p. 641). But here the context suggests that the meaning is 'modest and not self-assertive'. Certainly here, as elsewhere, it is God who insists on the uniqueness of Moses and resorts to stern measures to secure that recognition (see A. C. Welch, *Kings and Prophets of Israel*, pp. 45–62). There is considerable confusion between the two words *'ānāw* (humble, trustful) and *'ānî* (afflicted), both of them meaning 'poor', but the first denoting a state of mind, and the second a situation in life.

6–8. This oracle is in the regular 3:3 epic metre. The E-tradition is that God normally speaks to a prophet in dreams and visions, and often in enigmatic terms. Moses, however, is unique. God speaks to Moses directly, mouth to mouth and not in riddles.

6. a prophet among you: RSV here follows V, reading *nāḇî' bāḵem*. The Hebrew is 'if the Lord is your prophet', an obvious error.

7. my servant Moses: this term *'eḇeḏ* (servant, slave, worshipper) is used regularly of heroes of the faith: Abraham, Isaac, Jacob, etc., but mostly of David and Moses. It denotes an individual of particular devotion and loyalty to God. In Isa. 40–55, whatever the function of the Servant is, or his identity, certainly complete devotion of a unique kind is involved. Paul's New Testament equivalent is *doulos* (slave), but *pais* is used of the Holy Child, both from LXX.
entrusted with my house: this is a possible translation, meaning that Moses is in charge of the House of Israel, or, less likely, the sanctuary. Most prefer 'in all my house he is trustworthy'.

8. dark speech: following EVV. The Hebrew *ḥîḏāh* was a riddle, an enigmatic saying (LXX and V exactly) (cf. Arabic *ḥāda* (decline, turn aside, avoid)). Cf. 1 C. 13:12, where EVV have 'darkly' instead of the Greek 'riddle': RSV, in a mirror dimly.
the form: naturally the Versions avoid a strict translation here. LXX and S have 'glory'; V joins 'figures' with 'riddles'.

10. leprous: this is not true leprosy according to the levitical descriptions of 'leprous uncleanness' (Lev. 13.17), where, if a person is white all over his body, he is ritually clean. But the Hebrew does not say 'white as snow', merely 'as snow'. Only once is snow thought of as white in the Old Testament (Isa. 1.18). Usually snow is moist and wet, in which case 'like snow' could mean an open wound or ulcer, which is what is involved in Lev. 13. This fits in with 'flesh half-consumed' in verse 12, an effect of true leprosy.

11. Aaron acknowledges the supremacy of Moses and his uniqueness. But why was Aaron not punished also?

14. spit in her face: this is easily understood as a most insulting procedure (cf. Isa. 50.6; but Job 30.10 is different), but in Dt. 25.9 the public insult is part of the penalty. Here the seven days' exclusion is explained as public shame.

15. brought in again: LXX has 'was cleansed', connecting the isolation with the ritual of the cleansed leper (Lev. 14.9). The same word is used in 2 Kg. 5.6, 11 of Naaman being cured from his leprosy. The Talmud (*b. Soṭah*, 9b) says that the people waited for her as a reward for her having waited for Moses for a single hour when he was hidden in the bulrushes.

(g) THE SPIES 13.1–14.45

The story as we have it is composite, and doubly so. First, the J and E traditions have been woven together, and later the P-editor interwove a P-tradition. This P-tradition is found in 13.1–17a, 21, 25–26a (to 'Paran') 32 (to 'inhabitants') and 14.1–7, 10, most of 26–39. The JE-story is much the less ambitious. The twelve men, one from each tribe, set out from Kadesh and go as far as Hebron and the vale of Eshcol, whence they return with the wonderful bunch of grapes. They report a fruitful land, but say that the inhabitants are giants and too strong for them. Caleb alone is confident. His reward is to enter the land and for his descendants to occupy part of it (see also Dt. 1.36). In JE Caleb is a Kenizzite, and in 1 Sam. 30.14 the Negeb of Caleb is distinguished from the Negeb of the Cherethites and the Negeb of Judah. The JE-tradition continues with an abortive attack on the Amalekites and the Canaanites of the southern highlands. According to the P-tradition, the spies set out from the wilderness of Paran and penetrate the whole country as far as 'the entrance to Hamath'. They bring back a thoroughly bad account of the country, except for Joshua and Caleb, who report that it is fertile, 'a land which flows with milk and honey'. Joshua and Caleb. therefore, alone enter the Promised Land.

13.1–20. The spies are chosen, given their instructions, and sent away. These leaders, apart from Caleb and Joshua, are not mentioned elsewhere, though half the names are found elsewhere. It is by no means certain that the names have been preserved correctly. The probable meanings of the names are discussed in Gray *HPN*.

17. The Negeb is the rough waterless country south of Judaea, now irrigated on a large scale by Israeli determination. The word itself means 'dry, parched' (cf. Aramaic), but often it is used to denote the south. Hence AV has created confusion here by 'southward', whereas actually they were to move north into the Negeb.

19. camps or strongholds: Moses wanted to know whether the Canaanites lived in encampments (tents) or in towns with walls.

20. first ripe grapes: this fixes the time as the end of July.

21. This verse is from the P-tradition, but 22–24 are JE.

the wilderness of Zin: this is an area just over twenty miles south-west of the southern end of the Dead Sea and north-west of the Edomite hill-country of Seir. It is to be distinguished from the Wilderness of Sin (Hebrew *sîn* with a *sāmeḵ*; Zin is Hebrew *ṣin* with a *ṣāḏē*), which is said to be to the west of the Sinai peninsula, some fifty miles from the southern tip. See Grollenberg, *Atlas of the Bible*, map 9, p. 44, but this is assuming the southern site for Mount Sinai.

Rehob: or Beth-rehob (2 Sam. 10.6), is west of Hermon and close to the city of Laish-Dan (Jg. 18.27–29).

the entrance of Hamath: most modern scholars do not translate the Hebrew, and read Lebo-hamath as the name of the city, some sixty miles farther north-north-east from Beth-rehob along the valley between Lebanon and Anti-lebanon. The pass is eight or nine miles wide. Lebo-hamath is over the pass and close to the source of the Orontes, which flows north from here, and finally turns west to reach the sea about thirty miles north of ancient Ugarit.

22. This and the next two verses form JE's account of the spies.
Hebron is an ancient sacred site twenty miles south of Jerusalem. It is the modern *el-Khalîl* and was the ancient capital of the south. Here all three patriarchs were buried, and Sarah, Rebekah, and Leah. What Shechem was to the north, Hebron was to the south. Here David first set up his kingdom and reigned for seven years. The name itself means 'confederacy'; the earlier name was Kiriath-arba (city of four, Gen. 23.2; Jos. 14.15). Tradition said it was built seven years before the Egyptian Tanis (see Zoan, next verse).
the descendants of Anak: these were the 'long-necked ones' but M. Noth (*Joshua*, p. 63) thinks they were so called because they wore necklaces. Old Testament writers think of them as of enormous height, and LXX in verse 33 says they were giants. According to 2 Sam. 21.18–22 there were four descendants of these giants of old, all slain by David's warriors.

Zoan is identified with Tanis, as the Greeks called it. At one time it was Avaris, capital of the Hyksos Pharaohs (1720–1570 B.C.), who were expelled by Ahmose I, founder of the 18th dynasty. The fortifications were strengthened by Seti I (19th dynasty, 1308–1290 B.C.) and it was a royal residence in the time of Ramses II (1290–1223 B.C.). Here the giant statue of Ramses was found. The modern site is *Ṣân el-Ḥagar*. It is not possible to say what 'seven years before Zoan' means. The site is very ancient and much earlier than 2000 B.C.

23. the Valley of Eshcol: this is not certainly identified, but some think it is the modern *Beit Ishkahil*, about four miles north-west of Hebron. Eshcol means 'cluster'. Possibly the story is aetiological and the story arose because of the name of the valley.

26. Kadesh: this is the modern *'Ain Qadeis*, fifty miles south of Beer-sheba. In Num. 32.8 it is Kadesh-barnea, and so in D. In Gen. 14.7 it is *'Ain Mišpāṭ* (Well of Judgment), and in Num. 27.14 it is Meribah of Kadesh. Clay Trumbull (*Kadesh-Barnea*, pp. 272f.) re-identified the site eighty years ago, and found still two ancient wells and some pools. One of these pools is *'Ain Qedeirât*, where there are ruins of an early fort dating from the early monarchy. The site is now a successful experimental farm run by the Egyptian government (J. Gray in *DB*, p. 546). Kadesh, according to JE, was the centre round which the tribes settled for most of the time between Egypt and Canaan, and therefore many have thought that the site of Mount Sinai must be sought near here. The name means 'sanctuary' and there are at least three other places of this name in the Old Testament: Kedesh in Galilee (Jos. 20.7), Kedesh in Issachar (1 Chr. 6.72 (Heb 57)), and Kadesh, the great Hittite capital on the Orontes and the site of the famous battle between Ramses II and the Hittites (2 Sam. 24.6 (RSV, following LXX)).

27. flows with milk and honey: this is the traditional phrase for the fruitfulness of the Promised Land: and it is found in J first, then in D (seven times), once in H (Lev. 20.24), twice in Jeremiah, and twice in Ezekiel. Some say the origin is the idea that in earliest times 'milk and honey' were the food of the gods, like nectar and ambrosia, but such a suggestion looks like wishful anthropological thinking. Both the milk (*ḥālāḇ*, fresh milk) and the honey (*d*[e]*ḇaš*) are characterized by flowing freely. For **'honey'**, see Lev. 20.24.

29. The Amalekites: these were a nomad tribe of considerable strength who raided from the deserts south of the Negeb. They were there long before the Hebrews (24.20), and were always at enmity with them. Saul sought to massacre them all, and even Agag was struck down in the end (1 Sam. 15). According to 1 Chr. 4.42f. there were still Amalekites among the Edomites in the time of Hezekiah, but a band of Simeonites, 500 strong, destroyed them.

the Hittites: according to Hebrew traditions, these peoples were one of the seven nations of Canaan. It is only in comparatively recent times that it has been realized they were once a nation comparable in power to Egypt at its strongest. There are two traces only of this greatness in the Old Testament: Jos. 1.4 and Ezek. 16.3. The Hittite Empire was established in Asia Minor *c.* 1800 B.C. and was at its greatest from *c.* 1380 B.C. They conquered the Mitanni in Asia Minor and Upper Mesopotamia, and penetrated as far south in Syria as the Hamath-Kadesh pass, where the indecisive battle with the Pharaoh was fought in 1286 B.C. Their power declined from 1200 B.C. and it may well be that the Hittites whom the Israelites found in Canaan were the remnants of this once powerful people. It is said that the characteristic facial features of the Jew are Hittite rather than Semitic in origin, and this seems to be shown by a comparison of Hittite and Jewish bas-reliefs. See *DB*, p. 386.

the Jebusites: these were the original inhabitants of Jebus, or Jerusalem, and were still in possession of the city until David captured it (2 Sam. 5.5–9). The statement of Jg. 1.8 must be a later idealization.

the Amorites: these were one of the original peoples of Canaan; indeed the whole area was called Amurru by the Babylonians. Their original home was North Syria, but by the end of the nineteenth century they were masters of the whole of Mesopotamia. The great Hammurabi was an Amorite, and so also was Zimri-Lim of Mari, where in recent years French archaeologists have made many important discoveries. Many of the early codes of law, such as the famous Code of Hammurabi, were Amorite, and early Hebrew law was apparently based on it. The Hittites succeeded the Amorites as the dominant power, but remnants lived on. Og king of Bashan and Sihon king of Heshbon were Amorite kings. Solomon is said to have forced the remnants of the western Amorites into his labour gangs (1 Kg. 9.20f.). In the E- and the D-traditions 'Amorites' is the regular name for all the pre-Israelite inhabitants of Canaan; the J-term is 'Canaanite'.

the Canaanites: these were the inhabitants of the low country, that is, the coastal plain and the Jordan valley.

33. the Nephilim: this name occurs twice: here of the very tall men (LXX and V, giants) who were aborigines in Canaan, and in Gen. 6.4 of the demi-gods who were born to the sons of God by mortal women. Evidently the JE-tradition identified the Anakim as descendants of the mythical demi-gods.

grasshoppers: these locusts at the hopper stage were allowed as legitimate food

(Lev. 11.22). Whether John the Baptist ate these locusts or locust beans is a question which may never be settled.
and so we seemed to them: there is a suggestion to read not *kēn* (so) but *kēn* (gnats), as Isa. 51.6 (RSV, RVm) and the plural in Exod. 8.13.

How the People received the Report of the Spies **14.1–10**

Once more the people are full of complaints and wish they had never left Egypt: Exod. 14.10–12 E, 16.3 P; Num. 20.4–13 JE and P—thus from all three traditions. Here, in the P-tradition the rebellion is against Moses and Aaron, and they and Caleb and Joshua plead with the people. In the JE-tradition the rebellion is against God, and Moses and Caleb plead with the people.

3. little ones: the collective noun *ṭap* (root *ṭ-p-p*, take quick, little steps) includes all the little 'toddlers' (Dt. 2.34; Num. 31.17 (small boys), 31.18 (small girls)).
go back to Egypt: this is what the Israelites must never do (Hos. 11.5; Dt. 17.16). Egypt is always the source of Israel's greatest woe, and the final punishment is to be driven back there with whips (Dt. 28.68). Thus one of the most remarkable passages in the Old Testament is Isa. 19.23–25, where Israel, Egypt, and Assyria are united.

4. captain: following EVV. Hebrew is *rō'š* (head, leader).

5. fell: the verb strictly means a swift, sharp descent: Am. 3.5 of the sudden swoop of a bird into a trap; in Gen. 24.64 (RSV alighted from) of Rebekah's hurried descent from her camel. Here, Moses and Aaron fling themselves on the ground in agonized appeal: V and DV have 'fell flat (*prone*) on the ground'.

9. they are bread for us: in modern colloquial English, 'they are our meat'.
protection: the Hebrew *ṣal* (shadow) is a metaphor for protection which has much more meaning for those who live under a tropical sun than for us. See Isa. 32.2.

10. the glory of the Lord: this is P's regular phrase for a theophany. In so far as God may be said to have a body (which definitely is not so), it is this Splendour, this Magnificence, which serves both to display his glory and shroud his *numen*.

11. believe in me: the Hebrew *he'ᵉmîn* means 'rely upon, trust in', and not 'believe in' in the sense of assent. This is why Paul uses *pistis* to mean 'faith' in the sense of trust, full reliance.
signs: the word *'ôṯ* (sign) has a special meaning as a sign or token of God's power for good or for ill. Particularly, as in the exodus stories, it is a sign of the presence and activity of God the Saviour. This is the sense in which the miracles of the Gospel according to St John are signs (*sēmeion*). Thus, both the rainbow (Gen. 9.12 P) and circumcision (Gen. 17.11 P) are signs of the covenant, which is the instrument through which God exercises his saving grace on behalf of Israel both in salvation and in preservation. See further, C. A. Keller, *Das Wort OTH als 'Offenbarungszeichen Gottes'* (1946).

12. the pestilence: LXX has 'death', following an earlier meaning of *deḇer* (Arabic *dabr*, departure, death). The rendering of RSV is from V through EVV.

The Black Death was the pestilence which caused such havoc in England in the fourteenth century A.D.

13–26. Moses pleads with God on behalf of the people. Moses and Samuel are the two great intercessors (Jer. 15.1; Sir. 46.16). Some moderns think this section is later than the rest, perhaps early seventh century, but such comments belong rather to the strictly literary type of criticism. The section is certainly pre-P.

13. It is perhaps better to treat this verse as the protasis of a hypothetical sentence, with verse 14 as the apodosis. 'If the Egyptians . . . (for thou . . . them), they will tell. . . .' (S. R. Driver, *Hebrew Tenses*, pp. 185–87: double perfect-with-*waw*-consecutive).

14. face to face: here and Isa. 52.8 are the only two places where this phrase is found (Dt. 19.21 is *lex talionis*). The phrase means 'close-up' in the photographic sense, and is expressive of closest intimacy, God's absolute imminence. For the important difference between 'imminence' and 'immanence', see *ET* 68, 1956–57, 68–71.

14b. It is thought that this verse contains elements from various sources (Exod. 13.21, 33.9f.; Num. 10.34), and the similarity between verse 18 and Exod. 34.6f. J has suggested 'a late JE' date for the section.

15. thy fame: cf. Isa. 53.1 where the translation is 'what we have heard'. Certainly something more is required here than the ordinary 'report, news, what we have heard'. LXX has 'thy name', possibly reading the consonants *š-m-k*, possibly deliberately ignoring the letter *'ayin*.

16. has slain them: LXX has 'scattered them' (cf. the exactly similar variation in the story of the quails, 11.32).

18. This verse is a shortened version of Exod. 34.6–7. V follows the Hebrew but the other ancient versions keep closer to Exod. 34.6–7.

slow to anger: the Talmud (*b. San.*, 111a) tells a story of how Moses expected this to be towards the righteous only, but God insisted it was towards the wicked also and there would come a time when Moses would need the latter. This 'forbearance' of God is a most important element in God's dealings with men.

steadfast love: the word *ḥeseḏ* traditionally has been translated 'lovingkindness, mercy' under the influence of LXX *eleos* and V *misericordia*. Modern scholars recognize a basic element of constancy, steadfastness embedded in the word (*DIOT*, pp. 94–106, *DB*, p. 595). G. A. Smith favoured 'leal-love' as including two essential elements of love and loyalty. H. G. May (*Peake's Commentary on the Bible*, rev. ed., §251i) says it 'has overtones of loyalty and commitment'. A. R. Johnson in his important article 'ḤESEḎ and ḤĀSÎḎ' (Mowinckel Festschrift, *Interpretationes ad Vetus Testamentum* . . ., etc., 1955, pp. 100ff.) favours the meaning 'devotion', though sometimes it has overtones of compassion or sympathy. The range of the word therefore is generally agreed to be between 'steadfastness, reliability' on the one hand and the 'lovingkindness, mercy' of EVV, but inclining more towards the former meanings. The word comes to stand for God's unchanging love for erring and undeserving Israel, and for God's determination to be faithful to the covenant however unfaithful Israel may be. This develops into the NT *charis*, with its additional emphasis on the fact that all God's favour is undeserved. Further, since to the Hebrew 'truth' (*'ᵉmeṯ*) is not a proposition to be accepted so much as something to be relied upon, we often get *ḥeseḏ* and *'ᵉmeṯ* together (cf. 'grace and truth' Jn 1.14).

forgiving iniquity: much here depends on the translator's theory of the atonement. The word translated 'forgive' is the root *n-ś-'* (lift up, carry, carry away) and *'āwôn* (iniquity), like the other words for 'sin', can mean the consequences of it. The meaning can be 'taking away the punishment', which may be best here, since the next phrase has to do with clearing the guilty. The meaning may be 'carry away the sin', so that it is no longer between man and God (cf. the sin-offering ceremony). Further, the 'but' could at least as easily be 'and'.

transgression: the word *peša'* means 'rebellion', an important difference, since 'transgression' tends to involve breaking rules, but 'rebellion' is against a person.

the guilty: following EVV and ultimately LXX, which add this. V and DV have 'leaving no man clear'. The root is *n-ḳ-h*, used in Semitic languages generally in ritual senses, e.g. Accadian 'pour a libation'. But see Isa. 3.26; Zech. 5.3 (twice), where the word is used of clearing out liars and perjurers. Here, he will not endlessly purge them out, but limits the penalty to the fourth generation.

visiting: in the P-tradition this root *p-ḳ-d* means 'appoint, muster, number', but not 'visit' in this sense of divine intervention. The P-editors are transcribing earlier sources.

19. forgiven: possibly a double meaning is intended, since the verb *nāśā'* can mean 'forgive' a person and also 'carry, bear', its primary meaning. Cf. Exod. 19.4; Dt. 32.11, God carrying Israel as on eagle-vulture's wings.

21. RSV rightly follows RV here in making the whole of this verse the binding element in the oath. The 'because' in EVV at the beginning of verse 22 is wrong. The *kî* introduces the substance of the oath, as RSV has seen.

22. put me to the proof: this is much better than the 'tempted' of EVV. The word *nisseh* is a neutral word and means 'put to the test' with either good or bad intent, and similarly the Greek *peirazō*. This sometimes means 'test' (e.g. the noun, Mt. 6.13) and sometimes 'tempt' (Mt. 4.1) in the sense of entice into sin. The Satan of the Old Testament started by being the Tester, but by the time of the prologue of Job he had become cynical. In Zech. 3.1 he is man's accuser, and by 1 Chr. 21 he is active against God, ultimately to become the king of the counter-kingdom of evil.

these ten times: meaning 'over and over again' (Gen. 31.41, etc.). But the Rabbis actually enumerated ten times when Israel tested God: twice at the Red Sea, twice over the manna, etc (*b. Arakh.*, 12a).

23. At the end of this verse LXX has a passage based on Dt. 1.39, anticipating verse 31.

24. he has a different spirit: this is a modernization of the original, which has 'because another *rûaḥ* was with him'. He was controlled by a different spirit from that which motivated the rest. See note on 11.17 for this psychological use of *rûaḥ*.

25. These were not the Amalekites and the Canaanites of the hill-country (verse 45), but those who dwelt in the two valleys, the maritime plain (called a 'valley' *'ēmeḳ* in Jg. 1.19, 34) and the Jordan valley (Jos. 13.19, 27). There is no need for any interpolation. The people had to set out southwards, so as to go round the Amalekites and come into Canaan from the east.

28. says the Lord: this is the famous 'Thus saith the Lord' *n^{e}'ûm '^{a}ḏōnāy* of the Prophets, found rarely elsewhere, but often there, especially in Jeremiah (162 times). The word *n^{e}'ûm* is found in the Balaam oracles in Num. 24, which see.

as I live: this is the common form of the oath when God is represented as the speaker. It is found twice only (here and verse 21) in the Pentateuch, but is common in Ezekiel (sixteen times). The common form as used by men is 'as the Lord liveth', and this is common in 1 and 2 Samuel, 1 Kings, and Jeremiah.

30. I swore: lit. 'I lifted my hand', the usual gesture in many countries and times of swearing an oath.

31. they shall know: LXX has 'they shall possess it' which may well be right; reading *w^{e}yār^{e}šû*, which is not markedly different from *w^{e}yāḏ^{e}'û* so far as the Hebrew consonants are concerned. The alternative is to think of the root *y-d-'* as involving intimate personal knowledge, so that they 'knew' the land as men know the Cotswolds (J. B. Priestley, *The Good Companions*, ch. 2: 'man . . . has been content. Yes, these two [i.e. Nature and man] signed a peace here, and it has lasted a thousand years').

33. shepherds: the Jewish exegesis is 'wanderers', whence V and then EVV, possibly all influenced by 32.13.

shall suffer for your faithlessness: lit. 'shall bear the penalty of your whoredoms'.

34. displeasure: all the versions had difficulty with this word *t^{e}nû'āṯî* (my opposition, frustration). Ancient Jewish tradition insisted it means not 'my estrangement from you' but 'your estrangement from me'. LXX boldly paraphrases with 'the anger of my wrath', and V has 'my vengeance'. Heb certainly involves active opposition on God's part.

36–37. The ten spies died of a sudden plague, a clear sign of the divine displeasure.

39–45. The people determine to do what they ought to have done at first, but it is now too late, and they meet with disaster.

44. they presumed: following EVV. There are two roots *'-p-l*; the first corresponds to the Arabic *'afala* (? swell), whence *'ōpel* can mean 'tumour' and 'rounded hill', and the second corresponding to the Arabic *ǵafala* (be reckless, headstrong), which is most likely the meaning here. The ancient versions guess, and Rashi's 'insolence' is good.

45. pursued: the root is *k-t-t*, crush by beating. LXX has 'cut them in pieces', but Rashi is right: 'pounded them, blow upon blow'.

Hormah: the word means 'complete destruction'. The masculine form is *ḥērem*, the sacred ban which involved a complete massacre. The place has been tentatively identified with the modern *Tell el-Mishash*, ten miles east of Beer-sheba (Grollenberg, *Atlas of the Bible*, map 14, p. 65).

(h) RULES CONCERNING SACRIFICES, AND OTHER MATTERS **15.1–41**

The P-editors have grouped five sets of instructions: 1–16, the necessary quantities of flour, oil, and wine for the various offerings; 17–21, details of first-fruit cakes; 22–31, some rules about the sin-offering largely independent of Lev. 4.1–3 and chapter 13; then 32–36, the fate of the sabbath-breaker; 37–41, the tassels to be worn on the fringes of cloaks. The first four are from the P-tradition, but the latter may well contain H-elements.

The Proper Grain- and Drink-offerings **1–16**

There were occasions when a *minḥāh* (grain-offering) was presented independently, but this section deals with those which accompanied the *'ôlāh* (whole-offering) and with the accompanying drink-offering. There is another list of quantities in Ezek. 46.5–15, in which all the quantities are standardized, though the amount required with the lamb was voluntary. See the comparative list in Gray, *ICC*, p. 170. In the Numbers list, the quantities increase with the size of the animal: one tenth ephah for a lamb, two tenths for a ram, three tenths for a young bull. Similarly for the oil: one quarter hin for a lamb, one third for a ram, one half for a bull. The quantities of wine for the drink-offering are exactly similar. In the Ezekiel list there is a standard one sixth ephah of grain, and a standard one hin of oil. There is no drink-offering in this list.

3. The *'iššeh* (offering by fire) includes everything that was burnt on the altar, the whole body of the *'ôlāh* (whole-offering), or the independent *minḥāh* (grain-offering), or any token taken from a *minḥāh*. The *neḏer* (vow) and the *nᵉḏāḇāh* (freewill) are types of the *zeḇaḥ* (sacrifice) none of which went to the altar, apart from the blood and the fat.

5. **the drink offering:** nothing is said in the Old Testament concerning the manner of this rite. In ancient Greece and Rome the custom was to pour the wine over the sacrificed animals, and some have assumed that this was the Israelite custom also. According to Sir. 50.15 and Josephus (*Ant. Iud.* III, ix, 4), the drink-offering was poured out at the foot of the altar.

13–16. Once again it is laid down that the 'stranger', the foreigner who has settled permanently in Israel, has both equal rights and corresponding obligations. This word *gēr* later became the regular term for the proselyte, the convert to Judaism from paganism, and this is the regular rendering of LXX.

16. one law and one ordinance: this phrase is inclusive, involving both *tôrāh* (law: a new judicial decision) and *mišpāṭ* (ordinance: a decision based on precedent).

The Offering of the First Kneading **17–21**

This offering was a *ḥallāh* (perforated cake) from the first meal, straight from the threshing floor. This is the type of cake in common use in the Temple: eaten in the shared meal, constituted the shew-bread. It was not burned on the altar, but was a *t^e^rûmāh*, i.e. it was the perquisite of the priesthood as a whole.

20. the first: Jewish tradition says that the first action on proceeding to prepare the meal for baking must be to set aside the proper portion. This is fixed by the Mishnah (*Ḥull.*, i, 1; ii, 7) as one twenty-fourth for home baking and one forty-eighth for the public baker.

coarse meal: following RVm, and depending on the Syriac *'arsānā'* (hulled barley). The meaning of the Hebrew *'^a^rîsāh* is uncertain. LXX and so EVV depend on the Talmudic use of *'arsān*, which is a dough made from barley-meal or wheat-meal and suitable for invalids and children. Another meaning is 'kneading-trough' or 'a batch of loaves from one kneading trough', and this seems best: from the first batch of your baking.

Laws Concerning the Sin-offering **22–31**

The general opinion is that here are laws older and less developed than those of Lev. 4.1–35, 5.7–13, and they come from a different group. Here there are two types of offender, the whole people and a particular individual. In Leviticus there are four types. Here, the victim is always a yearling goat, a male or a female; there the victims are graded according to the status of the offender. Here there is no provision for the poor; in Lev. 5.7–13 there is provision made for the poor. The fact that no whole-offerings are mentioned in Lev. 4.1–5.13 is of no account, since in that section the editors are concerned with sin-offerings only and do not mention any other offering except when they must (Lev. 5.7). There is another possible explanation for the differences between the two passages, and it is as follows: the Leviticus passage is dealing with sin-offerings in general, but this particular passage is dealing with unwitting mistakes to do with the offerings of the kneading-trough, verses 17–21.

25. make atonement: i.e. perform the cleansing, propitiatory rite.

30. with a high hand: the phrase means 'proudly, triumphantly' in Exod. 14.8; Num. 33.3, but here deliberate sin, done arrogantly against God. It is the sin of pride, one of the seven deadly sins, but actually the greatest sin of all, since it is the insolence (the Greek *hubris*) of the man who sets himself up against God. Almost all the great Greek tragedies are concerned with man's *hubris* and the inevitable disaster it brings. Basically this is why, in ancient Israelite law, the offender is cut off from the people. It is not so much because his sin is deliberate as that it is defiant. See Gen. 11.1–9; Isa. 14.13f.

The Man who Broke the Sabbath **32–36**

Here is an example of 'sin with a high hand' and the story is added here by way of example. A similar piece of legislation is given in Lev. 24.10–23. The case is adjourned until an oracle (*tōrāh*, instruction from God) can be obtained, and when this decision has been given, it stands as a 'judgment' (*mišpāṭ*) for future guidance.

The penalty of stoning to death avoids the shedding of blood and the consequent blood-guilt. The deliberate hubristic nature of this offence is the point of the saying in Lk. 6.5 (cod. D) to the man who was working on the sabbath: 'Man, if you know what you are doing, you are blessed: but if you do not know, you are accursed, and a transgressor of the law.'

34. made plain: see Lev. 24.12 where the same root is used, but there translated 'should be declared'. Rashi says that the Israelites knew very well that the penalty was death, but they had not had explained to them what was the manner of death.

The Law concerning Tassels **37–40**

This section is held to be H in origin, in view particularly of verse 41. There is a double tradition concerning the *ṣîṣîṯ*. Some say it means 'fringe' and others say it means 'tassel'. LXX has *kraspeda* (edges, hems) and so T. Hence the 'hem, border' of EVV in Mt. 9.20, 14.36 (RSV has 'fringe'). In Ezek. 8.3 the meaning is 'lock', though the Arabic *naṣîyat*, which is sometimes quoted, means either 'lock' or 'fringe' (bang). In Dt. 22.12 the name is *geḏîlîm* (RSV 'tassels'). This word means something that is twisted as a string of onions is twisted, and it is used of the festoons worked on the capitals of columns (1 Kg. 7.17). Rashi says they are called *ṣîṣîṯ* because they hang down, but this explanation seems to have no ancient support. The Hebrew *kānāp* (here translated 'corner') means anything like a wing: extremity, corner, edge, hem, but all as flying out. Gray (*ICC*, pp. 184f.) is in no doubt about the matter and says it was a tassel and not a continuous fringe. There were tassels on Egyptian garments and fringes on Assyrian garments. The most likely solution of the problem is that the *ṣîṣîṯ* was a fringe round all four edges of the garment, but that the threads were twisted together in groups so as to form a fringe of tassels like the large overhanging cloths which covered Victorian and Edwardian tables, or like their counterpanes. According to Jewish tradition, there were eight threads and five knots in each tassel. This was because the numerical value of *ṣîṣîṯ* is 600, and this plus 13 makes 613, the number of the commandments of the Law. This, they said, is how verse 40 can be fulfilled. It is generally maintained that the custom was originally connected with the idea of amulets, but that, as in numerous other cases the Hebrews adapted it and provided a religious significance. See *HDB*, ii, pp. 68–70, and for modern times, *JEn*, ii, p. 76.

39. follow: the word is *tûr*, which is the word used of the spies spying out the land. The original meaning of the word was 'turn about, turn back', hence LXX 'turn back', and hence RSV here. But AV had 'seek after' (cf. RVm), which preserves some of the 'spy' nuance. Perhaps 'nose after' is better.

(i) THE REBELLIONS OF KORAH AND OF DATHAN AND ABIRAM **16.1–50** (Heb 16.1–17.15)

This is the opening chapter of the thirty-eighth *sidrah* (lesson) for the Reading of the Law in the synagogues, and the corresponding *haftarah* (reading from the Prophets) is 1 Sam. 11.14–12.22, which is the larger part of Samuel's speech at the renewing of the kingdom. He recounts the repeated rebellions of the people against God in that they wanted a king like the nations. The choice is governed by the idea that God alone is king over Israel, so much so that even in 2 Sam. 7, the seed-bed of the dream of the Davidic Messiah, the word 'king' is avoided. Further, to seek any other king is a rebellion against God equal to the great rebellion of Korah.

This chapter is certainly composite. The stories of two mutinies are interwoven. Korah and some Levites mutinied against the exclusive right of Aaron to the priesthood. Two Reubenites, incidentally descendants of Jacob's first-born son, rebelled against the authority of Moses. The rebellion of Korah is from the P-tradition; that of Dathan and Abiram is from the JE-tradition. The JE-material is in verses 1b, 2a, 12–15, 25–36, 27b–32a, 33–34. Dathan and Abiram complained that Moses had set himself up as prince. Further, he had not fulfilled his promises and duty, and brought them into the Promised Land with its fruitful fields and vineyards. Their punishment was that the earth miraculously opened and swallowed them up, they, their households, and all their property. The P-material is to be found in verses 1a, 2b–11, 16–24, 27a, 35–50. But in this there are two distinct strands. In what is apparently the older story, the claim is that all Israelites are equally holy, and no man has the right to exalt himself above the rest as having special status in the eyes of God (verses 2b–7). Korah and his 250 supporters take a censer each and stand at the entrance of the Tent of Meeting (verses 18–24), but fire bursts out from God and consumes them (verses 27a, 35). The people murmur at this slaughter and an angry God bursts out so that many die forthwith of the plague, but Aaron rushes forward with truly sacred incense burning on fire taken properly from the altar and the plague is stayed, though not until 14,700 are dead 'beside those who died in the affair of Korah' (verses 35, 41–50). In the later story, the protest is against some Levites who seek to exalt themselves above the rest of the Levites and made themselves exclusively the priests. This group is centred round Aaron (verses 8–11). As before, the malcontents take their own censers; and Moses and Aaron take up their own censers (verses 16–17). After the blaze, Eleazar son of Aaron picks up the bronze censers which Korah and his company had held, and hammered them out to make a bronze covering for the altar. The bronze on the altar is henceforth to be a perpetual reminder that no man who is not a proper priest, a descendant of Aaron, shall come near to the altar (verses 36–40).

It is probable that in this later P-story we have a reflection of the struggles of the immediate post-exilic period, when the Zadokites and the Aaronites established themselves as priests. See further, pp. 13f. The probability is that, being Levites, once the Korahites were full priests, but ultimately they had to be content to be doorkeepers (Pss. 42.4 'led the throng', 84.10). Certainly they were once Temple-singers (cf. the Korahite psalms, 42–49, 84, 85, 87, 88).

1f. Now Korah . . . took men: there is no word for 'men' in the Hebrew, and this (or some such word) has to be inserted because *l-ḳ-ḥ* (take) is a transitive verb. The ancient versions attempt to solve the difficulty in various ways, but the best solution is proposed by I. Eitan, *A Contribution to Biblical Lexicography*, 1924, and G. R. Driver, *Die Welt des Orients* I, pp. 235–36. This involves reading *wayyēḳaḥ* (for *wayyiḳḳaḥ*, same consonants, different vowels) from the root *w*(*y*)-*ḳ*-*ḥ* (Arabic *waḳaḥa*, be bold, insolent). Cf. the same root in Job 15.12, as Rashi realized, but he follows T and S and thinks the meaning is 'separate himself from'.

1. Korah: the meaning of this name is uncertain. There was a Korah who was a son of Hebron (1 Chr. 2.43), and Korah was a nephew of Hebron, Kohath's third son (Exod. 6.18, 21). In the later P-strand Korah is a Levite, but that means nothing except that in later times his descendants were Temple officials. Obed-edom was a Levite according to 1 Chr. 15.18, etc., but originally he was a Gittite (2 Sam. 6.10), and Samuel was an Ephraimite (1 Sam. 1.1; 1 Chr. 6.33–38 (Heb 18–23)), just as Zadok ultimately appears as a descendant of Eleazar son of Aaron (1 Chr. 6.8 (Heb 5.34)). These are genealogies of ecclesiastical descent in reverse.

On the son of Peleth does not appear again in the story and no reference is made to him anywhere else. The presence of the name here and its absence elsewhere are equally hard to explain. Some LXX MSS have Onan, a name found elsewhere as a son of Judah (Gen. 38.4, 46.12).

3. You have gone too far: cf. EVV. But LXX and V interpret it differently (cf. Dt. 1.6): why should anybody want anything more than that all should belong to God? That ought to be enough for you.

holy: here means belonging to God and having full access to him in holy things and holy rites. See Gray, *ICC*, pp. 209–11.

4. he fell on his face: as in 14.5 the meaning is that Moses flung himself down on the ground, but it was in entreaty to God, as elsewhere. The Rabbis noticed that this case was different. Moses was not interceding with God. It was because he felt himself helpless. This was the fourth time the people had offended, and on each previous occasion Moses had interceded for them (Exod. 32.11; Num. 11.2, 14.13). The *Midrash Tanḥuma* says it is as though a prince sinned against his father, and his father's friend interceded for him thrice, but the fourth time he felt himself powerless, thinking he could no longer trouble the king.

6. censer: see Num. 4.9, 14. The word is used for any flat pan for carrying burning materials, from a small snuff-dish to a large ash-pan.

9–11. We are here dealing with Levites and not with the whole assembly. This is not a lay movement against the sacerdotal group. It is a movement of the Levites against the Aaronic priesthood. There is great emphasis on the functions of the Levites in the Chronicler's writings, and possibly this section is an earlier phase of that struggle.

11. Murmuring against Aaron is alleged to be murmuring against God. See Exod. 16.2–8, where the people murmur against Moses and Aaron, whereupon Moses says it is really murmuring against God. Presumably the middle term of this logic is that Moses and Aaron have been directly appointed by God in this exclusive manner.

12. Here is the JE-story of a civic revolt against the authority of Moses. To have led the Israelites out of Egypt ought to satisfy any man's ambition; why should Moses proceed to set himself up as a prince. But actually Moses has failed, in that he has not led them into the promised fruitful land. Dathan and Abiram therefore refuse to obey Moses's summons.

14. put out the eyes: the Hebrew idiom is 'pierce, bore out the eyes' (1 Sam. 11.2; Prov. 30.17). Our English idiom is 'throw dust in the eyes'.

15. do not respect: following EVV. In modern English, this is 'do not look at, take no notice of'.

offering: the Hebrew certainly is *minḥāh* (tribute, grain-offering). If the text is correct, then the word is used as in Gen. 4.4, in the general sense of a sacrifice as a tribute-offering, and possibly also as part of the regular daily offering (*tāmîḏ*), in which a grain-offering was wholly offered on the altar (Exod. 29.41) and not a token only, as was usually the case. The *Midrash Tanḥuma* here refers to their share of the *tāmîḏ*, which was offered on behalf of the whole community of Israel. This offering has nothing to do with the incense of verse 7, since that is the P-story, and verse 15 is in the JE-story. Those who think there is a mistake in the Hebrew suggest reading *'anḥāṯām* (their groaning, moaning) for *minḥāṯām* (their offering).

I have not taken . . .: note the parallel between this and 1 Sam. 12.3. The he-ass is the traditional thing not to have taken (cf. 1 Sam. 8.16). LXX has *epithumēma* (things desirable), reading *ḥāmûḏ* for *ḥ^a^môr*, which involves only the slightest of changes in Hebrew.

18–24. This is the earlier P-story, according to which Korah summons the whole congregation in opposition to Moses and Aaron. Moses and Aaron intercede for the people that all do not perish for the fault of one. The congregation is bidden to stand aside from Korah. The 'dwelling' and 'Dathan and Abiram' in verse 24 belong to the JE-story which is taken up again at the next verse.

22. the God of the spirits of all flesh: this phrase is found only here and 27.16. Here is the somewhat advanced theology of P, but it is easy to assume a greater development than is actually the case. It may well mean little more than the God who sustains the physical life of every human being, or of all living creatures.

all flesh: this phrase is used in three ways: (1) all living things, Lev. 17.14, Num. 18.15 P and elsewhere; (2) animals, Gen. 7.15, 21, 8.17 P; (3) all mankind, Dt. 5.26, but no clear-cut instance in P.

shall one man sin: the strict translation is 'one man sins, and wilt thou . . .'.

25–34. This is the JE-story of Dathan and Abiram, except for the addition of 'Korah' in verse 27 and of 'and all the men . . .' in verse 32b.

26. be swept away: this is reading the root *s-p-h* (Arabic *safā*), used of the wind raising the dust and carrying it away. LXX seems to have read some form of *sûp* (come to an end), and so EVV; but V and DV paraphrase with 'lest you be involved'.

28. of my own accord: lit. ‘from my heart’. This is an excellent example of the way in which Hebrew uses ‘the heart’ as the central core of the individual, that centre from which all thought and all action proceed.

29. the fate of all men: it is best to read ‘and’ rather than ‘or’. ‘If these men die a natural death and the normal visitation of mortals is visited upon them’, the reference being to that action of God whereby every man must die. Cf. Job 12.10; Ps. 104.28: when God withdraws the *rûaḥ* (spirit, breath), then a man dies. See note on Lev. 18.25 for what is involved in ‘visitation’. Another way of expressing natural death is ‘died for his own sin’ (Zelophehad, Num. 27.3), i.e. from God’s ordinary intervention and not from any special and sudden invasion of destructive wrath.

30. creates something new: .. ‘creates a creation’. EVV follow V and have ‘make a new thing’. It is something both unprecedented and unexpected (cf. Jer. 31.22; Isa. 48.6; Exod. 34.10 J). It is a direct act of God contrary to the normal way he acts: what is called a miracle.
opened its mouth: in Dt. 11.6 the earth (*’ereṣ*, not *’ᵃḏāmāh* as here and Gen. 4.11) opens its mouth to receive Dathan and Abiram, but there is no mention of Korah: which is confirmation of the Korah story being completely distinct.
Sheol: this is the vast underworld which is the home of the dead. For the classical description of Sheol, see Job 3.17–19, 21.23–26; also Isa. 14.9–11 and Ps. 6.5. In the course of centuries the idea developed of different compartments in the abode of the dead, and it became the place where the spirits of men awaited the final judgment, though the three divisions of Enoch 22.1–14 (see also Lk. 16.22–25 for two of them) suggest that the judgment is virtually at death. The derivation of the word is unknown. See *DB*, p. 906.

35. The P-story of Korah and his company is taken up again here.

36–50. This is the P-story of the aftermath of the destruction of Korah and his company. In the Hebrew it belongs to chapter 17.

36–40. This is evidence of the composite nature of the P-tradition. According to Exod. 27.2, 31.2, Bezalel overlaid the altar with bronze when it was first made at Sinai. At Exod. 38.22 LXX harmonizes by saying that Bezalel used this particular bronze. The section is important for the understanding of Hebrew priestly ideas of holiness. Even though the censers had been used illegally by men in their presumption, they still were holy enough to be used on the altar and too holy for any non-holy person to touch them. We are in the world of *taboo* and this concept of holiness has nothing to do with ethics.

37. blaze: the ancient versions took *śᵉrēp̄āh* to be the burnt-out mass of men and censers, in which case it was the ashes that were scattered far and wide. The scattering of the fire is not so much to ensure that the fire is put out (since this is actually an excellent way of spreading it), but to make sure that no ‘common’ fire can be kindled from it. It is holy fire, though irregularly holy. Even the remains of the fire are *taboo*-holy.
for they are holy: LXX, S, and V rightly connect this phrase with the next verse.

'Because these sinful men consecrated the censers at the cost of their lives, they shall be made. . . .'

38. hammered plates: the word *paḥ* is used only here and Exod. 39:3, where EVV have 'thin plates' and RSV has the excellent 'gold leaf'. The bronze was hammered out into very thin layers (cf. the root *r-ḳ-'*, used of the firmament as a dome of brass, hammered out thin and stretched over the earth.

sign: this use of *'ôṯ* is somewhat different from that in 14.11, where it is a sign of the intervention of the Saviour God of Israel. Here it is not so much a positive reminder (verse 40 (Heb 17.5), *zikkārôn*) that the Aaronites are the only legitimate priests, as a warning (more like a *môpēṯ*, portent) of what will happen to whoever follows Korah's example and seeks to encroach upon the privileges of the priests.

39. Eleazar is the successor to Aaron as High Priest (20.22–29), and is the P-ancestor of the Zadokites. As High Priest, Aaron may have no contact with the dead (Lev. 21.10–15), but Eleazar, still not yet High Priest, is less circumscribed (Lev. 21.1–4).

40. reminder: a much better translation than the 'memorial' of EVV.

41–50. Aaron and Moses are not yet at the end of their troubles, for now the people blame them for the deaths of Korah and his company. The cloud of the Presence descends, and the splendour grows more intense. The bursting out of the blazing fire is imminent. Aaron dashes into the midst of the people carrying legitimate holy fire, and the slaughter is stopped, though not before 14,700 are dead.

46. wrath: see note on Lev. 10.6.

(j) THE STORY OF AARON'S ROD (Heb 17.16–28) **17.1–13**

Here is the final demonstration of the privileged status of the Levites. It is handed down in the P-tradition, attested by divine intervention and miracle. The story belongs to an early strand of P, since it exalts the Levites as against the other tribes and not Aaron as against the Levites. The rods are left overnight within the Tent of Meeting, and in the morning Aaron's rod has sprouted, budded, blossomed, and produced ripe almonds. Levi with Aaron as his representative is the chosen tribe. It is not clear how many rods there were, but V and DV make it thirteen by reading verse 6 as 'there were twelve rods besides the rod of Aaron'. The Hebrew is inconclusive. P usually thinks of Levi as distinct from the twelve secular tribes.

2. rods: both this word *maṭṭeh* and the word *šēḇeṭ* can mean both 'rod, staff', and 'tribe'. Every traveller had his staff. Moses the shepherd had his shepherd's staff. In Num. 21.18 the princes and the nobles have sceptre and staves (different words are used). Aaron certainly had a magic rod according to the P-tradition (Exod. 7.9, 19, 8.5, 16), though in the E-tradition it belongs to Moses (Exod. 4.17). It is impossible to say whether these twelve (thirteen) rods were ordinary pieces of dry stick, the kind of staff that every man had, or the staff which was the chief's badge of office. Gray (*ICC*, p. 217) gives instances of legends of trees miraculously growing from rods thrust into the ground: Joseph of Arimathea and his blackthorn at Glastonbury, the club of Hercules, the spear of Romulus, the angel's rod which grew into the terebinth of Hebron, etc. Such lists are misleading and due to the influence of folklorists who seize on similarities and neglect the differences. Aaron's rod was not thrust into the ground, and the double meaning of the word *maṭṭeh* makes it likely that the story developed from this double meaning: the dead *maṭṭeh* (stick) sprang to life and it represents the *maṭṭeh* (tribe) which God chose and blessed.

fathers' house: here the phrase means a whole tribe. Normally a father's house is a sept within a clan with so many clans to a tribe (1.2, 3.20). Probably the use here is unique because the play on the word *maṭṭeh* in the story prohibited the use of this normal word for 'tribe'; the story would have become impossibly confused. The Mishnah (*Taan.*, iii, 6, 7) says that there were twenty-four courses of priests, each course being on duty for one week (i.e. twice a year, not counting the four special sabbaths), and there were seven father's houses in each course, one for each day of the seven.

5. make to cease: the same root *š-k-k* is used of Noah's flood subsiding (Gen. 8.1), so perhaps it means here that God is going to settle this matter of choice and precedence once and for all.

8. almonds: the almond is the *šāḳēḏ*, the waker-tree (Jer. 1.11f.), being the first tree to blossom in the spring.

10. before the testimony: Aaron's rod was put back inside the tent, where the pot of manna was (Exod. 16.33; cf. Heb. 9.4). But 1 Kg. 8.9 says there was never anything in the Ark apart from the two tablets of stone.

12–13. These two verses supply an introduction to the next chapter. If everybody who goes near the Tabernacle meets with this fate, then we shall all perish. The reference is to the earlier strand in the Korah story.

(k) THE PRIESTS AND THE LEVITES: THEIR DUTIES AND THEIR PRIVILEGES **18.1–32**

The Aaronites are now firmly established in the priesthood and the Levites in the service of the priests. The dues of the people to Levites and priests, and of Levites to priests are carefully set out.

1–7. The priests are to serve the altar and fulfil the duties of the inner shrine. The Levites perform all other duties. Priests and Levites form a hierarchy distinct from the people, and the Levites are a secondary order within the hierarchy.

1. shall bear iniquity: EVV have 'the iniquity of the sanctuary', which is even more strange. What iniquity can be involved in connection with the sanctuary? One explanation is that they are to pay the penalty for all ritual errors, the Levite for any error in connection with the sanctuary as a whole, the priest for any in connection with the priesthood. But a better explanation depends on the two link verses at the end of the previous chapter. Any one who approaches the sanctuary does so at an awful risk and it is wrong for man to come near to the awful God. The priests and Levites have been chosen to approach God. They will take all the risks and pay whatever penalty may be incurred.

1. you and your sons means the Aaronic priests. **Your fathers' house** means the whole tribe of Levi.

2. that they may join you: the Hebrew has the passive 'that they may be joined'. This is the popular explanation of the name Levi: the root *l-w-h* (join) (Gen. 29.34 J).

3. The Levites are not to come near the altar or any of the holy vessels. The penalty is death to the Levite and death to the priest for allowing it.

7. as a gift: Heb 'a service of a gift'; LXX 'you shall perform the service, a gift of your priesthood'. The meaning is that this service is a privilege conferred on them by God himself.

Dues to the Priests from the People **8–20**

These dues are extensive. They include all holy-gifts, all grain-offerings except the *tāmîḏ* (daily offering), all sin-offerings (on behalf of individuals), all compensation-offerings, all so-called heave-offerings and wave-offerings, all first-fruits of wine and grain, all 'devoted' (*ḥērem*) things, and all first-born of living creatures whether man or beast.

8. Read: 'I have given you all that is reserved (*mišmereṯ*, kept, kept back) of the offerings made to me.' The word *mišmereṯ* usually means 'care of, responsibility for, guard', but here it means the portion which is kept back out of such offerings as the *zeḇaḥ* (shared-offering), of which the breast was kept back for the priesthood and the right thigh for the officiating priest.

consecrated things: these were the holy-gifts, the *ḳoḏāšîm*, gifts of the people which went to the Temple personnel, contrasted with the *ḳorbānîm*, which went to the service of the sanctuary.

as a portion: following RVm; cf. Accadian *masaḫu* (to measure) and Arabic *masaḥat*. This is one of a number of uncommon roots, known in this case to T and S, but lost in a very common root of similar appearance. It is found only here, and EVV (by reason of the anointing) derived it from the common root *m-š-ḥ* (anoint). LXX has *geras* (gift of honour) and Rashi has a similar idea when he says the word involves distinction.

9. reserved from the fire: these are the offerings of the people which did not go to the altar-fire: grain-offerings, sin-offerings, and compensation-offerings. They are 'most holy gifts', i.e. they must never go outside the Holy Place and must be eaten by the priests alone.

11. the offering of their gift: lit. the portion (*tᵉrûmāh*) of their gift. The term is here used in a general sense of all portions of offerings which were the share of the priesthood. Such gifts are 'holy' (not 'most holy') and include first-fruits and firstlings of domestic animals. Throughout this chapter the technical terms for the types and parts of sacrifices are not used in the normal way. We seem to be dealing with a different stratum of the traditions.

12. the first fruits: RSV preserves a distinction between these (*rēšîṯ*) and the *bikkûrîm* (first-ripe fruits) of the next verse, as EVV. For the technical difference between these two terms, see Lev. 2.14. But since this chapter is irregular in its use of technical terms, perhaps the distinction is between those first-fruits which went straight into the Temple store-chambers and those for which there was first a reception ceremony in the Temple (Neh. 10.35–37); see Gray, *ICC*, p. 225. The alternative is to regard all the terms as being somewhat loosely used, and so not to attempt any precise definition. For a detailed study of the dedication of first-fruits among peoples throughout the world, see Gray, *ICC*, pp. 225–29, and the relevant passages in Frazer, *The Golden Bough*, ii, pp. 318–30, 459–71.

14. devoted thing: this is the *ḥērem*, the ban or that which is banned from common use, either in war or as an offering given irredeemably (see Lev. 27.21).

15–18. The principle that lies behind the whole idea of first-fruits and the first-born is that all increase of every kind belongs to God, and this must be acknowledged by the presentation at the shrine of the first of the fruits and the first that is born. These are not 'given', but 'presented', since they are God's already. Thus at all harvest festivals, modern equally with ancient, the 'harvest-gifts' are God's gifts to men and not man's gifts to God. When all this has been acknowledged in the first-fruits ceremony, God permits men to use the rest for sustenance and enjoyment. The term here is 'to make *ḥôl* (common)', so that one form of this root *ḥ-l-l* comes to mean 'begin'. No first-fruits could be redeemed. They were the perquisite of the priests and were 'holy', i.e. they could be eaten by the families of the priests. All the first-born of men had to be redeemed at five shekels, which was the regular tariff for a male child one month old (Lev. 27.6). The first-born of clean domestic animals could not be redeemed. These became the property of the priests and were 'holy'. The first-born of uneatable animals such as the ass (Exod. 13.13) could be redeemed, but if not, they were destroyed. The custom of presenting first-fruits is a natural reaction of man all the world over. There was a time in Israel when the first-born son was actually sacrificed: Mic. 6.7; 2 Kg. 3.27 where the editor agrees that such a sacrifice in a time of direst extremity was valid and could be effective, even if made to a Moabite god. In modern times the custom is developing among some Jews of referring to a female first-born as a *b^{e}ḵôrāh*. The firstlings of herd and flock were not always the perquisite of the priests (Dt. 15.19–23), but at one time were eaten by the worshippers, at the central shrine if a perfect animal and at home if it was deformed.

15. opens: the word is *peṭer*, which means 'that which breaks through'. Elsewhere the verb is used of David breaking out and escaping from Saul (1 Sam. 19.10) and of the outspread flowers of the Temple decorations (1 Kg. 6.18).

all flesh: here this means all living creatures, both man and beast, as is evident from the next phrase.

redeem: the writer is exactly correct in using the root *p-d-h* (get by payment what was not his originally), and not the root *g-'-l* (get back what was his own originally).

16. at a month old is correct. The translators of EVV (from a month old) were

probably influenced by Dt. 15.20 according to which the firstlings of sheep and cattle were eaten by the worshipper annually at the central shrine.
the shekel of the sanctuary: this is the holy shekel, the old heavier coin (see Lev. 5.15).

17. sprinkle: as elsewhere, read 'fling'. The blood was flung against the corners of the altar. All blood was taken to the altar. Ritually clean blood was flung above the red line, ritually unclean blood below the red line ('at the foot').

19. holy offerings: these are the *ḳoḏāšîm*, the holy-gifts which the priests received as their due: if 'holy', the priest's family could also partake of them; if 'most-holy', only the priest could eat them.
covenant of salt: this is a covenant which must never be broken (Lev. 2.13).

Dues to the Levites from the People **21–24**

21. every tithe: according to Dt. 14.22–23 the Israelite ate his tithe at the central shrine, but every third year it went to the oppressed classes in Israel, those who had no rights of their own and no property in their own right. These were the Levite, the resident alien (stranger), the fatherless, and the widow (Dt. 26.12). But by the time of Num. 18 all the tithe went to the Levites, whatever the year. By the time of Lev. 27.30–33 and 2 Chr. 31.6 the tithe had been extended to cover cattle and sheep and no redemption of this tithe was permitted. For other details, see Lev. 27.30f.

22. The tithe is here represented as payment to the Levites for taking upon themselves the obligation and the risk of approaching holy things. The change from ancient practice needed an explanation.

23. iniquity: better 'responsibility', but see verse 1.

Dues to the Priest from the Levites **25–32**

What the people were to the Levites in the matter of tithes, the Levites were to the priests. The Levites had to take a tithe of the tithe as a *tᵉrûmāh* (verse 26, offering), that is, the part of an offering which goes to the priests. This tithe must be from the best (lit. from all its fat; cf. verse 12). When this best has been handed over to the priests, then what is left becomes *ḥôl* (common), that is, proper to be eaten by somebody other than the priest and his family. This nine-tenths of the original tithe is the Levites' reward for serving in connection with the Tent of Meeting. There will now be no penalty (verse 32, where RSV follows EVV with **sin**) for what they do in approaching holy things.

27. This *tᵉrûmāh* (offering, i.e. the part taken off from the tithe and given to the priests) of yours is so far as you are concerned parallel to the part (the original tithe) which the people took off their harvest.
fulness: this word *mᵉlē'āh* is used in Exod. 22.29 (Heb 28) to mean 'full harvest'. Possibly this is the meaning in the difficult Am. 2.13, 'as the cart [wheel] presses the harvest . . .'.

29. the hallowed part from them: the Levites are told that, out of all these gifts which they receive from the people, they have to give 'a portion to the Lord', a *t^e^rûmāh*, which is in fact a contribution to the priests, and this is further defined as the hallowed part of the gifts the Levites have received.

32. These holy-gifts of the people are not available for eating by the Levites (they must not 'profane'—make *ḥôl*—them) until they have taken off a share (*t^e^rûmāh*) and given it to the priests. Otherwise it would be just as much a sin for the Levites to eat the tithe as it would be for the ordinary man to eat anything of his harvest until he had given a tithe to the Levites.

(l) THE RED HEIFER: CONTACT WITH THE DEAD **19.1–22**

The reducing of the whole body of the red heifer to ashes is connected with the necessity of removing the ritual uncleanness which was associated with the dead. For parallel ideas and rites among other nations, see Gray, *ICC*, pp. 241–48. For the use of the colour red in such ceremonies, see Frazer, *The Golden Bough*, ii, pp. 142, 254f., 311. Some think that red represents the colour of fire as a cleansing agent, but this is not the normal Hebrew idea. The red has more likely to do with the colour of blood as a de-sinning agent (cf. the ceremony of de-sinning the altar (Lev. 4.7) and other similar ceremonies). Fire certainly destroys sin when there is no other way of getting rid of it (Lev. 4.1–12, 13–21), but it is not a normal cathartic agent, though cf. Num. 31.23. For details of the rite and suggestions as to its origin and significance, see *HDB*, iv, pp. 207–10, *DB*, p. 235, and the Mishnah tract *Parah*, which is a whole tract dealing with this particular matter.

2. the statute of the law: this double phrase is unusual, but see 31.21, and cf. 27.11 and 35.29. There is no *a priori* reason to suppose an error, though V has *religio victimae*, which in ecclesiastical Latin means 'the religious observance of the victim', whence some would read *happārāh* (the heifer) for *hattôrāh* (the law).

red . . . without defect: it is not always possible to be precise in these colours. The verb *'adama* (*'aduma*) in Arabic means 'be tawny', but in Isa. 1.18 the adjective is used of 'red like crimson', and in Ca. 5.10 it means dark and ruddy from exposure to the sun. The 'heifer' is due to LXX *damalis*, but V and DV rightly have 'a cow of full age'. It had to be between two and five years old. Jewish tradition says that 'without defect' refers to the redness, so that if there were but two black hairs on the animal it would be unsuitable (*Parah*, ii, 5). It had to be one which had never been used for secular purposes and never mounted.

3. Eleazar had to perform the cleansing rites. He was the second priest so long as Aaron was alive. Both the Midrash and the Talmud (*b. Yoma*, 42b) say that the ceremony had to be carried out by the Sagan (the second priest), who was the chief officer of the Temple (cf. an Anglican dean). No man could be High Priest unless he had been the Sagan (*b. Yoma*, 41a).

4. sprinkle: this is correct here. The verb is *hizzāh*, and it is a de-sinning rite. In later time the ceremony took place on the Mount of Olives. The gate in the eastern wall, the Upper Gate, the entrance to the Holy of Holies, and the floor of the Holy of Holies are said to have been virtually the same height as the outer wall, so that the man who was performing the sprinkling rite could look straight across to the porch of the Holy of Holies. He could thus be 'outside the camp' and yet 'sprinkle toward the front of the tent of meeting'.

seven times: here again is the sacred seven which is essential for the effectiveness of so many of these cleansing rites.

5. in his sight: it is unusual for this to be mentioned. A non-priest slaughtered the animal and Eleazar had to see that all was done with precise correctness. This is the only case of a sacred rite in which the blood was burned outside the camp, just as it is the only case of a victim associated with Temple rites being slaughtered 'outside the camp'.

6. cedarwood and hyssop and scarlet stuff: see Lev. 14.4, where another primitive rite has survived. Cf. the 'holy water' of Babylonian ritual, the efficacy of which was enhanced by cedar and other aromatic woods. In the red heifer rite the slip of cedar wood and the hyssop were not tied together with the scarlet thread and used for the sprinkling (Lev. 14.7, 51), but were all thrown into the burning mass.

8. wash his clothes: the word is *kāḇas* (Accadian *kabāsu* is 'tread down' and *kibsu* is a path). The word is used occasionally of an individual washing to cleanse from sin (Jer. 2.22, 4.14; Ps. 51.2, 7 (Heb 4, 9)), and Ps. 51.7 (Heb 9) has 'purge me [lit. de-sin] with hyssop'. The normal word for a person washing himself is *rāḥaṣ* (Accadian *raḫâṣu* is 'overflow'). These represent ancient distinctions which still survive, where, for instance, the washing of clothes is done by trampling on them, and where, as in India, it is considered dirty to get into a bathful of water. Washing should be done by pouring water on the body. Thus 'bathe his flesh' means pour water over his body.

9. ashes: this (*'ēper*) is light ash-dust that flies about everywhere (Arabic *'apira*, be agile). The word used for the ashes of a sacrifice is *dešen* (fat ashes).

the water for impurity: it is water to be used for the removal of the ritual uncleanness caused by contact with a dead body. This word *niddāh* is used of various types of ritual impurity, adultery, menstruation, etc., and itself means 'nasty, abhorrent'. The verb is used in the sense of de-impurifying (cf. root *ḥ-ṭ-'*, de-sin). LXX and V have 'sprinkling', either thinking in terms descriptive of de-impurifying rites or perhaps actually reading *nizzāh* for *niddāh*.

for the removal of sin: the Hebrew is 'it is a *ḥaṭṭā'ṯ*, sin-offering'. Commentators have found this difficult, because the rite differs from that described in Lev. 4. Hence RSV has avoided the technical term and has described exactly the purpose of the rite. It is indeed for 'the removal of sin'. The P-editors knew exactly what they were saying. The red heifer was a sin-offering in the sense that it was for the removal of sin, but it was not a sin-offering in the narrower sense of Lev. 4. Actually it was 'a burnt sin-offering' (verse 17).

11. seven days: once more we have the seven days of the passage rite (see Lev. 4.6).

13. thrown upon him: this is correct (*zāraḳ*, of flinging against the altar) and not *hizzāh* (sprinkle, as in de-sinning rites). But in verse 18 'sprinkle' is right.

14–19. Here are details as to what is to be done in particular instances of death. The section is from a different source, and this is a de-sinning rite with sprinkling. In the previous section and again in verse 20 the de-impurifying water is thrown over the man. But in verse 21 we have a reference to the sprinkling rite once more.

16. This is the law which led to the whitening of graves so that the ritually pious could avoid touching them inadvertently (Mt. 23.27). To call a High Priest a 'whitened wall' (Ac. 23.3) was certainly reviling him.

17. some ashes of the burnt sin offering: i.e. some of the dust from the burnt ash of the offering for the removal of sin.

21. until evening is the shortest time that ritual uncleanness can last.

(m) THE FINAL EVENTS AT KADESH **20.1–13**

This section is so thoroughly welded into one by the P-editors that some commentators do not care to analyse it precisely from the literary point of view. P thought the Israelites came to Kadesh in the fortieth year, but JE thought they went straight to Kadesh from Egypt. Thus in verse 1 the month of their arrival is given, but not the year. Miriam may have died at almost any time during E's nearly forty years' sojourn round Kadesh.

The Waters of Meribah **2–13**

Once more, when difficulties arise, the people wish they had never left Egypt, but this time it is not a case of 'murmuring'. It is a matter of 'striving' (contending, disputing: the verb *rîḇ* means 'strive, contend' in or out of the courts). This is one of the aetiological stories. It explains a place-name, in this case Meribah (strife, contention). In Exod. 17.7 Meribah is identified with Massah (testing), and both are identified with Rephidim and also with Kadesh, which is sometimes called Meribah-Kadesh (Num. 27.14, etc.). The parallel story (Massah: J and Meribah: E) is in Exod. 17.1–7.

3. died when our brethren died: this is with Korah and his company (16.35 and 49, 17.12f.).

8. the rod: this is the rod with which Moses struck the Nile and turned the water into blood (Exod. 7.20 E). With it he divided the sea (Exod. 14.16 E). But in the P-tradition it is Aaron who has this marvellous rod (Exod. 7.9, 20, 8.5 (Heb 1), 16 (Heb 12)).

the rock: this rock is famous in tradition and exegesis. There is a Jewish tradition which says that the water which gushed from the rock in Horeb followed the Israelites all the way to Canaan, stopped when they stopped, and moved on when they moved on. A variant is that the rock followed them all the way, and this tradition is used by St Paul in 1 C. 10.4. See also A. M. Toplady's hymn 'Rock of Ages, cleft for me' especially since the Hebrew *sela'* does mean 'crag, split off a rock'.

10. you rebels: Who were the rebels? The people had contended with Moses, not rebelled. Rashi offered two suggestions: *môrîm* is not from *mārāh* (rebel) but from *yārāh* (teach); or, it is the Greek word *mōroi* (fools); cf. Mt. 5.22 as a term of abuse. Modern commentators have suggested that Moses and Aaron were the rebels and that originally this speech was addressed to them. Part of the difficulty is to decide how it was that Moses incurred God's displeasure in this affair, especially since it was this which caused his exclusion from the Promised Land (verse 12). Some would translate 'can we bring forth water . . .' or 'must we bring forth . . .' showing either doubt or unwillingness in respect of the command of God (verse 8). Some say he struck the rock twice, showing either loss of temper or loss of faith. According to Ps. 106.32–33, the people made Moses bitter (Hebrew *mārar*) 'and he spoke words that were rash'. Rashi says that Moses ought to have done as he was told and spoken to the rock (verse 8), instead of which he struck the rock and even struck it twice. In Dt. 1.37, 3.26, 4.21 another reason is given: God was angry with Moses because the people refused to enter the Promised Land after the report brought back by the spies.

13. showed himself holy: it is not easy to see how God vindicated his holiness in any moral way. But if holiness here has to do with might and awesomeness alone, then this is vindication. The story is probably at least to some extent aetiological, since Kadesh is derived from the root *ḳ-d-š* (be holy).

THIRD SECTION **20.14–36.13** WHAT HAPPENED FROM KADESH TO THE PLAINS OF MOAB

(a) THE PEOPLE ARE REFUSED TRANSIT FACILITIES THROUGH EDOM **20.14–21**

The section is composite. The general opinion is that, according to the E-tradition, the Israelites turned south and went as far south as the Gulf of 'Aqaba in order to avoid crossing Edomite territory, and then came north again well to the east of Moab (Jg. 11.18). Then they came in from the desert north of the Arnon gorge. But the P-editor thought they went across northern Edom and across the Arabah south of the Dead Sea, then presumably up through the Moabite country (Num. 20.21, but see 21.10–13). The D-tradition makes them travel south along the western border of Edom, down south as far as the Gulf of 'Aqaba, but then up north along the Arabah and through Moabite territory immediately to the east of the Dead Sea (Dt. 2.1–13, 28–29).

14. brother Israel: Esau-Edom and Jacob-Israel are the twin ancestors of the two peoples, traditionally rivals ('divided' Gen. 25.23) from birth. The trouble historically seems to have begun when the Israelites were seeking a home in Palestine, and Am. 1.11f. may be an echo of Num. 20.20. The greatest enmity developed from the way in which the Edomites took advantage of the disasters of Judah in the sixth century, an enmity which never died, and nothing that Herod the Great (an Idumaean) did could diminish the hatred in which the Jews held him.

adversity: the 'travail' of RV is better, though now used only in a specialist sense: anguish, hardship, weariness. AV has the curious 'travel', originally the same word as that in RV, but it has been modernized in some editions.

16. an angel: this is dependent on Exod. 23.20 E rather than on Exod. 14.19, where the reference is to the Angel of God, the special manifestation of God. The idea of the angel-guide belongs to another way of thinking about God and his dealings with Israel.

17. the King's Highway: from V *via publica* and DV 'the common highway'. This is the regular caravan-route through Edom. The usual word for 'highway' is *mᵉsillāh* (Isa. 40.2), and *dereḵ* more often means 'caravan route', the road which people tread. Cf. the Old English use of 'way': the Icknield Way (see also Exod. 13.17f).

18. come out: i.e. to war (1 Sam. 17.20 and in Phoenician).

(b) THE DEATH OF AARON **20.22–29**

This is P's account of the death of Aaron and the investiture of Eleazar, his elder surviving son. The traditional site of Mount Hor is near Petra, the *Jebel Nabî' Hārûn*, fifty miles south of the Dead Sea, well into the Edomite country, but this must be wrong, even though the identification is as old as Josephus (*Ant. Iud.* IV, iv, 7). An alternative is the *Jebel Maḍurah*, not far from Kadesh and on the north-west of the Edomite border. According to Dt. 10.6 the name was Moserah.

26. garments: these are the special clothes of the High Priest (Lev. 8.7–9).

29. thirty days: the same period as for Moses (Dt. 34.8). The usual period was seven days, the passage time.

(c) THE FIGHT WITH A KING OF THE NEGEB **21.1–3**

This story is said to be from the JE-tradition, and records an abortive attempt to cross the Arabah just to the south of the Dead Sea, which is what P seems to think they did. Arad was a well-fortified settlement identified with the modern Tell Arad, about eight miles south of Hebron. Probably Atharim (the ancient versions, except LXX, have Tarim) is Tamar or Hazazon-tamar in the Arabah, a few miles south of the Dead Sea. The king of Arad heard they were taking this Atharim-road, rushed down from the hills, and took some of them prisoner. Hormah is usually identified with the modern *Tell el-Mishâsh*, west-south-west of Arad and near Beersheba. According to Jg. 1.17, this city was once called Zephath and was captured later by Judah and Simeon. Possibly 21.1–3 is a variant of the attack of 14.45.

(d) THE 'BRAZEN' SERPENT **21.4–9**

This story is of great importance to both Jew and Christian. It is important to the Jew because it was the last, but most dreadful, of Israel's apostasies; to the Christian because of the reference in Jn 3.14. See also Wis. 16.5–7, where the incident is the supreme evidence that God's wrath does not 'continue to the uttermost' and it is emphasized that it was not what they beheld that saved them but 'the Saviour of all'. See also *RH*, iii, 8. The story has been a favourite mine of typological treasure from Philo (*de Alleg.*, ii, 20; *de Agricul.*, 22) downwards.

According to 2 Kg. 18.4 king Hezekiah destroyed this serpent because the people were sacrificing (*ḳiṭṭēr* means 'sacrifice' in pre-exilic contexts) to it. Modern commentators think that this serpent was the original Jebusite fetish and Zadok the original Jebusite priest (H. H. Rowley, 'Zadok and Nehustan', *JBL*, 58, 1939, 113–41). Thus Num. 21.4–9 is an aetiological story designed to justify the continuance of the cult during the kingdoms by associating the serpent with Moses.

The site of the incident is Punon (21.10 and 33.43), identified with the modern *Feinân*, twenty-five miles south of the Dead Sea, where copper was mined in ancient times (Grollenberg, *Atlas of the Bible*, map 9, p. 44). The cult of the serpent was widespread in ancient times, not least in Palestine. A bronze cobra has been found at Gezer, serpent ornaments at Beth-shemesh; Beth-shan means 'house of the snake'; '*Ēn-hattannîm* (Neh. 2.13) means 'the serpents' spring'); see further, *RAPLA*, pp. 98ff. The association of the snake and healing is widespread, notably the cult of Asklepios, who appeared in the form of a snake in healing dreams (Walter Pater, *Marius the Epicurean*, chapter iii); also the badge of the Royal Army Medical Corps.

4. by the way to the Red Sea: i.e. by the Red Sea caravan-route which skirted the western border of Edom. The Heb has *yam-sûp*, which LXX identified with the *eruthra thalassa* (the Red Sea of EVV). This phrase originally referred to the Red Sea and the Indian Ocean (Herodotus), and later, when the Greeks discovered the Persian Gulf, it included that also (Xenophon); but Demosthenes used the term vaguely of distant unknown waters. The translation Sea of Reeds is modern, depending on the use of *sûp* (reeds) in Exod. 2.3, 5; Isa. 19.6.
became impatient: the Hebrew is 'the *nepeš* (here 'temper') of the people became short'. Once more hardship leads to complaints against Moses for ever bringing them out of Egypt. Jewish tradition finds a double crime here; it was also a complaint against God.

5. worthless: the EVV 'light bread' means something else today and is complimentary. This bread was 'vile' (RVm), miserable—almost any derogatory word will do.

6. fiery serpents: the adjective in Hebrew is *śᵉrāpîm*, the same word as that for the seraphim who are in attendance upon God in Isaiah's vision (6.2, 6); and in both cases the meaning is 'burning ones'. Some hold that the heavenly seraphim were originally serpent deities. Others think that the fiery serpents were serpent-demons and the heavenly seraphim are personifications of the lightning, just as the twin cherubim are the twin spirits of the thunderstorm. This latter explanation is much the more likely. In any case, there is no absolute need to assume that these serpents were anything other than snakes with a particularly venomous and burning bite.

9. bronze: the word *nᵉḥôšeṯ* means copper in Job 28.2, where it is a metal smelted directly from the ore. Copper and bronze utensils have been found at

Lachish (*Tell ed-Duweir*) and at Troy. Evidently the ancients hardened the copper with tin and made the alloy bronze. The word 'brass' (EVV, whence the traditional 'brazen serpent') was formerly the name of an alloy of copper with either tin or zinc, and occasionally with other metals; it was a general term for any alloy of copper. In modern times brass is an alloy of copper and zinc, and bronze (Italian *bronzo*) an alloy of copper and tin.

(e) THE JOURNEY FROM MOUNT HOR TO THE PLAINS OF MOAB **21.10–20**

Verses 10 and 11 are usually allocated to P, but the rest is from E and includes two very ancient songs, 14–15 and 17–18.

10. Oboth: water-skins. The site may be the modern *'Ain el-Weiba*, fifteen miles from the south end of the Dead Sea and west of Punon.

Iye-abarim: the ruins of Abarim, the regions beyond the river. Possibly this is the modern *Mahay*, at the south-east corner of Moab and near the head of the Zered gorge.

13. Arnon: this is the modern *Wady el-Mûjib*. The territory between the Arnon and the Jabbok (*Nahr ez-Zerqā*, fifty miles north) was disputed territory. The Ammonites claimed it as originally theirs, and that Israel took it (Jg. 11.13). Jephthah replied that it never was theirs, nor did it ever belong to Moab, and that the Israelites took it from the Amorites. The Ammonites certainly occupied this area in later times (Jer. 49.1f.); it is the area surrounding the modern *'Ammân*, the capital of the modern state of Jordan. The northern Moab border varied. Mesha (MI, *DOTT*, pp. 195–8) said that Omri took this territory from Moab early in his (Omri's) reign, but that Mesha occupied it in the latter half of Ahab's time. It contains the ancient capital of Moab, Dibon, the modern *Dibân*.

the Book of the Wars of the LORD: this and the Book of Jashar (the Upright, Jos. 10.13; 2 Sam. 1.18) were two ancient collections of early songs. They are part of the saga of Israel, the story of the fight for liberty against the enemies of Israel in the first days, and the Book of Jashar contained David's lament over Saul and Jonathan. Only three short pieces survive.

Waheb in Suphah: this is the opening phrase in a fragment from the ancient song-book. If the text is correct, they are two place-names in Moab or to do with the watersheds in that area. AV has followed V, 'as he did in the Red Sea, so will he do in the streams of Arnon', which depends on ancient Jewish exegesis. It involves reading *wāhēḇ* as the rare Hebrew root *y-h-b* (give: common in Aramaic, Syriac, Arabic), *bᵉsûpāh* as equivalent to *bᵉ(yam) sûp*, and the objective particle as introducing what to us is the subject, which does happen occasionally in Hebrew. LXX read *zhb* for *whb* and took *sûpāh* from the root *s-p-p* (burn, Aramaic).

15. slope: this translation is influenced by Dt. 3.17, 'the slopes of Pisgah'. The word probably means 'watershed'. The difficulties of this fragment can be judged from the great variations in translations, both ancient and modern.

16. Beer: this place is unidentified. It is 'the Well', some well-known well that was dug in ancient times. The word introduced 'the Song of the Well'.

17–18. This ancient song is introduced in a way almost exactly that in which the Song of the Sea (Exod. 15.1–18) is introduced. Both Talmuds (*b. RH*, 31a, *j. Meg.*, iii) say that this song was sung every third sabbath and the additional sabbath service, with Exod. 15.1–10 and 15.11–18 on the other two sabbaths; and Dt. 32.1–43 in six sections, one each sabbath, at the morning service.

18. and from the wilderness: Heb intends this to belong to the song: 'a gift from the wilderness' (Ps. 126.4).

19. The sites of these places are uncertain. Possibly Bamoth is the modern *Khirbet el-Quweiqiyeh*, five miles north of Dibon.

(f) THE VICTORIES OVER THE TWO AMORITE KINGS 21.21–35

The victories over Sihon and Og occupy a foremost place in the saga of Israel. They were the first victories of the newly emancipated people of God. See Dt. 2.20–3.11; Jg. 11.19–21; Ps. 135.11, 136.19–27.

21. Moses first seeks peaceful passage, as he had done with Edom (20.14–21). The overture for a peaceful settlement became fixed in Israelite law (Dt. 20.10–18).

23. Jahaz: not certainly identified, but it may be the modern *Khirbet Umm el-Idhâm*, five miles or so north of Dibon: so Jerome (*Onom.* 131.17). It was one of the four Levitical cities in the Reubenite country, but Mesha of Moab recaptured it in Ahab's time (MI 20).

24. Jazer: RSV follows LXX which says that Jazer was on the Amorite-Ammonite border, reading the consonants '*-z-r*. The Hebrew reads only '*-z*, and says that the Israelites did not at this time conquer any territory north of the Jabbok, because it was too strong ('*az*). Jazer is probably the *Khirbet Jazzir* near the modern *es-Salṭ*, twelve miles south of the Jabbok. It was once a Levitical city (Jos. 21.39), later it was Moabite (Isa. 16.8f.; Jer. 48.32) and Judas Maccabaeus captured it (1 Mac. 5.8).

25. Heshbon was Sihon's capital. Note the similar way in which a king's capital is mentioned regularly in the notices of the northern (Israel) kings (1 Kg. 15.33, 16.15, 23, etc.). It is the modern *Hesbân*, twenty miles east of the northern end of the Dead Sea. It was once a Levitical city (Jos. 21.39), later it was Moabite (Isa. 15.4, Jer. 48.2) and there were some famous pools there (Ca. 7.4). It is not mentioned on the Moabite Stone.

27. the ballad singers: these were the men who recited the *mᵉšālîm*, wandering from place to place like the bards, the minstrels who sang the sagas and the ballads. The *māšāl* (usually translated 'proverb') was properly a sentence constructed in parallel lines, or any pithy saying which involved a comparison. The root *m-š-l* means 'be like'. The term could include folk-songs, figurative sayings, and discourses, and even Balaam's oracles and Job's speeches. For the wide range of the term, see the contents of the Book of Proverbs: 10.1–22.16 contains mostly independent antithetical couplets; chapters 25–29 vary in content and length but are similes. The rest of the book is composed of longer and more miscellaneous pieces, but all to do with the pithy sayings of the wise.

27–30 is an ode celebrating the utter defeat of Moab, but by Sihon the Amorite king who conquered that territory before Israel came that way. Another explanation involves the omission of verse 29e as a gloss, and is that the ode celebrates Omri's conquest of Moab (*c.* 880 B.C.); cf. MI 4, 5. This may be so, but the present text undoubtedly thinks in terms of Sihon as the conqueror. It is thus now a satirical ode (so Ewald, *History of Israel*, Eng. tr., ii, pp. 205–07) saying to the Amorites: you once destroyed the Moabite country, setting out from Heshbon and burning everything. Now Heshbon is burnt out again, come and build it up again if you can.

28. the lords of: LXX has 'swallowed up', reading *bāl^{e}ʿāh* for *baʿ^{a}lê*, thus providing an admirable couplet.

heights: EVV have 'high places', taking the line to refer to the hill-shrines of Moab.

29. people of Chemosh: Israel is 'the people of Yahweh', and similarly Moab is 'the people of Chemosh'. Solomon erected a shrine to him (1 Kg. 11.7, 33; 2 Kg. 23.13).

30. This verse is corrupt beyond repair. **Their posterity** depends on LXX. The verse apparently tells of destruction from Heshbon to Dibon and on to Medeba. For a reproduction of the famous mosaic map found at Madaba, probably early sixth century A.D., see Grollenberg, *Atlas of the Bible*, p. 61.

33. The Israelites followed the caravan-route up into Bashan where they defeated and massacred Og king of Bashan, his family, and his people. Edrei is probably the modern *Derʿā*, forty miles east of the Jordan.

(g) BALAK AND BALAAM **22.1–24–25**

These three chapters contain the story of how Balak king of Moab was overcome with terror when he saw the hordes of Israelites on the borders of his country, and how he sent for Balaam to come and curse Israel so as to ensure their destruction. Balaam refuses the plea of the first company of messengers, saying that God has forbidden him to accompany them. He is persuaded by the second embassy. Then there follows the story of Balaam's ass, and later the turning of the curses into blessings, concluding with (24.17–24) a series of short oracles concerning the ultimate fate of Israel-Jacob and her neighbours. For a full analysis of these chapters see Gray, *ICC*, pp. 307–79. There are certainly two traditions. The reference to 'the elders of Midian' (22.4, 7) is strange and may be due to the P-tradition which connects Balaam with Midian (31.8) and blames him for the affair of Baal-peor (31.16, 25.1–16). God permits Balaam to go with Barak's men (22.20), but is then angry because he went (22.22). According to these chapters Balaam is entirely favourable to Israel, but in 31.7 and 16 he is Israel's enemy. Jewish tradition in general is heavily critical of Balaam. He was a bloody and deceitful man who died before half his time (*b. San.*, 106b). He has no place in the world to come (*San.*, x, 2; *Aboth*, v, 19). See also Philo (*de Vit. Mos.*, i, 48–55), Josephus (*Ant. Iud.* IV, vi, 2).

1. This verse belongs to the P-tradition into which all the wilderness traditions have been fitted. The people set out from Iye-abarim (21.12) and arrive at their last semi-permanent camp before entering Palestine. Here the P-editors sited the affair of Baal-peor, and the story of how Phinehas became 'third in glory' (Sir. 45.23); and from here Moses went up Mount Nebo to die.

the plains of Moab: this is a P-phrase. The reference is not to the high dry plateau east of the 'red wall of Moab', but to the flat plain east of the Jordan across from 'the plains of Jericho' (P: Jos. 4.13, 5.10). The whole area contains about fifty square miles of well-wooded, well-watered country. This is the '*ᵃrāḇāh* of D and P, not the arid desert-land of other traditions in south-west Judah and the Arabian desert. The translation 'plains' is from T and V.

Jericho: this is the first mention in the Bible of one of the best-known biblical sites, partly because of the ancient story of the walls of Jericho and partly because of the extensive modern excavations. It is the modern *Tell es-Sulṭân*. It was destroyed by Joshua (Jos. 6), and rebuilt in the time of Ahab (1 Kg. 16.34). The latest authoritative accounts of the excavations are Miss K. M. Kenyon, *Archaeology in the Holy Land* (1960), and in the archaeological journals. Miss Kenyon's book revises some of Garstang's conclusions (*Joshua, Judges*, 1931).

2–21. Balak sends messengers twice to Balaam and finally persuades him to set out to curse Israel. It is essential to recognize that both curses and blessings were regarded as having a compulsion of their own which ensured their being realized.

2. Balak: the name means 'destroyer, devastator', if, that is, it is indeed a Hebrew word. He is not known outside these chapters and Hebrew traditions which have grown out of them. The name *Zippor* (Heb *ṣippôr*) is from the root *ṣ-p-r* II (twitter, cheep), and means any small bird which cheeps, especially the ubiquitous sparrow (Arabic '*uṣpûr*). It is argued that names like this involve a primitive totemism, but cf. such British names as Bird, Sparrow, Starling, etc.

3. The double statement is generally supposed to indicate the interweaving of literary sources. The 'was distressed' of EVV is far too mild a rendering.

4. the elders of Midian: these are mentioned here and in verse 7, but never again.

5. Balaam the son of Beor: many identify him with the Bela of Gen. 36.32, a king of Edom. The difference in the names is only an afformative *mem*. The meaning is uncertain.

Pethor, which is near the River: if this means the Euphrates, then Pethor is probably Pitru, mentioned by Shalmaneser III (860–825 B.C.) and by Thothmes III (*c.* 1500 B.C.), the modern *Tell Aḥmar*, near the Euphrates, eighteen miles south of Carchemish. The Mesopotamian locale is supported by Dt. 23.4 (Heb 5). If Balaam travelled by ass, the journey was not the 400 miles which Pitru involves. It is best frankly to admit there are two traditions concerning Balaam's home. V translated Pethor as from the root *p-t-r* and made it *ariolus* (soothsayer).

in the land of Amaw: some authorities have 'Ammon', which fits in well with the tradition of Balaam riding on his ass for a comparatively short distance through fields and walled vineyards. Heb and LXX have 'of his own people', which scarcely seems right and is not informative. **Pitru** is in this area.

6. To curse the enemy effectively before the fight begins is to ensure victory.

7. the elders of Moab: in the next verses these are princes, another indication of more than one source in these chapters.

fees for divination: such fees, however small (1 Sam. 9.7f.), were essential. Hebrew here has simply 'divinations', whence Rashi supposes they carried the necessary materials in their hands, so that Balaam could not refuse to come on the ground that he had not the equipment. But Balaam is not tempted by gifts of money, neither at first nor later.

8. The Lord: there are continual changes in the divine Name throughout, and many variants from version to version. For a full study of these changes, see Gray, *ICC*, pp. 310f. Any use of the divine Name put into Balaam's mouth may mean almost anything: he was a true Yahweh worshipper; God does speak to even heathen in dreams (Rashi on Gen. 31.24); if the oracles were to be regarded as effective, the pious narrator would assume they came from the God of Israel.

15–20. Balaam agrees to go with the second embassy, not because it was larger and more honourable, but because God spoke to him in a dream (E-tradition).

Balaam and his Ass **21–35a**

This story is generally allocated to the J-tradition, and Balaam has with him only his two servants. Animals that speak are common in the folk-tales of most countries the world over.

22. the angel of the Lord: This is not a heavenly messenger, but a special manifestation of God Himself. We sometimes get variations in a narrative between 'the Angel of the Lord' and 'the Lord' (Gen. 16.7–13; Jg. 6.11–24; Zech. 3.1–5). The conception represents a stage in the development of God's transcendence, when it was no longer acceptable to think of God as speaking directly to men.

adversary: the word is *śāṭān*, later used as the personal name of the devil (cf. Arabic *Śaitân*). The Satan is first found as one of God's officers whose duty it is to check the pious professions of the faithful (Job 1). In Zech. 3 he is the prosecuting counsel; in 1 Chr. 21.1 (cf. 2 Sam. 24.1) he is the enemy of Israel. Ultimately he is king of the counter-kingdom of evil and has a host of helpers (see *The Jews from Cyrus to Herod*, pp. 132–9).

his two servants: the Palestinian Targum identified these with Jannes and Jambres, two of Pharaoh's magicians who withstood Moses (2 Tim. 3.8).

23. the field: this is a literal translation of Hebrew *śāḏeh* (LXX 'plain'). It is the untrodden country through which the track ran. It may or may not have been cultivated land. We would say 'open (hedgeless) fields'.

24. a narrow path: the Hebrew root means 'be deep', hence RV 'hollow way'. LXX assumes the ass has turned into a ploughed field and was 'in the furrows'. The path was a narrow way between the walls of vineyards. There is a famous walled garden in early Muslim history, the Garden of Death at the battle of al-Yemana, in which the Faithful exterminated the rebels with great loss to themselves among the Readers and the Companions of the Prophet.

32. perverse: after EVV. As RVm points out, the word means 'precipitate'. LXX has *ouk asteia* (not seemly). Probably the meaning is that Balaam was continuing recklessly, taking no notice of the warnings. The word may, however, refer to the steep sides of the road, the walls which prevented any turning aside.

34. I have sinned: this is not a deliberate act against God. Read therefore, either 'I have made a mistake' or 'I have been in the wrong'.

Balak Welcomes Balaam **35a–40**

He meets him at the boundary of his territory and escorts him to **Kiriath-huzoth** (city of streets), site not known.

36. the city of Moab: it is better not to translate but read 'Ar of Moab' (21.28), the frontier city perched on the south side of the gorge of the upper Arnon.

on the boundary formed by the Arnon: the word is *g^e^bûl* (boundary), but cf. the Arabic *jabal* (mountain). Perhaps the word originally means 'precipitous mountain, cliff' and came to mean 'boundary' because a cliff or a ravine would often be the boundary. Hence translate 'cliff, ravine', but 'boundary' at the end of the verse.

38. This is the true theory of prophecy. The prophet is the mouthpiece of God. Cf. Exod. 7.1; Aaron is prophet to Moses, and Moses is god to Aaron in the sense that the words are the words of Moses, but Aaron speaks them.

40. sacrificed: the root *z-b-ḥ* does not always mean 'slaughter for sacrifice'. The primary meaning is 'slaughter'. This meal was a shared sacrificial meal in which all the flesh was eaten by Balaam and the princes.

Balak's First Attempt to Ensure the Curse **22.41–23.12**

Balaam requires all proper provision for an effective oracle and Balak willingly complies. Balaam has to see the people he is required to curse. There have to be seven altars, and seven bulls and seven rams to be sacrificed, seven being the sacred number which ensures success in these magico-religious affairs.

41. Bamoth-baal: possibly the Bamoth of 21.19, destroyed by Israel but rebuilt by Mesha of Moab (MI 27). It is said to be near the modern *Khirbet el-Quweiqiyeh* to the south of the *Jebel en-Nebā* (Mount Nebo). The name means 'high-places (shrines) of Baal'. There was a whole range of hill-tops in the area, many of which, if not all, were sacred places dedicated to various gods: Baal, Nebo, Peor, etc.

the nearest of the people: the word is *ḳ^e^ṣēh*, which means 'end of, extremity of'. The translation depends on which end of the people is intended. RSV says the nearest; EVV say the farthest away and so the whole people, following V. LXX says 'a part'.

23.3. to a bare height: following RV, supported by such passages as Job 33.21; Isa. 41.18, 49.9, and six cases in Jeremiah. The 'solitary' of AVm is from T.

LXX has a doublet: *eutheian*, straight, open; and another reading which involves taking the first three Hebrew consonants as the first letters of three words: to-ask the-face-of God.

Balaam's First Oracle **7–10**

It is in the epic 3.3 rhythm, and almost wholly in synthetic couplets.

7. discourse: EVV have 'parable'. The word is *māšāl* (see 21.27).

Aram: some want to read 'Edom', partly because occasionally 'Aram' is an error for 'Edom' (2 Sam. 8.12 and 13; 1 Chr. 18.11), and partly to assimilate the two traditions as to Balaam's home. But the second line of the couplet shows that 'Aram' is right. Nothing is gained by altering the text to make the two stories agree.

the eastern mountains: the east (always *ḳeḏem* in this connection) is the traditional home of wisdom.

9. mountains, hills: the parallelism is closer and more elegant than this. The similarity is in the heights, and the contrast between the rocky mountains and the rounded hills.

10. the fourth part: some would read *riḇᵉḇôṯ* (ten thousands of) for *rōḇa'*, and possibly this is the origin of the 'peoples' of LXX. But there is a root *r-b-'* meaning 'dust', and probably this is what is intended here (cf. RVm 'dust clouds').

Balak's Second Attempt to Secure the Curse **13–24**

He chooses another site, seven new altars are built, and seven bulls and seven rams are sacrificed. But the result is the same.

13. This time Balaam can see only part of Israel, not the whole mass of them.

14. the field of Zophim: i.e. of the Watchers, some unknown spot on the Pisgah highlands, overlooking the Jordan valley and the plains of Moab where the Israelites are.

Balaam's Second Oracle **18–24**

This like the first, is in the epic 3:3 metre and, once again, it is in carefully constructed synthetic couplets.

18. Rise: this and the 'rise up' of EVV are literal translations, but the word is strictly introductory: 'attention', 'listen', '*Achtung*'.

19. lie: this is the usual meaning of the word, and so in all versions, but see Isa. 58.11 of a spring failing, and Hab. 2.3 of an oracle not coming true.

a son of man: this is the idiomatic use of *ben* (son of) to denote a member of a class or group. It is better here to translate the phrase by 'mortal man'. See the similar parallelism in the couplet of Ps. 8.4 (Heb 5). There are many instances of this idiom: *ben-mešeḳ* (Gen. 15.2), 'son of possession', means 'heir'; *ben-māweṯ* (2 Sam. 12.5), 'son of death', means either 'deserves to die' or 'doomed to die' (*moriturus*). The phrase 'a son of man' is to be distinguished from the title 'The Son of Man' (see commentaries on the Book of Enoch and the Gospels).

repent: the fundamental meaning of the root *n-ḥ-m* in Hebrew involves the idea of 'change of mind', arising from an earlier idea of 'breath of relief'. It can mean 'comfort', but comfort out of sorrow rather than comfort in sorrow. Here the meaning is 'change his mind', and this forms a good parallel to the previous line, which refers to an oracle which God has spoken and it will come true. For the meaning of the root *n-ḥ-m*, see *ET*, 44, 1932–33, 191f.; 57, 1945–46, 47–50. V has 'be changed', evidently realizing that the earlier meaning has survived, as often happens, side by side with more developed meanings.

21. he has not beheld: the subject of the verb is usually taken to be God, but S and T assume the speaker to be the subject. It is best to think of an indefinite subject, which we express by the passive or by 'one' (cf. French *on*, German *man*). T and V understand this verse to refer to idols and makers of idols.

the shout of a king: T understands this to be triumph shout of God, the divine king. LXX finds difficulty in this and has 'the glories of rulers'. Rashi takes *tᵉrûʿāh* to be from the root *r-ʿ-h* II (be friendly, a companion) and so sees here an expression of God's kindness towards Israel; he refers to Jg. 15.6 and 2 Sam. 15.37. But the Hebrew *tᵉrûʿāh* is used of the blast of a trumpet, the shout of battle, the shout of victory, and even of the acclamation at the crowning of the king (the *Königsjubel*: our 'God save the Queen'). This acclamation of victory and coronation triumph is probably the meaning here, since the next verse refers to the triumphant exodus from Egypt. We are here involved in the triple time-content of the Kingship of God: he became king when he created the world; he becomes king (as here) after an act of salvation; he will become king for ever at the end of days.

22. horns of the wild ox: the *rᵉʾēm* is the wild ox, the great *rîmu* of the Assyrian bas-reliefs. The nearest European equivalent is the wild and strong aurochs of the German forests, now extinct, which Caesar called *urus*. T and Rashi thought of the root *rûm* (be high), and so of God's towering strength and height. LXX and V similarly have 'strength'. The word *tôʿᵃpôṯ* certainly has to do with 'towering heights', but probably not so much of mountains as of the towering horns of the aurochs (cf. of highland cattle), symbol of the towering strength and power of God demonstrated in his rescue of Israel from Egypt and his care of them through the desert. Read 'he (God) was to him (Israel) like the towering horns of an aurochs'.

23. enchantment, divination: here are two words for consulting God by means of signs and omens. Both methods depend on the careful observance of happenings not caused by human agency: the flight of birds, and various ancient equivalents of throwing dice. The first word *naḥaš* has to do with the observance of birds (so LXX) or of omens generally (V *augurium*; the observer of birds is *auspex*), and the second word *ḳesem* refers to the casting of lots, e.g. by arrows (Ezek. 21.21 (Heb 26)). There are two possible explanations of the couplet: it can mean there is nothing of this kind of thing in Israel and that Israel therefore is worthy of God's guardian care (AVm and RV): it can mean Israel is so well protected by God that no divinations can have the slightest effect (AV, RVm, RSV). The choice is largely subjective.

25. Barak has had enough and dismisses Balaam, but the next verse reopens the matter.

23.26–24.2 is an introduction to the oracles of the next chapter. These are of different origin and style and are usually ascribed to the J-tradition, though with editorial modifications.

Balaam's Third Oracle **24.1–9**

Balaam still asks for a bull and a ram to be sacrificed on each of seven altars, but no longer goes away to 'be met with' by God.

1. the wilderness: which way was he looking? The word *y*^e^*šîmôn* is used in Dt. 32.10 and five times in the Psalms of the scene of the wanderings; also in Isa. 43.19 of the return from Babylon. Hence, some commentators think Balaam was looking east and south across the desert which Israel had just crossed. So T, followed by Rashi; they are convinced that Balaam was Israel's enemy all along, and he was looking back to the Golden Calf, Israel's greatest apostasy, as though here was a basis for an effective curse on Israel. But see 1 Sam. 23.19 and 24, 26.1 and 3, where David spent some time as a fugitive in Jeshimon, and there was a Beth-jeshimoth (Num. 33.49) below in the plains of Moab where Israel camped. Balaam is still looking west across the Arabah.

2. the Spirit of God: 'spirit' is best not printed with a capital S, lest it should be thought to refer to the Third Person of the Trinity (see EVV).

3. oracle of: here (thrice) and also in the fourth oracle (15–19) this word *n*^e^*'ûm* is used. These six instances and 2 Sam. 23.1 (twice), with perhaps Ps. 36.2, are the only cases where this word is used before a non-divine name. It is the frequent phrase of the prophets: 'Thus *saith* the Lord'. Some authorities parse the word as a noun (utterance of) and others as a passive participle of the root *n-'-m* (sigh, groan), but always in Hebrew of divine or oracular declarations.

whose eye is opened: this is a noted crux. LXX and T have 'see truly'. V has 'closed' (assuming *š-t-m* equals *s-t-m*), and so AVm, RV, understanding his eye to be originally closed, but uncovered (verse 4) after he had seen the divine vision. There is a Mishnaic and Aramaic root *š-t-m* which is taken to mean 'unseal, open', hence AV, RVm, RSV, and S. The word is used of boring a hole through the seal of a wine-jar and inserting a tube through which to draw the wine. The Rabbis were persistent in denigrating Balaam, and say (*b. Nidd.*, 31a) that his eye was bored out so that the socket was open, and he was blind in one eye (*b. San.*, 105a: the singular is used, and not the plural).

4. Almighty: this word *šadday* is of uncertain origin and meaning. The English equivalent comes from LXX and V. Jewish tradition makes it a composite word, 'He who is self-sufficient'. Other explanations are 'rain-giver' (*š-d-h*, pour forth), high god (Accadian *šadû*). The name is found mostly as an archaism, notably thirty-one times in Job, particularly as the author's second choice when he needs a second divine name in a parallel couplet.

falling down: LXX interprets this to mean 'in sleep (*hupnos*)', this being the *tardēmāh*, the deep, supernatural, hypnotic sleep during which the god appears (Gen. 15.12, Job 4.13; also p. 279). For *n-p-l* (to fall down) as involving sometimes sudden descent (see Lev. 9.24).

uncovered: the root *g-l-h* is a strong word with overtones of 'revealed, stark naked'. LXX has the verb *apokaluptō*. His eyes are stripped naked of all else as he lies prostrate before the mighty God and sees the vision of the Almighty.

6. valleys: there are two distinct words *naḥal*: a valley, river-bed, a torrent of rushing water in the time of heavy rain (Accadian *naḫlu*); and palm-tree (Arabic *naḫl*). The latter is better here, because of 'gardens' in the next line, and a garden of the Near East involves trees to a much greater extent than an English garden. All four lines of this verse are concerned with trees.

gardens: LXX has *paradeisos*, which is the Hebrew *pardēs* (a tree park), itself the ancient Persian name for those gardens which contained every kind of tree (Neh. 2.8) which were the delight of the Persian kings. They influenced the glowing descriptions of fertility in Isa. 41.19 and ensured the name Paradise for the Garden of God at both the beginning (Gen. 2) and the end (Rev. 22.2) of time. The British modern equivalent is Kew Gardens.

aloes: this is the lofty eaglewood (*aquilaria agollocha*), native to Cochin-China, north India, and Malaya, which sometimes gives off a pleasant smell, as the cedar does always. LXX read other vowels and translated 'tents which God has pitched', and so V and DV. Some scholars, knowing that this tree is not native to Palestine, interchange two consonants and read 'terebinths'. But if we are thinking in terms of exotic trees, there is no reason why we should not retain 'aloes' and even think, as Rashi did, of the aloes which God planted in Eden.

7. This verse is difficult and the Versions differ considerably (see Gray, *ICC*, pp. 363–6). LXX makes the whole verse messianic. The first couplet refers to irrigation buckets and plenty of watered land; Modern Israel shows what can be done by irrigation.

Agag: the ancient Versions, except V, have 'Gog' (Ezek. 38 and 39); but this makes the verse late, unless Gog is part of a legend older than we know. Agag (1 Sam. 15.32f.) was the first king to be destroyed by the 'new' Israel. LXX has: 'A man shall issue from his seed, and he shall have dominion over many peoples; and he shall be higher than the kingdom of Gog, and his kingdom shall be exalted.'

8. The first two lines are a virtual repetition of 23.22. Most commentators would omit one of the remaining three lines so as to obtain a couplet. Many omit the second of these three lines as too short, but this line could be reckoned as having three stresses, since the first word is very long. In this case omit the last line, which definitely is short. An alternative is to read *ḥ^{a}lāṣāyw* (his loins) for *ḥiṣṣāyw* (his arrows), and retain the line as a variation from the regular metre.

Balaam's Fourth Oracle **10–19**

Barak is angry and bids Balaam hurry home, but Balaam explains his helplessness. He must speak the word which God gives him. The first three couplets follow the pattern of the third oracle. Indeed, we probably should repeat the second line of verse 16 in verse 4.

10. he struck his hands together: this is a sign of derision (Lam. 2.15; Job 27.23). The rites have been ineffective (altars, sacrifices, etc.), and Balaam has been made a failure who deserves neither honour nor monetary reward.

17. shall crush the forehead of Moab: this is what David did (2 Sam. 8.2).

a star shall come forth: lit. 'shall march forth'. The only other use of a star as a metaphor for a king is Isa. 14.12, but it is a frequent Near East metaphor. T has 'king'; see also Rev. 22.16, 'the offspring of David, the bright morning star'. The leader of the great revolt in the time of Hadrian was styled Bar-kokba (son of a star). The link with Mt. 2.2 is obvious.

sceptre: the Versions interpreted: LXX (man), S (prince), T (Messiah). The modern suggestion is 'comet', continuing the metaphor of the first line.

break down: some would read *ḳoḏḳōḏ* (skull) for *ḳarḳar* (corner, forehead), which involves only the slightest of changes and secures an admirable couplet (cf. Jer. 48.45).

the sons of Sheth: following AV, RVm, and the ancient Versions. T interprets the descendants of Sheth (Gen. 4.25) to be all mankind. But some suggest that the Hebrew *šēṯ* should be *šᵉ'ṯ* (? tumult cf. Jer. 48.45), and others *śᵉ'ēṯ* (pride).

18. Seir was the ancient capital of Edom (cf. Jg. 5.4). This verse and the next have suffered in transmission: perhaps 'and Edom shall be a possession, and Seir shall be a possession; and Israel shall do valiantly, and one from Jacob shall trample his enemies; and the (last) survivor shall perish from Ar (of Moab)'.

Oracle against Amalek **20**

The Hebrews regarded Amalek as a very ancient people, and the oracle makes full use of this to provide the antithesis between 'first' and 'his last'.

Oracle against the Kenites **21**

They were traditionally descended from Cain. Tradition associates the Kenites closely with Israel (Moses's father-in-law; also Jg. 4.11) and Saul gave them a friendly warning when he was going to massacre the Amalekites (1 Sam. 15.6). The point of the oracle is that the *ḳēnî* (Kenites) is like a *ḳēn* (nest) set high on a crag.

22. Asshur: no one is happy about this reference. One proposal is that the reference is to a local tribe (Gen. 25.3), but this tribe is as much too small here as Assyria is too big.

Oracle against Asshur and Eber **23–24**

The first two lines (23b and 24a) of the oracle make a couplet, but the text is uncertain. Possibly, with assistance from the versions: 'Alas, who shall come to be (Sam) from the north, and is coming forth to war (LXX) from the direction of Kittim?' But all must be tentative. 'The north' is the traditional direction from which trouble was expected (esp. Jeremiah, Ezekiel).

24. Kittim is Cyprus, which the Greeks called Kition. This reference to 'ships from Kittim' is interpreted in Dan. 11.30 to refer to the Roman galleys. The oracle was thus taken as a sure guarantee of the destruction of Rome. Eber is the eponym ancestor of the Hebrews. In the Dead Sea Scrolls the Kittim are 'a foreign power of the author's own day' (1QpHab and 1QM), but also elsewhere. They are either the Seleucid kings of Syria and his people or the Romans. The Kittim of Assyria and the Kittim of Egypt in 1QM are certainly the Seleucids and the Ptolemies. But everything depends on the date of the scrolls (see Millar Burrows, *More Light on the Dead Sea Scrolls*, 1958, pp. 194–203).

(h) THE AFFAIR OF BAAL-PEOR 25.1–5

This is a double story: verses 1–2, sexual intercourse with Moabite women and worship of Chemosh, the Baal of Moab—J-tradition; verses 3–5, the whole people joining in the worship of the local baal of Peor—E-tradition.

1. Shittim: the word means 'acacia trees', and is probably the modern *Tell Kefrein*, ten miles east of Jericho and east of the Jordan, the last halt of the Israelites before the crossing (Jos. 2.1, 3.1).

2. sacrifices: these were sacred feasts, wherein the victims were eaten by the worshippers.

their gods: there is general agreement that this should be 'their God', Chemosh the national god of Moab.

3. yoked himself: LXX, here and in the similar Ps. 106.28, has the verb *teleō*, which is used by Herodotus (iv, 79) to mean 'initiated into the mysteries', and so V and DV.

Baal of Peor: the local fertility god, worshipped as the lord of fertility with joyful feasts and usually religious prostitution. He is a localization of the great god Baal, the rain-god of Canaan (cf. Ugarit tablets).

4. hang them in the sun: the mode of execution is uncertain. The simple form of the verb is used of Jacob's thigh (?hanging limp) at Penuel (Gen. 32.25 (Heb 26)); and of one person alienated from another (Jer. 6.8; Ezek. 23.17, 18). The causative form of the verb is found here and of Saul's seven sons in 2 Sam. 21.6, 9. LXX and Sym have 'expose', Aq has 'impale', V and DV have 'hang on gibbets'. Rashi says it means 'hanging', and he quotes 2 Sam. 21.6 and *b. San.*, 34b. He says that death for idolatry was by stoning, but they were hung up afterwards. But the corresponding Arabic word means 'fall down', and we know from 2 Chr. 25.12 that men were executed by being thrown over a cliff and smashed (cf. Lk. 4.29). The most likely solution is: they were thrown over a cliff and their broken bodies left unburied, exposed to the sun.

5. his men: each section of each tribe had its own chiefs who were its judges (Exod. 18.25f.).

(i) THE ZEAL OF PHINEHAS **25.6–18**

This deed gained Phinehas the succession to the priesthood, and he became famous for his zeal (Sir. 45.23f.). The Zadokites claimed their descent from Eleazar through Phinehas (1 Chr. 24.3). The incident has nothing to do with what happened in the previous verses. This is concerning immorality with Midianite women (P-tradition) and the reference to Peor in verse 18 is a harmonizing addition.

7. Phinehas: the name is Egyptian and apparently means 'Negro'. There was another Phinehas, a son of Eli (1 Sam. 1.3). It is not possible to draw any conclusion from the name, but there is a tradition that Moses married an Ethiopian (Num. 12.1).

8. the inner room: the word *ḳubbāh* means 'a vaulted tent' (cf. Arabic *al-ḳubbāt*, whence the English 'alcove'). V has *lupanar* (brothel).

through her body: Jewish tradition is that he drove the javelin through the private parts of them both. The Talmud (*b. Hull.*, 134b) says that the priesthood received the cheeks and the *ḳēḇāh* (fourth stomach of a ruminant: Greek *enustron*), because Phinehas thrust the woman through her *ḳēḇāh*. It was supposed to be a great delicacy (Aristophanes, *Equites*, 356, 1179). This is the only time this particular part is mentioned, and it may have been a perquisite of the priests only for a short time.

11. jealous: or zealous (cf. on 11.29).

12. my covenant of peace: with a change of vowels this could be 'my covenant (of the priesthood) as a reward (*šillûm*)'. The priesthood is to be vested entirely and perpetually in the descendants of Phinehas son of Eleazar. This does not acknowledge the Aaronite priests descended through Ithamar (see pp. 13f.).

(j) THE SECOND CENSUS **26.1–65**

The first census was taken at the beginning of the Wandering by Moses and Aaron (Num. 1, P); the second at the end by Moses and Eleazar (also P). The order is the same, except that here Manasseh precedes Ephraim. The LXX order is that of Gen. 46, except for Levi. For variations in the numbers, see chapter 1. Simeon must have met with some disaster, having lost two thirds of its fighting men, but Manasseh has increased by seventy per cent.

9–11. Normally in this list the mention of the families (clans) is enough, but here is an addition to explain that Dathan and Abiram, grandsons of Pallu, were destroyed with Korah the Levite. The verses depend on the composite narrative of Num. 16.

11. A realistic note is added to say that whatever Num. 16 says, there were Korahites in post-exilic times (1 Chr. 26.1–19). There were 'the sons of Korah' who once were Temple-singers (see the titles of Pss. 42–49, 84, 85, 87, 88, and cf. the titles of Pss. 50, 73–83 with the mention of Asaph, 1 Chr. 16.7, etc).

12. There are variations in the names of some of the Simeonite clans, but no greater than one would expect. The changes are without significance so far as this commentary is concerned.

33. the daughters of Zelophehad are not mentioned in Gen. 46 or Num. 1. Their case involved new legislation; but see Num. 27.1–11, 36.1–12.

52–56. Two principles are enunciated here: the land was allocated according to lot and the land was allocated according to the needs of the tribes. Perhaps P thought of the general locality as decided by lot, and the exact limits by need. Rashi says that the fertility also was taken into account.

57–62. The Levites were numbered separately, as before (1.47, 3.14–43), and the number was virtually unchanged—an increase of one thousand on twenty-two thousand. According to Num. 3.17 and 26.57 there were three main families, Gershon, Kohath, and Merari. Num. 3.18–20 divides these into groups of two (Libni and Shimei), four (Amram, Izhar, Hebron, Uzziel), and two (Mahli and Mushi), whereas Num. 26.58 disregards any threefold division, and equally has nothing of eight sub-families. It has five Levitical families, Libni, Hebron, Mahli, Mushi, Korah. Four are found in the other list as grandsons of Levi, but Korah is new, in spite of Num. 16 (see 26.11). Evidently there was more than one tradition as to the constitution of this tribe of Levi, and these variations are probably due to changes in the personnel of the Temple service. Obed-edom was once a Gittite (2 Sam. 6.10) but was later reckoned as a Levite (1 Chr. 15.18). This paragraph concludes with family details of Moses, Miriam, and Aaron, ending with another explanation of how the priesthood came to be carried on through the two younger sons of Aaron.

63–65. The conclusion of the story of the second Census. There are two names only common to both lists, Caleb and Joshua.

(k) THE DAUGHTERS OF ZELOPHEHAD **27.1–11**

Ancient Israelite law recognized only sons as heirs, and was very firm concerning the rights of the first-born (Dt. 21.15–17). He was the heir even if he was borne by the less-favoured wife. If the man died without a son, his brother must take his wife, and her first son was to be the deceased's heir (Dt. 25.5–10). To refuse to 'build up his brother's house' is a matter of public shame. The land must remain in the family, and any attempt to alienate the land from the regular male line met with deep-rooted opposition (1 Kg. 21.1–25). The levirate marriage is the basis of Gen. 38, so the custom must be very ancient indeed. In the story of Ruth the levirate marriage is assumed for the time of the judges, though there are strange features in the story, probably to be accounted for by the comparatively late date of the Book of Ruth. It is usually said that the P-tradition knows nothing of the levirate marriage, but Lev. 18.16 and 20.21 deal with adultery, intercourse with a brother's wife whilst the brother is still alive. If this story of the daughters of Zelophehad has really to do with inheritance, then we have a new law which abrogates the levirate marriage. The law is: in default of a son, the daughter inherits; in default of a daughter, the deceased's brother inherits; failing him, the heir is the next male kin.

But did daughters ever inherit the property of their deceased father? Supposing the widow who inherited the property was too old to bear children, did the daughters inherit, or was it the nearest male kin? The only other ancient evidence we have is concerning the property left by Elimelech, Naomi's husband (Ru. 1.3). Presumably whatever property there was in Bethlehem, two portions went to Mahlon as the first-born (he is mentioned first) and one portion to Chilion. Apparently Ruth was the wife of Chilion, the younger son. Presumably, therefore, the next of kin should have married Orpah. But all this does not matter, because evidently Naomi was regarded as a widow with one daughter and no sons (Ru. 4.3), and it was the next of kin who first had the duty to redeem the property (Ru. 4.4). Then comes the condition that he must marry Ruth. This is all the wrong way round, and it looks as if the next of kin understood the rule of inheritance to be: in default of a son, the next male kin inherits and the property is his. This makes sense of the statement that by marrying Ruth he would destroy his property. If he married Ruth, he would have to give her son property which had actually become his own. Thus the story of the daughters of Zelophehad cuts across all that we know of the laws of inheritance. Our suggestion is that it is really a story told to account for the tribe of Manasseh possessing territory to the west of the Jordan (Jos. 17.1–6). The territory allotted to Manasseh lay east of the Jordan. They did not receive the ten portions until four generations from Machir, who was one of the three clans that conquered the eastern lands (32.39 and 27.1). They receive an inheritance 'among their father's brethren' (verse 7), which we take to mean to the west of the Jordan. Normally the heir receives two portions (Dt. 21.17), but here the five daughters are represented as all being heirs, and so we get the five daughters receiving 'ten portions'. From a strict point of view this makes little sense, but it makes no sense at all any other way. In any case Num. 27.1–11 had to be emended (36.1–9), and even then a wrong reason was given (36.4) because the law concerning the reversion of property at the jubilee referred to land sold and not to land inherited. See *VT* 16, 1966, 124–7.

3. died for his own sin: the meaning is that he shared only in the general sin of all Israelites who came out of Egypt and died in the wilderness. He was not involved in any special act of apostasy. The rabbinic identification (by Aqiba) that Zelophehad was the sinner of Num. 14.32 is exactly what is not intended.

11. his kinsman: the word can mean either 'survivor' (Arabic *sa'ara*) or 'blood relation' (Arabic *ṯa'r*). The latter is better.

(l) JOSHUA IS CHOSEN AS MOSES' SUCCESSOR 27.12–23

Moses receives warning of his impending death and is bidden to choose his successor. P's account of Moses going up the mountain is in Dt. 34, the only part of Deuteronomy, apart from 1.3, which contains any element of the P-tradition.

12. this mountain of Abarim: this is 'the mountain range on the other side', east of the Jordan. These stand high and red as one looks east across the river. According to Dt. 32.49 the particular peak was Mount Nebo, generally identified with the *Jebel en-Nebā* (2,740 feet), twelve miles east of the mouth of the Jordan.

13. your people: more strictly, 'your father's kin'.

14. you rebelled . . .: this reference is back to Num. 20.1–13, 24 (see also Dt. 32.51).

during the strife: the word is *mᵉrîḇaṯ*, and 'the strife' was at Meribah of Kadesh (Heb Meribath-kadesh; so RSV at Dt. 32.51).

15. God of the spirits of all flesh: see 16.22. He is the God who gives physical life to all living creatures.

17. go out . . . come in: the phrases are used of being busy with ordinary adult affairs (1 Kg. 3.7), but often refer more specifically to military and punitive expeditions (1 Sam. 18.13, 16; Jos. 14.11), or even taking up religious guard duties (2 Kg. 11.9). The next phrases definitely refer to leadership in time of war.

sheep which have no shepherd: the same picture of a leaderless and consequently scattered people, subject to marauding enemies, is used in Micaiah's description of his vision (1 Kg. 22.17).

18. in whom is the spirit: this is not the spirit of prophecy and it has nothing to do with any sort of ordination. Joshua already has the God-given ability. Moses lays his hand upon him before Eleazar the priest and the whole assembled people in order visibly to lay his last commands upon him.

19. commission him: EVV have 'give him a charge'. The intensive form of the root *ṣ-w-h* is used giving one's last will and testament (Gen. 49.29, etc.).

20. invest: this phrase, like the previous 'commission' is a good translation (lit. give), except that both words are used in modern times with special ecclesiastical significance.

authority: this is the only case where the word *hôḏ* occurs in the Pentateuch. It stands for the honour, glory, prestige, authority of a king, and especially of God who is clothed with honour and majesty (*hôḏ wᵉhāḏār*, Ps. 104.1, seven times in all). This is the special honour and prestige with which God endowed Moses to a special degree, and some of this splendour (not all, since Moses was unique) was to descend on Joshua.

21. Moses needed no intermediary (Exod. 33.11, face to face), but Joshua must seek God's word through the High Priest who shall cast the sacred lot. This is the P-tradition.

Urim: this is the sacred lot (see Lev. 8.8).

(m) THE LIST OF OFFERINGS **28.1–29.40**

Here is a list, more detailed than that in Lev. 23, of offerings to be brought, each at its appointed time.

1. My offering: the word is comprehensive and includes all that is brought; hence LXX and S have the plural. These offerings when burned on the altar (*'iššeh*, fire-offering) are God's food, made into the smoke of that pleasing odour which he loves. It is not possible to say how far such phrases are entirely figurative.

3–8. The daily offering (the *tāmîḏ*). See Exod. 29.38–42; Lev. 6.19–23 (Heb 12–16). This offering is the basis of the whole sacrificial system, and Exod. 29.43–46 shows how important it is. The custom varied in details. In the time of king Ahaz (2 Kg. 16.15), the animal was offered in the morning and the grain in the evening. RSV has apparently followed this with 'the time of the oblation *minḥāh*' (1 Kg. 18.29 and 36) for the evening offering, and 'the time of the offering of the sacrifice *minḥāh*' (2 Kg. 3.20) for the morning offering. But in Ezek. 46.13–15b there is a morning offering of a yearling ram with fine flour and oil. Yet again, in Exod. 29.38–41 and here in Num. 28, the offering is two yearling rams, one in the morning and one in the evening, one tenth ephah of fine flour and one fourth hin of oil, with a drink-offering of one fourth hin of wine. According to Lev. 6.20–23 (Heb 13–16) the fine flour was divided into two portions, one for the morning and one for the evening. This is the only grain-offering which was completely burned on the altar (Lev. 6.22 (Heb 15)). Josephus (*Ant. Iud.* III, x, 7) confirms the double rite, one lamb and half the grain morning and evening, the grain being supplied by the High Priest.

3. continual: better, 'regular'. In Ezek. 39.14 the phrase 'men of *tāmîḏ*' means 'men in regular employment'.

4. in the evening: lit. 'between the two evenings' (see Lev. 23.5). Tradition varies with one theory 'between noon and sunset' and the other 'between sunset and dark'. The ninth hour (3 p.m.) as the proper time for the evening offering depends upon the former tradition 'between noon and sunset'.

6. continual burnt offering: this includes both the animal and the grain, both of which were completely offered up on the altar and comprised the *'iššeh* (fire-offering).

pleasing odour: see Lev. 1.9.

7. the holy place: the drink-offering was poured at the foot of the altar (Sir. 50.15), so that 'the holy place' here is the inner court beyond the Upper Gate, where the altar of burnt-offering was and where the priests ate the sin-offering. Whatever went into this area never came out again; it was either burned on the altar or eaten by the priests. But in Num. 18.10 this area is called 'the most holy place' (*ḳōḏeš ḳoḏāšîm*), a phrase which sometimes means the innermost sanctuary of all. There is considerable confusion in this matter. It is due to the differences in the ground-plan between Solomon's Temple and the post-exilic Temple. Solomon's Temple consisted of the 'house' (*bayiṯ*) and the inner shrine (*dᵉḇîr*), with the altar outside in the courtyard. In the post-exilic Temple there was the eastern gate (the Beautiful Gate) which led in from the Court of the Gentiles to the Court of the Women. Then there was the Upper Gate with its fifteen steps which led up into the Court of Israel and the Court of the Priests. The Court of the Priests was sometimes called 'the holy place', and it was here that the altar was situated, outside the innermost shrine of all, the Holy of Holies. This is said to have been divided into two areas corresponding to the two areas of the whole of Solomon's Temple, but sometimes it was called simply 'the holy place' (*ḳōḏeš*).

strong drink: the word *šēḵer* everywhere else is not wine, but other intoxicating drink. The drink-offering was certainly wine. Hence some LXX MSS (but no major MS) add 'wine', and V translates by 'wine'. But in Babylonian texts *šikaru* is the technical word used in connection with the drink-offering, and it may well be that here we have a relic of ancient Semitic custom with the ancient word surviving. Was there a drink-offering in orthodox worship before the exile? The only instance outside P and kindred literature is Gen. 35.14 E, and that is concerned with the setting up of an altar which involved pouring oil on it. (Both the drink-offering and the oil are mentioned in Gen. 35.14.) The references to drink-offerings in pre-exilic literature are to the cults of other gods. Either, the custom was ancient and so well-established as to need no mention, or the drink-offering was a post-exilic innovation (cf. incense). The Talmud (*b. B. Bath.*, 97a) explains the word as meaning that the wine must be intoxicating and not wine straight from the press (*'āsîs*, cf. the modern fruit-juice).

8. like the cereal offering: the word *minḥāh* here must mean the whole of the offering, both animal and grain. The second lamb must be offered 'between the two evenings' as a fire-offering, like the morning offering *minḥāh*) with its drink-offering. As before, the whole-offering (*'ôlāh*) is not the animal only, but the animal and the grain. Both together are a fire-offering (*'iššeh*). In all other cases, only a token at most of the grain-offering went to the altar. The priests (the whole company or the officiant) received the rest (Lev. 7.9, 10).

The Sabbath Offerings 9–10

Extra offerings are to be made on special days. The sabbath whole-offering consisted of two yearling male lambs, each with its normal grain-offering of one tenth ephah of fine flour mixed with oil and the proper drink-offering. In Ezek. 46.4, 5 the proposed sabbath offering is to be by the prince and to consist of six lambs with whatever grain-offering he can afford, and a ram with a fixed grain-offering of one ephah, plus one hin of oil for every ephah of flour.

The New-month-day Offerings 11–15

These were considerable: two young bulls, one ram, seven yearling male lambs as whole-offerings, all with the regulation grain- and drink-offerings. In addition there was a male goat as a sin-offering, a survival of the *taboo* nature of the days of the new moon when the demons were supposed to be active in the darkness (*JNYF*, pp. 22, 129). In Ezek. 46.6, 7 a different scheme is proposed: one young bull, six lambs, and one ram, with a grain-offering of one ephah for the bull and the ram, whatever is possible for each lamb, and one hin of oil per ephah.

16. The Passover is mentioned, but there is no mention of any sacrifices (cf. Lev. 23.5). There were no Temple sacrifices for Passover, since it was essentially a home festival. There is confusion in Ezek. 45.21, 22, where the Passover seems to be regarded as the first of the seven days of the Feast of Unleavened Bread, and a young bull is prescribed as a sin-offering for the first day.

The Offerings for the Feast of Unleavened Bread **17–25**

The first and seventh days are 'holy days' (Lev. 23.7, 8), the proclamation being that no 'servile work' (Lev. 23.8) is to be done. On each day there are two young bulls, one ram, seven lambs, each with its appropriate grain-offering. The proposals of Ezek. 45.23, 24 are seven young bulls, and seven rams, with the usual accompanying grain- and oil-offerings. Both authorities insist on a he-goat every day as a sin-offering.

The Offerings of the Feast of Weeks **26–31**

This feast is not mentioned in Ezekiel. It was 'the day of first-fruits' and was a one-day feast, though in later times there were two days because of difficulties of distance. See Exod. 34.22 J; Deut. 16.10; Exod. 23.16 E. The prescribed offerings were two young bulls, one ram, and seven yearling male rams. According to Lev. 23.18, the offerings were one young bull, two rams, and seven yearling male lambs, together with two loaves of fine flour, leavened and baked. In addition there was to be one male goat as a sin-offering (so also Num. 28.22) and two yearling male lambs for a sacred feast. The commentators (e.g. Kennedy, *Century Bible*, p. 154) think that the original requirements were two yearling lambs for the sacred feast and two loaves of new bread. Pentecost (Weeks, Harvest) never had the importance of the other two pilgrimages, *Maṣṣôṯ* (Unleavened Bread) and *'Āsîp-Sukkôṯ* (Ingathering, Tabernacles). In later times (T, Josephus, *Ant. Iud.* III, x, 6) it was called the *'ᵃṣereṯ* (closing), because it marked the end of the fifty days of harvest rites.

The Offerings for the First of the Seventh Month **29.1–6**

See Lev. 23.23–25. The day is a 'holy convocation', which means no work of any kind. It is called 'a day of *tᵉrû'āh* (trumpet-blowing)'. In addition to the normal offerings for the new moon (28.11–15) there are to be one young bull, one ram, and seven yearling male rams, all with the appropriate grain-offerings. There is also the male goat for the sin-offering. This day is not mentioned in Ezek. 45, 46, nor is the tenth day of the seventh month. The rearrangements due to the change of the calendar had not been finally fixed by that time (see on Lev. 23.23–25).

The Offerings for the Tenth of the Seventh Month **7–11**

This day came to be known as *Yôm Kippûr*, the Day of Atonement (see on Lev. 23.26–32). It was a day for special summoning as a holy day, a day of fasting, and no ordinary work to be done. In Ezek. 40.1 it is called *Rō'š-hašŠānāh*, New Year's Day. In fact, it is 'old New Year's Day' (see *JNYF*, p. 139). The offerings are those required for the first of the seventh month.

The Offerings for the Feast of Booths **12–38**

See Lev. 23.33–36, where the name of the feast is given. In Ezek. 45.25 the offerings are those for the Feast of *Maṣṣôṯ* (Unleavened Bread), seven young bulls, seven rams for whole-offerings with the proper grain-offerings, and one he-goat for a sin-offering—all this for each day. But here there are thirteen young bulls for the first day and one less on each succeeding day, fourteen lambs and two rams each day with the proper grain-offerings, together with the one he-goat for a sin-offering. By this time an eighth day (an *'ᵃṣereṯ*, closing day) has been added to the original seven-day feast (Lev. 23.36). This eighth day is not mentioned in Ezek. 45, and no length is given in J (Exod. 34.22) or in E (Exod. 23.16), not, in fact, until Deut. 16.13–15 with its seven days. It is possible that the period was always seven days, because of the importance of the sacred seven. The prescribed offerings for the eighth day are those of the first and the tenth days of the seventh month.

The Rabbis take full advantage of the numbers of animals sacrificed at the Feast of Booths. There were seventy, an allusion to the seventy nations on earth, who like the number of the young bulls will gradually decrease. There were ninety-eight lambs to avert the ninety-eight curses of Deut. 28.15–68. On the eighth day there were to be one young bull and one ram. The word *'ᵃṣereṯ*, said they, means 'restriction' from leaving Jerusalem. This eighth day was for one nation only. It is as though a king ordered a feast for all his courtiers, but on the last day he said to his bosom friend, 'Now you make a modest banquet for me, so that I may enjoy myself with you.'

39–40. The first of these concluding verses is to say that all the above-mentioned offerings are additional to vows and freewills. In Heb the second verse is 30.1.

(n) THE VALIDITY OF VOWS, ESPECIALLY WOMEN'S VOWS **30.1–16**

This section discusses when a vow is binding. Other aspects are dealt with in Num. 6 (P), Nazirite vows; Lev. 5.4–5, the rash vow; Lev. 27, redemption of persons and property that have been vowed; Dt. 23.21–23 (Heb 22–24), the importance of keeping vows. Here, in Num. 30, there are two types of vow, those made by a person who is wholly responsible at law for his own actions, those made by persons who are not responsible at law, unmarried daughters living in their father's house and wives subject to the authority of the husband. These were represented in court by the man, father or husband. In the first type, the man who utters the vow is unconditionally bound by it, if, that is, he has passed the age of thirteen, which, according to Jewish law, is the age of responsibility. In the second category, if the father/husband repudiates the vow immediately on hearing it, then the vow is not valid. If he does not repudiate it, then it is binding and he is liable. The whole matter of vows is discussed in the Mishnah tract *Nedarim*.

2. The vow must be kept without exception and without concession, but the person or piece of property vowed can be redeemed (bought back, root *g-'-l*) at the proper value (Lev. 27).

bind himself by a pledge: the word translated 'pledge' is *'issār* (root *'-s-r*, bind). This word is new with the P-tradition. Previously the word *neḏer* (vow) included all kinds of vows and pledges, but now *neḏer* involves the positive vow whereby a man binds himself to give something, whilst *'issār* is the negative vow whereby a man binds himself to abstain from something. Under earlier usage both Jephthah's vow and the Nazirite vow are a *neḏer*, but under later use Jephthah's vow was a *neḏer* because he gave his daughter, and the Nazirite's vow is an *'issār* because he places restrictions on himself. In Mishnaic Hebrew the root *'-s-r* means 'prohibit' and the corresponding Syriac root can mean 'penance'.
all that proceeds out of his mouth: this meant whatever he said must stand, whether he intended it or not. This is based on the theory that a word spoken under such conditions, presumably when winged with the name of God, has a life of its own. This is the counterpart of the belief that blessings and curses have powers of their own, and that there is in the spoken words the power which ensures its fulfilment. Cf. Isaac's blessing, Gen. 27.33–35. Later Jewish thought saw the strangeness of such beliefs, and it is laid down in the Mishnah (*Terumoth*, ii, 8) that a man's 'word remains void until mouth and heart agree'. The actual instance quoted is: a man says the wrong word when he presents an offering—he says 'tithe' when he intends to say '*teRûmāh* (so-called heave-offering)'.

The Vow of an Unmarried Daughter **3–5**

The plain meaning is 'young unmarried, but marriageable'. The number of older unmarried women in Israel must always have been very small indeed, so small that the number was negligible. But the Rabbis interpreted the word *bin'ûreyhā* (**in her youth**) to mean the first stage of womanhood. She is not a minor (*ḳeṭannāh* and she is not a full-grown woman (*bôḡereṯ*: a woman of twelve and a half years of age, the nipples of whose breasts have become wrinkled: *bāḡar*, to be rough). After this age, a father no longer has authority over his daughter (*b. Ned.*, 47b) in these matters. All this is post-biblical usage. In the Old Testament a *na'arāh* (young woman) is of any age from infancy to young womanhood and need not be a virgin. Thus the difference between *na'arāh* and *'almāh* (Isa. 7.14) is that the *'almāh* may be married and the *na'arāh* probably not married (but neither necessarily one or the other), and the *'almāh* is a woman past puberty and able to bear a child, whereas the *na'arāh* includes this, but is a much wider term: any female who is young, even as young as a baby. But neither word necessarily involves virginity.

4. hears of: this is correct, and EVV are wrong. He must repudiate what she has said, not if and when he hears her say it, but when he hears about it (cf. verse 5, 'on the day that he hears of it'). The father must register his objection forthwith (V *statim*), otherwise all must stand.

5. expresses disapproval: the Hebrew *nû'* is stronger than this, and means 'frustrate, forbid': EVV 'disallow', and so LXX and T.
will forgive her: presumably she is not to be penalized for not fulfilling her vow, because her father intervened and cancelled the whole thing. This does not satisfy

Rashi. He says that the woman who needs forgiveness is the one who did not know that her vow has been cancelled, assumed that the vow was valid and yet broke it. The Talmud (*b. Kidd.*, 81b) puts it differently: if a woman whose vow has been cancelled requires forgiveness when she breaks the vow, how much more those whose vows have not been cancelled and they have transgressed.

The Vows of a Married Woman **6–15**

This section includes all women who have been married. The widow and the divorced woman are independent and must abide by their vow. The principle is the same for a married woman as for an unmarried daughter living in her father's house. If the husband repudiates the vow as soon as he hears of it, then the vow is not valid.

6–8. It is sometimes assumed (cf. AV) that these verses refer to a married woman, so that verse 9 has to be treated as a parenthesis, after which the writer reverts to the cases of married women making vows. But, as Rashi points out, the phrase 'if a woman belongs to a man' (RSV 'married') includes a woman who is betrothed but has not yet gone to live in her husband's house. This is correct. We thus have three separate categories: one, the betrothed woman who utters a vow, her father does not hear about it, and her husband hears about it after she has gone to live with him; two, widows and divorced women who have now no husbands; three, the normal case of the married woman. Thus verse 9 is not a parenthesis, but is the second of three categories.

6. thoughtless utterance: LXX has 'through the dilatation of her lips', in modern popular speech 'opens her mouth wide'. It must have been common for people to utter rash vows (Prov. 20.25; Ec. 5.2; Sir. 18.23), and perhaps this is what Ps. 15.4 is about.

10–15. These verses have to do with what the Talmud (*b. Ned.*, 70a) called 'fully married' women. In Jewish law there were two stages in marriage, the betrothed woman (virgin) who had not yet gone to live with her husband, and the woman who lived in her husband's house (cf. Mt. 1.18).

13. to afflict herself: normally the phrase means 'fast' (Lev. 16.29), but here it involves any kind of self-abstinence. The Sifre and the Talmud (*b. Ned.*, 76b) interpret this to mean that vows of abstinence are the only vows a husband can disannul.

(o) THE HOLY WAR AGAINST MIDIAN **31.1–54**

Followed by regulations concerning the return of survivors and the allocation of booty.

The Midianites were not massacred. The story is a *midrash*, a story invented to illustrate a theme, a law or a regulation. Jerubbaal-Gideon fought against the Midianites (Jg. 6–9), and Isa. 60.6 speaks of dromedaries from Midian. The story belongs to the P-traditions and has grown out of Num. 25.6–18, the story of how Israel was led astray by the Midianite women and how they were saved from the worst effects of the consequent plague by the zeal of Phinehas (cf. also Sir. 45.23–24). The importance of the story of Phinehas and the Midianite plague is that it is given as the basis of the perpetual priesthood of the Aaronite-Eleazar priests (Num. 25.13; Sir. 45.23f.), and these were the Zadokite priests, who even after the exile comprised two-thirds of the 'Aaronite' priests. Further, we have the regulations concerning the ritual cleansing of those who had killed others in battle and so come into contact with the dead, and also the regulations concerning the disposal of the booty. The ritual cleansing of warriors home from the wars is an age-old custom, but is here revised in accordance with P-traditions as to ritual cleanness. The rule by which booty taken in war is divided between those who fought and those who stayed behind was instituted by David (1 Sam. 30.21–25), but here the regulations are traced back to Moses, though with allocations to the priesthood in accordance with the greatly increased demands made by the post-exilic priesthood. A remarkable feature of the story is that 12,000 Israelites annihilated every fighting man among the Midianites. This must have been a considerable number, since there were 32,000 virgins among the Midianites. The Israelites also brought back over 800,000 animals, and from first to last not one Israelite lost his life (verse 49). But the story is *midrash*.

The Story of the Campaign **1–12**

This was a 'holy war' (cf. the *jihâd* of Islam). It involved the complete extermination of Yahweh's enemies: it was 'the Lord's vengeance'. It is represented as the last action of the Israelites directed by Moses before his death. Possibly this is the way in which the P-editors indicate a late tradition.

3. arm men . . . for the war: there is division of opinion concerning the root *ḥ-l-ṣ*. Some say there are two roots: one, draw off, draw out, withdraw; the other arm, equip for war. But it is probable that there is one root only meaning 'withdraw' and that the use of the root in connection with *ṣāḇā'* (campaign, RSV war) means 'release for the campaign'. The word therefore does not mean 'strip for battle' by drawing off one's ordinary clothes and putting on armour (which most Israelites would not have), but 'being withdrawn, seconded' for a particular holy campaign.

4. a thousand from each of the tribes: cf. Jg. 20.8–11, where one tenth of the fighting men of each tribe is sent against Benjamin, and this also in a sort of holy war.

6. Phinehas leads the expedition. He was at that time the son of the priest (P's pre-exilic High Priest). The priest himself cannot lead the army since he must have no contact whatever with the dead. So his son leads the army. Cf. 16.37 (Heb 17.2), where Eleazar is deputed to deal with the ritually unclean censers, his father Aaron being the priest at the time. It is proper that Phinehas should lead the host in this 'holy war'.

the vessels of the sanctuary: some commentators have thought this means the sacred garments. But in 4.15 the same phrase is translated by RSV as 'the furnishings

of the sanctuary' and this is what the phrase means. The writer is wanting to say that Phinehas took the Ark with him (1 Sam. 4.4; Num. 14.44, 10.35f.). See 1 Chr. 9.20; 2 Chr. 5.5; also 2 Chr. 20.20–23, where Jehoshaphat marches out against Ammon, Moab, and Edom with the Levitical choirs at the head of the column, singing 'with a very loud voice' (verse 19), with the result that the enemy are utterly routed with no loss to Judah.
the trumpets: these are the long, slender metal tubes with flared ends. According to the P-tradition only the priests used them (Num. 10.3ff.; 2 Chr. 13.12).
for the alarm: not necessarily, since the word *tᵉrûʻāh* means 'a trumpet call'. It is here for a call in battle, either to sound the charge, or, as in the Temple ritual, to call on divine aid.

8. the five kings of Midian: these are mentioned also, together with Balaam son of Beor, in Jos. 13.21f., where they are called both 'the leaders of Midian' and 'the princes of Sihon', and are said to have been defeated by Moses at the same time as Sihon king of the Amorites.

10. cities . . . encampments: the first is a permanent walled settlement, and the second a nomad's encampment (LXX *epaulis*, a place to spend the night in). The 'goodly castles' of AV is from V.

11. spoil . . . booty: both words are used in a general sense of booty captured in war, but more strictly the first has to do with flocks (Arabic *ṯallat*) and the second is 'that which is seized'. LXX has 'foray' and 'spoil stripped from the slain'.

The Warriors Return **13–24**

Moses is angry because the army has brought back the children and all the women. He demands the slaughter of every male child and all the women except the virgins. The reason given is that the whole trouble at Peor was caused by the women. This reason is based on 25.16, which combines the traditions concerning the Moabite women in 25.1–5 and the Zimri-Cozbi incident of 25.6–15. The old custom was to secure the extinction of the defeated people; this new reason is more 'religious'.

19. These are the rules of Num. 19.12, 16–19, but the de-sinning rites of the next verses go far beyond this. It is difficult to justify de-sinning by passing through fire from what we know of Israelite custom, though such de-sinning rites can be paralleled among other nations.

The Distribution of the Booty **25–54**

Moses, Eleazar, and the chiefs deal first with the virgins and the animals, which are divided, half for the warriors and half for the people. This corresponds with 1 Sam. 30.24f., but the taxes levied in verses 28ff. are new. Such a tax is doubtless ancient. Mohammed required one fifth for God, for his apostle, kindred and orphans, poor and wayfarer (Koran 8.42).

28. tribute: the word *mekes* is 'tax' in Aramaic. LXX has *telos*, which can mean 'tax'.

29. One five-hundredth of the women and children allotted to the returning warriors is taken as an offering to the Lord (*tᵉrûmāh*) and given to Eleazar which he receives on behalf of the whole company of priests. The Levites received one fiftieth from the people's half of the booty.

32. the booty remaining: following AV. This will be the cattle and sheep remaining after the army had been fed on the way home. The alternative is that the booty which each man had stripped from the slain was his own property (verse 53) and so was exempted from the half-and-half allocation. This would consist of such jewels as are listed in verse 50. This is how RSV understands the verse, and it seems to be the better interpretation.

50. offering: the word is *ḳorbān*, here used in its strict and narrow sense: that which is brought near as a gift to the Temple and allocated to the Temple service, and not like the 'holy gifts' (*ḳoḏāšîm*) for the use of the priests.

each man: it is not clear whether this refers to the officers or to every man in the army.

armlets: AV has 'chains' and RV 'ankle chains', and so Rashi. This is based on the root *ṣ-'-d* (step, march), but 2 Sam. 1.10 says that Saul's *'eṣ'āḏāh* was on his arm, and so LXX here. V has 'garters'.

bracelets: all are agreed that this was an ornament which encircled the arm, though T has *sibbᵉḇîn* (ornaments that sparkle), which explains the 'tablets' of DV. These are ornaments 'of precious metal or jewellery of a flat form worn about the person' (*OED*), mentioned in the first half of the seventeenth century.

beads: AV has 'tablets' and RV 'armlets' (so RSV in Exod. 35.22) with 'necklace' in the margin. All versions, ancient and modern, mostly guess, but the corresponding Arabic word *kumzat* is 'bunch, heap', so we probably have a cluster of small ornaments, and 'beads' is satisfactory, provided they are thought of as a cluster rather than a necklace.

to make atonement for ourselves: cf. Exod. 30.12, where each man is to give a *kōper* (ransom) for his life, so that he may be spared at the Census (cf. 2 Sam. 24). Here again, men's lives have been spared. It is thus better to think of the root *k-p-r* here not in the usual atonement-sense of P, but as a denominative verb from *kōper* (ransom): 'to give a ransom for our lives before the Lord'.

51. The value according to pre-1914 standards was over £34,000 sterling, but the purchasing value would be very much greater indeed.

53. This is a note to explain how the men came to have all this treasure. Some understand the verse to mean that the common soldiers retained their booty, and the gift made to Moses and Eleazar was by the officers only.

54. memorial: this is comparable to the altar-plates of Num. 16.40 (Heb 17.5) P or the crown (crowns) of Zech. 6.14, reminders to the people of an incident they must remember.

(p) REUBEN, GAD, AND HALF MANASSEH SETTLE EAST OF THE JORDAN **32.1–49**

Reuben and Gad ask to settle on the good grazing land east of the Jordan. Moses thinks this means a weakening of the solidarity of the tribes, and that once again the people will be discouraged, as they were by the reports of the spies (Num. 13–14). When the Gadites and the Reubenites promise to take their full share in the assault, Moses grants their request. Verses 33–42 introduce the half of the tribe of Manasseh and connect the story with Num. 21.21–35 and the campaigns against Sihon and Og, which in the earlier traditions (JE and D) are regarded as being wholly independent of this request of Gad and Reuben.

Reuben and Gad ask to settle East of the Jordan **1–5**

1. the land of Jazer: this is the land east of the Jordan and to the south of the Jabbok, the northern half of the territory between the Jabbok and the Arnon. Thus the land of Gilead here must mean the southern half of this territory, though in verse 29 it includes the whole area between the two rivers. All the places mentioned in verses 3, 34–37, except Jazer (see 21.24, where the name is not in Heb), are in the southern half of this area. Verses 39–42 are from a different tradition, and 'Gilead' (not 'the land of Gilead') is the area north of the Jabbok, between that river and the Yarmuk, which flows into the Jordan a little to the south of the Sea of Galilee.

3. Ataroth is said to be the modern *Khirbet ʿAṭṭarûs*, eight miles north-west of Dibon and eight miles east of the Dead Sea. It is mentioned on the Moabite Inscription (MI 10), where it is said that 'the men of Gad dwelt in Ataroth from of old', that the king of Israel built it for himself, but that Mesha took it and massacred the inhabitants. **Dibon** is the modern *Dibân*, four miles north of the Arnon, twelve miles east of the Dead Sea and Mesha's capital. **Nimrah** (Beth-nimrah, house of the leopard) is, apart from Jazer, the most northerly of all these sites, ten miles north-north-east of the mouths of the Jordan, close by the modern *Tell Nimrin*. **Heshbon** is the modern *Ḥesbān*, sixteen miles east of the mouths of the Jordan and the capital of Sihon (Num. 21.26ff.). **Elealah** is the modern *el-ʿÂl*, a small ruined village near to Heshbon to the north-east. The location of **Sebam** is not known neither is that of **Nebo**, though it is mentioned on the Moabite Inscription. Mesha captured it from Israel and massacred the 7,000 population. It was a shrine and Mesha took 'the vessels of Yahweh and dragged them before Chemosh', the god of Moab. **Beon** (probably Beth-baal-meon) was rebuilt by king Mesha (MI 30) and is the modern *Maʿîn*, ten miles south-south-west of Heshbon and ten miles east of the Dead Sea.

7. discourage the heart: lit. 'make the heart to waver'. V has 'subvert the minds'.

The Gadites and Reubenites explain **16–27**

16. sheepfolds: lit. 'sheep-walls', the drystone walls such as are to be seen in Palestine today and in Britain on the northern fells and moors.

17. Take up arms: see note on 31.3.

ready: EVV have 'ready armed' following LXX (fully armed; perhaps reading *ḥ^amūšîm* for *ḥūšîm*) and V 'armed and girded for battle'. The Hebrew apparently means 'hastening', and so T.

22. free of obligation: cf. Dt. 24.5, where the meaning is 'freed from the obligation to serve in the army or on any public business'.

Agreement is Reached **28–32**

If the Gadites and the Reubenites take part in the invasion of Canaan, they are to have the land of Gilead. Otherwise they must inherit with the rest. It is a little difficult to see how the P-editors thought this would be accomplished.

34–36. Some of these cities are mentioned in verse 3: Dibon, Ataroth, and Beth-nimrah. As for the others, **Aroer** (juniper, or cypress) is the modern *'Arâ'ir* on the southern edge of the Arnon gorge and three miles south-west of Dibon. In Jos. 13.9 it is the southern boundary town of Israelite territory east of the Jordan. Mesha (MI 26) built the city in connection with the highway he made by the Arnon. The site of **Atroth-Shophan** is not known. **Jogbehah** is considered to be the modern *Jubeihât*, five miles north-west of Rabbath-Ammon, the ancient capital of Ammon and now the modern *'Ammân*, capital of the state of Jordan. **Beth-haran** or Beth-haram is south of Beth-nimrah and both are on the eastern edge of the Jordan valley.

37–38. All these places, except **Kiriathaim**, are mentioned in verse 3. Kiriathaim is the modern *Khirbet el-Qureiyât*, three miles north-west of Dibon. Mesha (MI 10) built it when he built Baal-meon.

39–42. This is a record of the capture of territory east of the Jordan by three Manassite clans, Machir, Jair, and Nobah. Apparently this was the original Manassite territory, though, according to Jos. 17.14–18 J, Manasseh received a share of the Josephite territory to the west of the Jordan, the dividing-line from Ephraimite territory being through Shechem, south to Tappuah, and then west along the Kanah valley to the sea. North of this belonged to Manasseh. See 27.1–11, where the daughters of Zelophehad received 'ten portions' west of the Jordan four generations later. It is generally assumed that these raids by Machir, Jair, and Nobah were from the west, but Machir's sons were reckoned as sons of Joseph (Gen. 50.23), and it was they who conquered the Gilead country. This apparently means that Manasseh's eastern territory was the earlier.

41. their villages: if this is correct, there is no antecedent for 'their'. It is better to read 'the villages of Ham', which he renamed 'the villages (**Havvoth**) of Jair' (Jos. 13.30; Jg. 10.3–5; 1 Kg. 4.13). The Arabic *hawâ'* is 'a circle of tents'. Ham is mentioned in Gen. 14.5 as the place where Chedorlaomer and his allies defeated the Zuzim. The site is twenty-five miles east of the Jordan and north-west of Ramoth Gilead.

42. Nobah is not known apart from this passage, either as a personal or as a tribal name. According to Jg. 8.11 it was near Jogbehah (verse 35) and there was a caravan route to the east of it running north–south. Possibly it is the modern

Qanawât, the Kanata of the Decapolis, but this is too far east if there is any close association with Jogbehah

(q) THE ITINERARY FROM EGYPT TO THE PLAINS OF MOAB **33.1–42**

This is the itinerary according to the P-tradition. The people journeyed in eleven stages from Rameses to the wilderness of Sinai; twenty stages to Ezion-Geber, one to the wilderness of Zin (Kadesh, 33.36), and nine stages to the plains of Moab. It is difficult to judge the factual value of the list. Twenty-two of the places are not mentioned elsewhere, and the list bears little relation to that in Num. 21.10–20. No mention is made of Massah-Meribah and Taberah, where major incidents occurred. The list can scarcely be complete, since wherever Sinai is there must have been more than one stage from Ezion-geber to Kadesh. For further problems, see the larger commentaries, especially Gray, *ICC*.

3. Rameses: see Gen. 47.11; Exod. 12.37. It was one of two cities (Exod. 1.11) which the enslaved Hebrews built for the Pharaoh of the Oppression. The site is disputed, but if it was in the land of Goshen, it was probably the modern *Qanṭîr*, the ancient Tanis.

triumphantly: better 'defiantly' (Exod. 14.8). The phrase is used in Num. 15.30 of sins that are presumptuous against God (lit. 'with a high hand').

5. Succoth: cf. Exod. 12.37. There is no certain identification.

6. Etham is said to be on the edge of the desert of Etham which stretched out for at least a three days' journey. The name is Egyptian and means 'wall, fortification'. This also is the meaning of the Hebrew word *Shur* (Exod. 15.22). Probably both names refer to the fortifications which the Egyptians built along the line of what is now the Suez Canal to make some sort of defensive line against raiding nomads. See map 5 (p. 30) in Grollenberg's *Atlas of the Bible*.

7. turned back to Pi-hahiroth: this turn brought them round to the west of the Bitter Lakes (Exod. 14.2), so that they were trapped by the Egyptians. If they had marched straight east from Etham there would have been no stretch of water to cross.

8. from before Hahiroth: the Masoretes have a *s^e^ḇîr* (unofficial correction) here and rightly read Pi-hahiroth.

through the midst of the sea: the Israelites do not reach the Red Sea until verse 10, where they camp beside it after leaving Elim. It is not generally realized how rarely it is said that the Israelites passed through the *yam-sûp*, whether this is to be translated Red Sea or Sea of Reeds. The tradition of the crossing of the Red Sea depends on Exod. 15.4. The other statements belong to the D-tradition (Dt. 11.4; Jos. 2.10, 4.23), and to the developed legend (Neh. 9.9; Pss. 106.7 (?), 106.9, 22, 136.13, 15). But the statement is not found in J, E, and P. The usual statement is that they passed 'through the sea'. See *VT* 15, 1965, 395–8.

three days' journey: this is the distance they talked about when they first asked permission to keep their feast (Exod. 3.18; see also Exod. 15.22; Num. 10.33).

Marah: the word means 'bitter', and the place is three days' journey from the Bitter Lakes. If Mount Sinai is in the southern tip of the peninsula, then the site is the modern *'Ain Ḥawâra*, twenty-five miles down the east coast of the Gulf of Suez. If they followed the Shur caravan route, then they travelled roughly parallel to the Mediterranean coast some twenty to thirty miles south of it.

9–11. The theory of the southern site for Mount Sinai depends on the reference in these verses to the encampment by the Red Sea. Otherwise both Marah and Elim would be away in the wilderness of Etham, and all due east of the Bitter Lakes, which is the JE tradition. The identifications of such stopping-places as **Dophkah** (? *Serābîṭ el-Khâdim*) and **Alush** (? *Wady el-'Eshsh*) depend upon what theory is accepted concerning Mount Sinai.

9. twelve springs: twelve springs and seventy palm-trees is a notable find in the desert and worthy a place in any desert tradition. It is to be expected that Jewish exegetes saw here one spring for each tribe and one palm-tree for each elder of the Sanhedrin.

10. the Red Sea: presumably the Gulf of Suez is here intended.

14. Rephidim: if the Hebrews travelled along the eastern shore of the Red Sea, then Rephidim is the modern *Wady Refâyid*, thirty miles north-north-west of the southern tip of the peninsula (Exod. 17.1, 19.2, both P). But the JE-traditions identify Rephidim with Massah and Meribah (Exod. 17.7), and this makes it near Kadesh, where according to the earlier traditions the Hebrews settled for thirty-eight of the forty years between Egypt and Canaan.

16. Kibroth-hattavah, Hazeroth: see 11.34f.

18–29. These twelve places are not mentioned elsewhere. Any identification is entirely speculative, and depends primarily on which tradition is followed: JE, due east, or P down towards the southern tip.

30–34. The P-tradition is here dependent on Dt. 10.6f., and this may well be a remnant of the old E-tradition. Moserah (? Moseroth) is where Aaron died (Dt. 10.6), but the P-tradition cites Mount Hor (Num. 33.38); all seem to be agreed that he died near Kadesh on the Edomite border.

36. Ezion-geber is at the head of the Gulf of 'Aqaba. It is the modern *Tell el-Kheleifeh*, near the modern Israeli port of Elath, though some think the coast-line has changed and the site is some fifteen miles to the north. It is rather more than fifty miles from Ezion-geber to Kadesh.

40. This verse depends on 21.1, a JE-passage which stands immediately after the P-account of Aaron's death. The editor evidently had chapters 20–21 in front of him when he constructed this itinerary.

43f. Punon, Oboth, Iye-abarim: the editor is still following Num. 21. The first two of these places are in the Arabah, the depression to the south of the Dead Sea. **Iye-abarim** (the ruins of Abarim) is up the Zered gorge in the Moabite country, and so is Dibon-gad, Mesha's capital (MI 1, 21, 28), rebuilt by Gad (Num. 32.34).

46. Almon-diblathaim: this is usually identified with the Beth-diblathaim of

Jer. 48.22 and MI 30. But we probably have two names here, Baal-meon (Num. 32.38) and Beth-diblathaim (cf. S).

49. Beth-jeshimoth is in the Jordan valley, twelve miles south-east of Jericho on the east side of the river. It is identified with the modern *Tell el-'Azeimeh*. The camping-site stretched from here on the west to Abel-shittim on the east (Num. 25.1, etc.), the modern *Tell Kefrein*, in the highlands east of the Jordan, about five miles from the river.

(r) FINAL INSTRUCTIONS BEFORE CROSSING **33.50–56**

The inhabitants are to be driven out entirely and all traces of their religion are to be destroyed. An empty land is to be divided by lot.

52. figured stones: see Lev. 26.1. AV 'pictures' is due to LXX *skopos* (something on which one looks). V has *tituli*, tablets such as can be seen on house-walls in Italy and in the Canton Valais. T thinks of 'places of worship'. Probably carved figures in stone are intended.

high places: these are the hill-shrines of Canaan. The custom of building shrines on hill-tops is common in many lands, making them earthly counterparts of the mountains of the gods surmounted by their palaces. The word *bāmāh* is not found in Ugarit except in the ordinary sense of high hills.

55. pricks: anything that pricks or pierces. The Arabic equivalent *šawkat* is a thorn. V has 'nails'.

thorns: see also Jos. 23.13 D. The reference is to something sharp, either a thorn or a barb. T thinks of *ṣinnôṯ*, which can mean either 'hooks' or 'shields' (cf. Am. 4.2) where there is the same dispute, since *sîrôṯ* also can mean 'thorns' or 'pots'.

(s) THE IDEAL BOUNDARIES OF CANAAN **34.1–29**

Compare another idealistic description of the borders of Canaan (Ezek. 47.13–23). The southern boundary is roughly the southern boundary of Judah, as one would expect, but the Israelites never occupied any of the sea-coast until Simon the Maccabee captured Joppa in the second century B.C. The northern boundary is difficult to identify, whilst that on the east may be expected to be indefinite as it shades off into the desert.

3–4. The line runs from the south end of the Dead Sea through Hazazon-tamar (Ezek. 47.19, the modern *'Ain el-'Arûs*), south-west out of the Arabah by the **Ascent of Akrabbim** (Scorpions), the modern *Naqb eṣ-Ṣafā*), and continues south-west as far as **Kadesh-barnea** (the modern *'Ain Qadeis*). This is the most southerly point. Then it runs west through the unidentified **Hazar-addar** (Settlement of Addar) and **Azmon** (? the modern *Quṣeimeh*, some sixty miles almost due south of Gaza). From there the boundary circles round to come out at the sea by **the Brook of Egypt**, the modern *Wady el-'Arîsh*.

6. its coast: this coastal strip was never occupied by the Israelites except for the short period when Hezekiah revolted against the Babylonian supremacy and imprisoned Padi of Ekron in Jerusalem.

7–9. The northern boundary began at some unidentified place on the coast and ran east to an unidentified **Mount Hor.** Probably it was intended to start from between Tyre and Sidon and run east to the foot of the Lebanon range. Thence it went north-east up to Lebo-hamath. After this all is uncertain. Possibly **Hazar-enan** is the modern *Qaryatein*, the last oasis before Palmyra, which is twenty-four hours farther on.

8. the entrance of Hamath: see 13.21. The name is probably Lebo-hamath, by the head of the Orontes.

10–12. It is impossible to trace this eastern frontier. All is uncertain until the mention of the shoulder (ridge) east of the Sea of Galilee (**Chinnereth,** harp-shaped).

13–15. This territory is outside the Promised Land.

16–29. One leader from each tribe is to assist Eleazar and Joshua in the allocation of the land. None of the names, except Caleb and the two chief assessors, are found elsewhere. They work from south to north, Dan being still in the south.

(t) THE CITIES OF THE LEVITES 35.1–8

This section is wishful thinking on the part of the P-editors. The allocation never took place. It contravenes the tradition that the Levites were never to own landed property (18.23, etc.), but there did come a time when Levites could own property (Ac. 4.36). According to Ezek. 48.8–14 the priests and Levites were to have strips of territory across the middle of the country, but evidently they did not get all they planned. There were to be forty-eight plots, 2,000 cubits square, with each square including a walled town. See Joshua 21 for a description of the allocation. The Aaronic priests were to receive thirteen cities, nine from Judah-Simeon and four from Benjamin. The Levitical families received the rest: the Kohathites, ten from Ephraim, Dan, and west Manasseh; the Gershonites, thirteen from Issachar, Asher, Naphtali, and east Manasseh; the Merarites twelve from Reuben, Gad, and Zebulun. See 1 Chr. 13.2; 2 Chr. 11.14, etc., where the Chronicler assumes that the Levites did possess these cities. Eight of the cities were cities of refuge (verses 9ff.).

2. pasture lands: these are lit. 'places of cattle driving', free range.

4. The pasture lands are to extend for 1,000 cubits (500 yards) from each city wall, the city being exactly square. But if the length of each outer boundary was 2,000 cubits, then the measurement must be from the centre of the city. But verse 5 can be taken (see Rashi) to mean 2,000 outwards from the city wall, and Maimonides understood this 2,000 to be additional to the 1,000.

(u) THE CITIES OF REFUGE AND THE LAW OF HOMICIDE 35.9–34

These laws are an attempt to modify the traditional 'avenger of Blood' custom in a developing society. The old rule was: 'Whoever sheds the blood of man, by man shall his blood be shed' (Gen. 9.6), and it was immaterial whether the killing was deliberate or accidental. The custom still holds among the Marsh Arabs of

Mesopotamia (W. Thesinger, *The Marsh Arabs*). The prime necessity was to distinguish between accidental homicide and wilful murder, and some system of temporary sanctuaries was needed. This gave time for inquiries to be made. If it was wilful murder the man was handed over; if it was homicide, the man could stay on in the city of refuge. Only after the regnant High Priest is dead may the man safely leave his city of refuge. The execution of justice has not yet become the duty of the state.

13. The six cities are listed in Jos. 20.7–8. They were **Bezer** (MI 27; possibly the modern *Umm el-'Amad*, fifteen miles east of the mouths of the Jordan), **Ramoth-gilead** (near the modern *el-Ḥoṣn*, twenty miles east of the Jordan and south-east of the Sea of Galilee), and **Golan** (the modern *Saḥem el-Jōlân*, eighteen miles east of the Sea of Galilee). The three west of the Jordan were **Kedesh** in Galilee (the modern *Tell Qades*, five miles north-west of Lake Huleh), **Shechem** (the partly excavated *Tell Balâṭa*, near *Nâblus*, in the centre of the country), and **Hebron** in the far south (the modern *el-Khalîl*, seventeen miles south-south-west of Jerusalem).

16–21. These verses define what constitutes wilful murder.

22–38. These verses define what is accidental homicide. It may have been a sudden affair without any previous ill-will, or the man may have been hit accidentally. In the British courts the incidents in verse 22 might still be murder, but the rest would be manslaughter, death by misadventure or accidental death. In some of these cases the slayer might be acquitted in a British court, but not in all.

Further Details **29–34**

There must be more than one witness. There must be no favour by bribery. No blood-price may be paid by the slayer to secure immunity. The homicide cannot buy his freedom and return to his home and property. He must stay in the city of refuge as long as the High Priest is alive. The whole legislation is based on the pollution of shed blood, and the only way effectively to cover the land on which the blood was shed was to shed the blood of the shedder of blood on top of it. Apparently the anointing of the new High Priest with holy oil and the special de-sinning rites could cover blood accidentally shed.

(v) THE DAUGHTERS OF ZELOPHEHAD **36.1–13**

This curious chapter purports to legislate that property inherited by women shall not go outside the tribe, and to ensure this they must marry within their tribe. What is curious is that ancient Israelite custom was firm that the male line alone inherits, and hence we have the custom of the levirate marriage (Dt. 25.8–10) whereby the deceased brother takes the widow and her son becomes the heir. But even if this chapter is an attempt to put right the situation created by Num. 27.1–11, which was bad law, it still is wrong, because 36.4 assumes that the reversion of property at the jubilee is concerned with inherited land. This is not so; it dealt only with land that had been sold. The story of the daughters of Zelophehad has to do with the Manassite territory west of the Jordan. They received their inheritance 'among their father's brethren' (Num. 27.7), which means west of the Jordan (Jos. 17.4) (see further, *VT* 16, 1966, 124–7).

4. Some take this verse to be a mistaken gloss, but even this does not do away with the strangeness of the chapter.

13. This is the subscription to the body of laws which has just preceded it, i.e. Num. 27–36 (cf. Lev. 27.34).

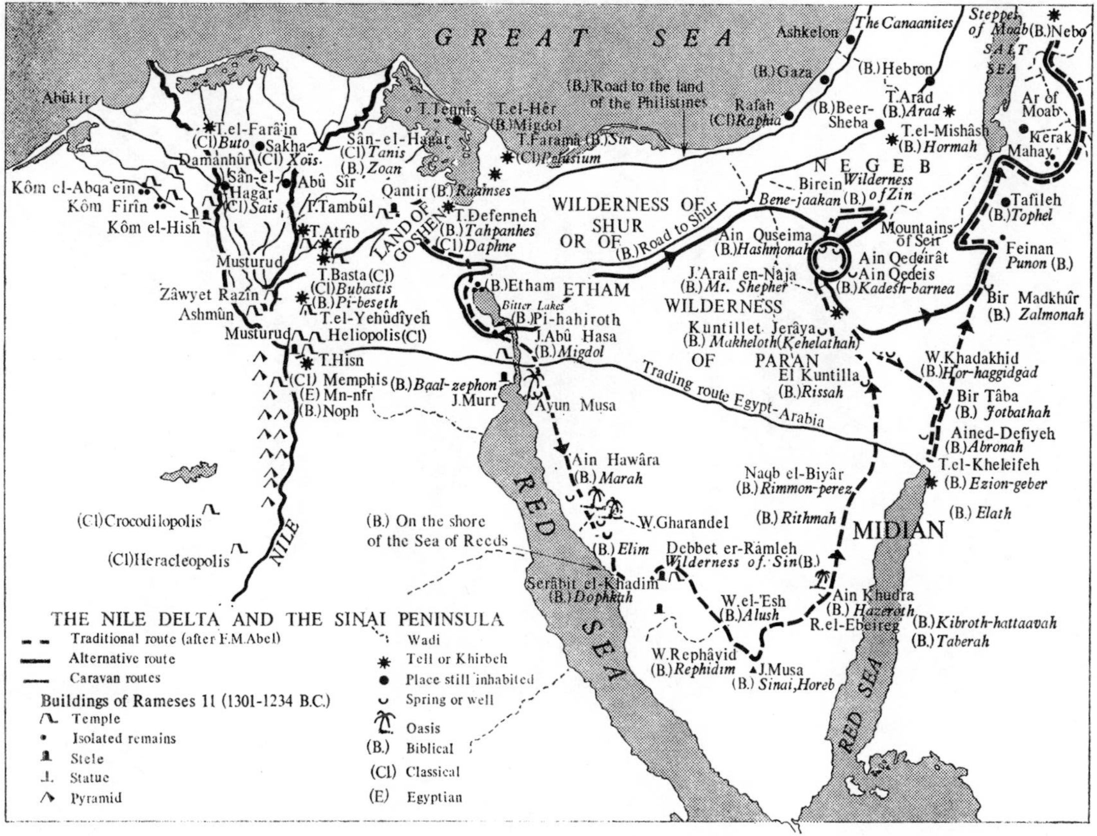

GREAT SEA
RED SEA
RED SEA
NILE
MIDIAN
NEGEB
WILDERNESS OF SHUR OR OF ETHAM
WILDERNESS OF PARAN
Abûkir
T.el-Farâ'in
(Cl) Buto
Sakha
(Cl) Xoïs
Damanhûr
Sân-el-Hagar
(Cl) Sais
Abû Sir
Kôm el-Abqa'ein
Kôm Firîn
Kôm el-Hish
T.Tambûl
T.Atrîb
Musturud
Zâwyet Razin
Ashmûn
T.Basta (Cl)
(Cl) Bubastis
(B.) Pi-beseth
T.el-Yehûdîyeh
Heliopolis (Cl)
T.Hisn
(Cl) Memphis
(E) Mn-nfr
(B.) Noph
(Cl) Crocodilopolis
(Cl) Heracleopolis
T.Tennis
Sân-el-Hagar
(Cl) Tanis
(B.) Zoan
Qantir (B.) Raamses
T.el-Hêr
(B.) Migdol
T.Farama (B.) Sin
(Cl) Pelusium
T.Defenneh
(B.) Tahpanhes
(Cl) Daphne
LAND OF GOSHEN
(B.) Etham
Bitter Lakes
(B.) Pi-hahiroth
J.Abû Hasa
(B.) Migdol
(B.) Baal-zephon
J.Murr
Ayun Musa
(B.) Road to the land of the Philistines
(B.) Road to Shur
Trading route Egypt-Arabia
Rafah
(Cl) Raphia
(B.) Gaza
Ashkelon
The Canaanites
(B.) Hebron
(B.) Beer-Sheba
T.Arad
(B.) Arad
T.el-Mishâsh
(B.) Hormah
Birein
Bene-jaakan (B.)
Wilderness of Zin
Ain Quseima
(B.) Hashmonah
Mountains of Seir
Ain Qedeirât
Ain Qedeis
(B.) Kadesh-barnea
J.'Araif en-Naja
(B.) Mt. Shepher
Kuntillet Jerâya
(B.) Makheloth (Kehelathah)
El Kuntilla
(B.) Rissah
Steppes of Moab (B.) Nebo
SALT SEA
Ar of Moab
Kerak
Mahay
Tafileh
(B.) Tophel
Feinan
Punon (B.)
Bir Madkhûr
(B.) Zalmonah
W.Khadakhid
(B.) Hor-haggidgad
Bir Tâba
(B.) Jotbathah
Ained-Defiyeh
(B.) Abronah
T.el-Kheleifeh
(B.) Ezion-geber
(B.) Elath
Ain Hawâra
(B.) Marah
W.Gharandel
(B.) Elim
(B.) On the shore of the Sea of Reeds
Serâbit el-Khadim
(B.) Dophkah
Debbet er-Râmleh
Wilderness of Sin (B.)
Naqb el-Biyâr
(B.) Rimmon-perez
(B.) Rithmah
W.el-'Esh
(B.) Alush
W.Rephâyid
(B.) Rephidim
J.Musa
(B.) Sinai, Horeb
Ain Khudra
(B.) Hazeroth
R.el-Ebeireg
(B.) Kibroth-hattaavah
(B.) Taberah
THE NILE DELTA AND THE SINAI PENINSULA
Traditional route (after F.M.Abel)
Alternative route
Caravan routes
Buildings of Rameses 11 (1301-1234 B.C.)
Temple
Isolated remains
Stele
Statue
Pyramid
Wadi
Tell or Khirbeh
Place still inhabited
Spring or well
Oasis
(B.) Biblical
(Cl) Classical
(E) Egyptian

INDEX

Aaron, 20, 49f., 161f., 168, 170
Aaronite priests, 13f., 58
Abiathar, 51
Abomination, 48, 88, 89
Alopecia, 71f.
Altar of burnt offering, 15f., 38f., 57, 81
Altar of incense, 39, 81
'am hā'āreṣ, 41
Amalekites, 149, 182
Amorites, 149
Anointing of priests, 21, 37, 54
Aqiba, 91
Ark, 28f., 80, 139
Atonement, 30, 40, 55f., 135
Augury, 94
Azazel, 77–83

Balaam, 10, 174–183, 195
Balak, 174–180
Ballad singers, 173
Ban (sacred), 117f.
Bethel, 9, 14
Binding of Isaac, 56
Blasphemy, 110
Blessing (priestly), 131
Blood, 15, 29f., 36, 48, 84f.
Book of the Covenant, 22
Breastpiece, 52
Brazen serpent, 170f.
Burnt (whole) offering, 14f., 16, 28–32, 44f., 102

Caleb, 152
Cedarwood, 73
Cereal offering, 14, 17, 42–46
Chemosh, 174
Cherubim, 78, 133
Circumcision, 68
Clean, 19, 62–83
Cloud (theophanic), 137, 143
Compensation (guilt) offering, 14, 17, 36f., 41–44
Concession for the poor, 31f., 42
Congregation, 40
Covenant, 20
Curse, 96

D (Deuteronomic Code), 6f.
Daily Offering (Tamid), 16, 45f., 57
Dathan and Abiram, 156–61
Daughters of Zelophehad, 21, 185f., 203f.
Day of Atonement, 20, 55, 77–83, 107f., 190
Dead, Cult of, 93f.
Dead Sea Scrolls, 13
Discharges, 76f., 106–109
Distribution of Booty, 195f.
Drink Offering, 154

E (Elohist tradition), 6, 9f.
Eczema, 71
El-'Olā, 12
Eldad and Medad, 143f.
Eleazar, 13, 170, 195, 202
Engnell, Ivan, 8
Ephod, 51
Episkopos, 93
Ever-burning fire, 45
Ezekiel, xl–xlviii, 7, 11f., 18f.

Fat, 15, 31, 35, 36, 40, 48
Feast of Booths (Tabernacles), 15f., 191f.
Feast of Trumpets, 107, 190
Feast of Unleavened Bread, 105, 190
Feast of Weeks, 106f., 190
Feast of Wood-offering, 44f.
Fire of the Lord, 140

Fire Offering, 12, 48f., 154, 187f.
First fruits, 16, 34f., 163f.
Firstborn, 125
Flood, 19f.
Frankincense, 33, 109
Fungus in houses, 72

Gate of Nicanor, 29
Gezer, 36, 114
Gilgal, 8
Gilgamesh epic, 31
Gleaning, 90
Glory of the Lord, 56, 150, 161
Golden Calf, 14, 50, 55f.
Grain Offering, 14, 16, 32–35, 42, 45f., 61f., 154, 159
Guilt Offering, 14, 17, 36f., 42–44, 46f., 75

H (Holiness Code), 3, 7, 10, 20, 22f.
Habdalah, 8, 60, 67f., 92
Heave Offering, 16, 17, 47, 55, 61, 102
Heave Offering of ashes, 44
Hebron, 9, 148
Hepatoscopy, 35f.
Herod Agrippa II, 53
ḥesed, 151
High Places, 115
High Priest, 13, 37, 38, 45, 50f., 52f., 78f., 102
Hittites, 149
Holiness, 19, 46f., 58f., 60, 67f., 98
Holy of Holies (Most Holy Place), 29, 38f., 62, 77, 80–113, 188
Holy Place, 28f., 36f., 38f., 40, 45, 55, 61f., 80f., 188f.
Holy Things (gifts), 17, 33, 42f., 61f., 101f., 128, 163, 166
Holy War, 193
Homicide (law of), 202f.
Horeb, 24
Horns of the altar, 38f.
Hyssop, 73f.

Idols, 89, 114
Impetigo, 72
Incense, 17, 31, 39, 58, 80, 180f.
Incest, 96f.
Interest, 113

J (Jehovist tradition), 6f., 9f.
Jealousy (Ordeal of), 20f., 128f.
Jericho, 175
Joshua, 143f., 150, 186f., 198
Jubilee, 111

K tradition (Morgenstern), 7
Kadesh, 18, 23, 25, 49, 148, 168f.
Kenites, 182
Korah, 158f., 184

L tradition (Eissfeldt), 7
Lampstand, 109, 126f., 134
Laver, 53f.
Layman, 58f.
Leprosy, 58, 69–72, 72–76
Leucoderma, 69
Levi, Levites, 12, 124f., 134f., 202
Levirate marriage; 185f.
Lex talionis, 110
Locusts, 65
Luther, 23, 78, 91

Manna, 140f.
Mediums, 94f.
Memorial, 16, 45
Mercy seat, 78
Meribah, 168
Midian, 193f.
Mildew (clothes), 72
Molech, 87f., 95f.
Moserah, 24
Moses, 139, 145f., 168f., *et passim*

Most Holy gifts, 17, 33, 34, 61, 125f., 163
Mount Hor, 25, 170, 200

Nadab and Abihu, 58f., 101
Nazirite, 130f.
Nea Tearia, 9
Necromancy, 94
Neighbour, 91f., 111
Nephilim, 149
Nicanor, Gate of, 129
Noth, Martin, 8
Numinous, 91, 150

Ordination, 54
Otto, Rudolf, 59, 60, 91

P (Priestly tradition), 3f., 7–10, 18–21
Paran, 24, 138
Passage Times, 38, 55, 74, 93, 130
Passover, 7, 20, 104f., 135f.
Peace Offering, 14, 16, 35f., 47–49, 55, 61, 83, 89, 102, 104
Pedersen, Johannes, 7f.
Pentateuch, 6–8
Phinehas, 13, 184, 193f.
Pillar (stone), 114
Pole (wooden), 114
Priests, 11–14, 48f., 49–62, 78f., 98–103, 124f., 158
Prophets (ecstatic), 143f.

Quails, 140f.
Qumran Scrolls, 13

von Rad, G., 8
Ransom, 92
Red Heifer, 73f., 166f.
Red Sea, 199f.
Redemption of property, 112f.
Refuge cities, 202f.
Repent, 179
Rephidim, 25, 200
Resident alien, 95
Righteousness, 91
Ringworm, 71
Rock, 168
Rod, 161f., 168
rûah, 128, 142

Sabbath, 103f.
Sabbath of solemn rest (Sabbaton), 83, 104, 111
Sabbath breaking, 155f.
Sabbatical Year, 110
Salt, 34
Satan, 152
Scapegoat, 79
Servant, 146
Seven, 38, 55, 60, 68, 74, 103f., 167, 177
Seventy elders, 142
Shared Offering (see Peace Offering)
Shechem, 8f.
Shekel of the Sanctuary (holy shekel), 43
Shekinah, 56, 78, 137
Sheol, 160
Shewbread, 109, 125f.
Shiloh, 12f., 48f.
Shingles, 71
Shur, 24
Signs, 150, 161
Sihon, 173
Simeon, 12
Sin, 101
Sin Offering, 14, 16, 36–42, 46f., 82, 155
Single Sanctuary, 22
Slavery, 113
Son of man, 178f.
Song of the Well, 172
Spies, 146f.
Suez Canal, 25

Tabernacle, 20, 28f.
Taberah, 140
Taboo, 35, 48, 63, 68f., 74, 84, 93, 103, 130, 160
Tamid (Daily Offering), 16, 45f., 57, 105, 127, 187f.
Tassels, 156f.
Ten Commandments (Words), 22, 80
Tent of Meeting, 21, 28f., 81
Teraphim, 51
Testimony, 80
Tetrateuch, 8
Thank Offering, 89, 102
Tithes, 116f., 165
Torah, 136
Transfiguration, 56
Trumpets (silver), 137

Ugarit, 15, 29, 30, *et passim*
Unclean, 19, 62–83
Unleavened cakes, 33, 47
Uppsala 'school', 7
Urim and Thummim, 52
Uzziah, 58, 69

Veil, 29, 38f., 126
Visit, 88
Vitiligo, 71
Vows, 116–118, 191–193

Wave Offering, 16, 17, 47–49, 55, 57, 61, 75, 131, 135
Wave of the Omer, 106
Whole (burnt) Offering, 14f., 16, 28–32, 44–49
Witchcraft, 94f.
Wrath of God, 59

Year of Release, 22

Zadokites, 11, 13f., 58
Zelophehad, daughters of, 185f., 203f.
Zin, Wilderness of, 26, 147